Published by

THE BIBLE FOR TODAY PRESS
900 Park Avenue
Collingswood, New Jersey 08108
U.S.A.

Church Phone: 856-854-4747
BFT Phone: 856-854-4452
Orders: 1-800-John 10:9
e-mail: BFT@BibleForToday.org
Website: www.BibleForToday.org
fax: 856-854-2464

We Use and Defend
the King James Bible

March, 2007
BFT3085BK

Copyright, 2007
All Rights Reserved

ISBN #1-56848-055-5

Acknowledgments

**I wish to thank and to acknowledge the assistance
of the following people:**

- **The Congregation** of the Bible For Today Baptist Church, for whom these messages were prepared, to whom they were delivered, and by whom they were published. They listened attentively and encouraged their Pastor as he preached;
- **Yvonne Sanborn Waite**, my wife, who encouraged the publication of these sermons, read the manuscript several times, suggested the various boxes, and gave other helpful suggestions and comments;
- **Dianne W. Cosby**, for typing these messages from the original cassette tapes and put them in computer format;
- **Daniel S. Waite**, the Assistant to the Bible For Today Director, who kept my computer working, guided the book through the printing process, and made important suggestions;
- **Barbara Egan**, our Bible For Today secretary who proofread the manuscript and, as usual, offered valuable suggestions and comments.
- **Loretta Smith**, a former attender of our Bible For Today Baptist Church, having moved out of state, volunteered to continue reading the manuscript and offered her valuable suggestions chapter by chapter throughout the book.

𝔉𝔬𝔯𝔢𝔴𝔬𝔯𝔡

- **The Beginning**. This book is the **seventh** in a planned series of books based on expository preaching from various books of the Bible. It is an attempt to bring to the minds of the readers two things: (1) the **meaning** of the words in the verses and (2) the practical **application** of those words to the lives of both saved and lost people.
- **Preached Sermons**. These are messages that have been preached to our **Bible For Today Baptist Church** in Collingswood, New Jersey, broadcast over radio, over the Internet by streaming, and placed on our Website as follows:

  (http://www.BibleForToday.org/audio_sermons.htm)

This site is for people all over the world to listen to, should they wish. As the messages were originally preached, I took half a chapter during our Sunday morning services, spending about forty-five minutes on each message.

- **Other Verses.** In connection with both the meaning and application of the verses in this book, there are many verses from other places in the Bible that have been quoted for further elaboration of Paul's discussion. One of the unique features of this study is that all the various verses of Scripture that are used to illustrate further truth are written out in full for easy reference.
- **A Transcription.** It should be noted that this book is made up largely from the transcription of the tape recordings of the messages as they were preached. These recordings are available in both audio and video formats (**Audio is BFT#3085/1-3**; or **Video is BFT #3085VC1-2**). Though there has been some editing, the words are basically the same as the ones I used as I preached the sermons. Though different in emphasis, this was also the method Dr. H. A. Ironside used in his Bible exposition books.
- **The Audience.** The audience intended is the same as the audience that listened to the messages in the first place. These studies are not meant to be overly scholarly, though there is some reference to various Greek words used by Paul. My aim and burden is to try to help believers to understand the Words of God. It is my hope that I can get as many as possible of my expositions in print so that my children, grandchildren, great grand-children, and many others might profit thereby.

Yours For God's Words,

D. a. Waite

Pastor D. A. Waite, Th.D., Ph.D.
Bible For Today Baptist Church

Table of Contents

First Timothy
Chapter One

Introductory Remarks

Though there is a dispute as to whether Paul was in the prison in Rome one time or two times, I believe the evidence points to two imprisonments. This letter was written between these two confinements. The early churches needed some instructions about proper church order. For this reason Paul wrote this

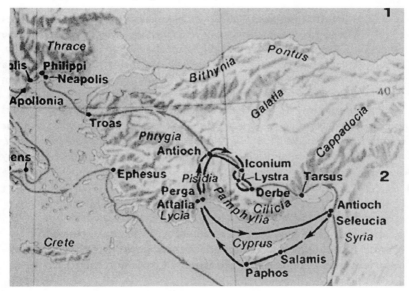

letter and that of 2 Timothy and Titus as well. These three letters are called the Pastoral Epistles because they were written to two pastors of the early church, Timothy and Titus.

According to tradition, Timothy was the pastor of the church at Ephesus. From the map above, you can see that Ephesus was located in Asia Minor which is now called Turkey. It was a major seaport in the Mediterranean Sea in its day. Timothy evidently had been led to the Lord Jesus Christ by Paul and is referred to as "*my own son in the faith*" (1 Timothy 1:2).

Timothy joined Paul when Paul visited the areas of Lystra and Derbe (Acts 16:1). Timothy's mother was a Jewess and his father was a Gentile. Timothy accompanied Paul in the events from Acts 16:1 through at least 20:4 where his name is mentioned.

In this book, Paul lays down many principles that were to be followed in the sound, Bible-believing local churches in his day as well as in the future days of the church age, including our own. It is sad but true that many of these principles have not been followed in our local churches today. For this reason there is a great spiritual poverty in altogether too many churches.

1 Timothy 1:1

"Paul, an apostle of Jesus Christ by the commandment of God our Saviour, and Lord Jesus Christ, *which is* our hope;"

In the first part of this chapter, we will be discussing about fifteen reasons for laws. We must keep the laws of man provided they do not conflict with the laws of God. This letter was written by the apostle Paul to his son in the faith, Timothy. Timothy was at that time the pastor of the local church at Ephesus, a large city in Asia Minor. Paul was writing Timothy in order to prepare him properly for his ministry at Ephesus.

Paul did not say he was a self-appointed apostle, nor did other apostles appoint him to that office. He was appointed *"by the commandment of God our Saviour, and Lord Jesus Christ."* Notice he said, *"and Lord Jesus Christ, which is our hope."* The Lord Jesus Christ is *"our hope."* There are many verses on *"hope."*

- Acts 23:6
  But when Paul perceived that the one part were Sadducees, and the other Pharisees, he cried out in the council, Men *and* brethren, I am a Pharisee, the son of a Pharisee: **of the hope and resurrection of the dead I am called in question**.

The Sadducees did not believe in the *"hope"* of the resurrection.

- Romans 5:2
  By whom also we have access by faith into this grace wherein we stand, and **rejoice in hope of the glory of God**.

If we are saved, we have the hope of the Glory of God by and by.

- Romans 15:4
  For whatsoever things were written aforetime were written for our learning, **that we through patience and comfort of the scriptures might have hope**.

- **Romans 15:13**
  Now the God of hope fill you with all joy and peace in believing, that ye may abound in hope, through the power of the Holy Ghost.

God wants us to abound in "*hope*."

- **1 Corinthians 15:19**
If in this life only we have hope in Christ, we are of all men most miserable.

There is a "*hope*" beyond this life. Paul was persecuted greatly and it would not have been worth it had there not been a "*hope*" beyond the grave.

- **Ephesians 2:12**
  That at that time ye were without Christ, being aliens from the commonwealth of Israel, and strangers from the covenants of promise, **having no hope, and without God in the world**:

Our condition before we were saved was one of "*no hope*."

- **Colossians 1:5**
  For the hope which is laid up for you in Heaven, whereof ye heard before in the word of the truth of the gospel;

For those who are born-again, there is a glorious "*hope*" waiting for them in Heaven.

- **Colossians 1:27**
  To whom God would make known what *is* the riches of the glory of this mystery among the Gentiles; which is **Christ in you, the hope of glory:**

Christ Indwells the Saved Ones

No one will be in Heaven without Christ dwelling within them. While we usually think of only the Holy Spirit indwelling the Christian (1 Corinthians 6:19-20, it is also true that the Lord Jesus Christ and God the Father also dwell within saved people as taught in this verse and in John 14:23 as well.

- **1 Corinthians 6:19-20**
  What? **know ye not that your body is the temple of the Holy Ghost *which is* in you,** which ye have of God, and ye are not your own? For ye are bought with a price: therefore glorify God in your body, and in your spirit, which are God's.

It is also true that the Lord Jesus Christ and God the Father also dwell within saved people as well.

- **John 14:23**
  Jesus answered and said unto him, If a man love me, he will keep my words: and my Father will love him, and **we will come unto him, and make our abode with him.**

- **Titus 1:2**
  In hope of eternal life, which God, that cannot lie, promised before the world began;

God promised eternal life as a "*hope*" to those who come to His Son by genuine faith. God always keeps His promises.

- **Titus 2:13**
  Looking for that blessed hope, and the glorious appearing of the great God and our Saviour Jesus Christ;

The Lord Jesus Christ is coming back again in the rapture for the born-again Christians to transform corruptible bodies into incorruptible, and mortal bodies into immortal, and then to take them to Heaven to be with Him forever.

- **Titus 3:7**
  That being justified by his grace, **we should be made heirs according to the hope of eternal life**.

- **1 Peter 1:3**
  Blessed *be* the God and Father of our Lord Jesus Christ, which according to his abundant mercy **hath begotten us again unto a lively hope by the resurrection of Jesus Christ from the dead,**

"*Hope*" in the Scripture is not "*I hope so, I guess so, I think so.*" "*Hope*" is a future event that is assured without any question.

1 Timothy 1:2

"Unto Timothy, *my* own son in the faith: Grace, mercy, *and* peace, from God our Father and Jesus Christ our Lord."

Evidently Paul had led Timothy to a saving knowledge of the Lord Jesus Christ. Therefore, Timothy is called "*my own son in the faith*." Either Timothy or Timotheus, which is another spelling of his name, is mentioned seventeen times in the New Testament.

- **Acts 16:1-3**
  Then came he to Derbe and Lystra: and, behold, a certain disciple was there, named Timotheus, the son of a certain woman, which was a Jewess, and believed; but his father *was* a Greek: Which was well reported of by the brethren that were at Lystra and Iconium. Him would Paul have to go forth with him; and took and circumcised him because of the Jews which

were in those quarters: for they knew all that his father was a Greek.

- 1 Corinthians 4:17
  For this cause have **I sent unto you Timotheus, who is my beloved son, and faithful in the Lord,** who shall bring you into remembrance of my ways which be in Christ, as I teach every where in every church.

Are We "Faithful in the Lord"?

Are we who are saved really *"faithful in the Lord"* like Timothy was? If not, we should be.

- 1 Timothy 1:18
  This charge I commit unto thee, son Timothy, according to the prophecies which went before on thee, that thou by them mightest war a good warfare;

Again Paul called Timothy his *"son."* He was not a physical son, but a spiritual son.

- 2 Timothy 1:5
  When I call to remembrance the unfeigned faith that is in thee, which dwelt first in thy grandmother Lois, and thy mother Eunice; and I am persuaded that in thee also.

Timothy was a believer in Christ as his Saviour. He was a young man who was selected by Paul to accompany him on his many missionary journeys. Timothy was faithful to the Lord and faithful to Paul as well. When Timothy was called to be the pastor of that church at Ephesus, Paul wrote Timothy some things that this pastor ought to know. That is why 1 Timothy, 2 Timothy, and Titus are called pastoral letters. Paul's greeting to Timothy was threefold. It involved *"Grace, mercy, and peace."*

"Grace" and "Mercy" Defined

"Grace" is getting something we do not deserve. That is Heaven and God's forgiveness of all our sins. *"Mercy"* is not getting something we do deserve. That is the Lake of Fire for all eternity.

One definition of Christian peace is *"the tranquil state of a soul assured of its salvation through Christ, and so fearing nothing from God content with its earthly lot, of whatsoever sort that is."* This is God's perfect peace indeed.

1 Timothy 1:3

"As I besought thee to abide still at Ephesus, when I went into Macedonia, that thou mightest charge some that they teach no other doctrine,"

Paul wanted Timothy to stay at *"Ephesus"* while he *"went into Macedonia."* *"Ephesus"* was, at that time, a major port in Asia Minor, which is now Turkey [**See the map of Ephesus above in the Introductory Remarks.**] The purpose for which Paul wanted Timothy to abide at *"Ephesus"* was *"that thou mightest charge some that they teach no other doctrine."* That word *"charge"* is not like a *"charge account."* It is a command. Notice how God uses that word *"charge."*

- **1 Thessalonians 5:27**
  I charge you by the Lord that this epistle be read unto all the holy brethren.

That is an urgent and solemn command.

- **1 Timothy 1:18**
  This charge I commit unto thee, son Timothy, according to the prophecies which went before on thee, that thou by them mightest war a good warfare;

This command is a weighty command.

- **1 Timothy 5:21**
  I charge *thee* before God, and the Lord Jesus Christ, and the elect angels, that thou observe these things without preferring one before another, doing nothing by partiality.

- **1 Timothy 6:13**
  I give thee charge in the sight of God, who quickeneth all things, and *before* Christ Jesus, who before Pontius Pilate witnessed a good confession;

- **1 Timothy 6:17**
  Charge them that are rich in this world, that they be not highminded, nor trust in uncertain riches, but in the living God, who giveth us richly all things to enjoy;

Pastor Timothy was to warn wealthy Christians and tell them plainly. It is not a problem of having *"uncertain riches."* The problem is *"trusting in uncertain riches."* Riches are certainly *"uncertain."* Look at the fluctuations in the stock market day by day. It is up and down daily, weekly, and monthly.

- 2 Timothy 4:1

I charge *thee* **therefore before God, and the Lord Jesus Christ**, who shall judge the quick and the dead at his appearing and his kingdom;

In the present verse (1 Timothy 1:3), God told Timothy through Paul to charge some and to be sure *"that they teach no other doctrine."* Doctrine is important.

In this verse we come to what I call a *"stop sign."* The Greek structure of *"that they teach no other doctrine"* is a present tense prohibition.

Two Kinds of Greek Prohibitions

In Greek there are at least two major kinds of prohibitions or negative commands:

1. The Greek aorist tense prohibition means to not even begin an action.

2. The Greek present tense prohibition means to stop an action already in progress.

Paul is saying here that he wants some of those in Ephesus to stop teaching other doctrines. Some in Ephesus were teaching doctrines contrary to the will and Words of God, and Paul wants Timothy to attempt to stop such false doctrinal teaching.

The Greek verb for *"teach no other doctrine"* is HETERODIDASKALEO. It is a compound verb consisting of HETERO (meaning *"another of a totally different sort"*) and DIDASKALEO (meaning *"to teach, or instruct"*) Taken together, the verb means *"to teach other or different doctrine; deviating from the truth."*

"Doctrine" is another word for *"teaching."* It refers to the teaching of the Words of God. We here in our 𝔅𝔦𝔟𝔩𝔢 𝔉𝔬𝔯 𝔗𝔬𝔡𝔞𝔶 𝔅𝔞𝔭𝔱𝔦𝔰𝔱 ℭ𝔥𝔲𝔯𝔠𝔥 teach and preach the various Bible *"doctrines"* as we come to them in our verse-by-verse method of preaching and teaching the Scriptures.

Why Do Pastors Desert Doctrine?

Many pastors in their sermons seek to stay away from *"doctrine."* They believe it confuses people and might divide them. Many of them either go in for psychological talks or sermons that abound in stories which some have called *"skyscraper sermons,"* that is, one tall story after another. *"Doctrine"* is mentioned many times in the Bible.

- Matthew 15:9
  But in vain they do worship me, **teaching *for* doctrines the commandments of men.**
- Matthew 16:12
  Then understood they how that he bade *them* **not beware of the leaven of bread, but of the doctrine of the Pharisees and of the Sadducees.**

The Lord Jesus warned His disciples about the false teaching and *"doctrine"* of the Pharisees and Sadducees.

- Mark 1:22
  And **they were astonished at his doctrine**: for he taught them as one that had authority, and not as the scribes.
- Mark 12:38-40
  And **he said unto them in his doctrine, Beware of the scribes,** which love to go in long clothing, and *love* salutations in the marketplaces, And the chief seats in the synagogues, and the uppermost rooms at feasts: Which devour widows' houses, and for a pretence make long prayers: these shall receive greater damnation.

The Lord Jesus Christ named names and exposed the teachers of false doctrine, which we should do as well. Faithful pastors and Bible teachers must do the same today.

- John 7:16
  Jesus answered them, and said, **My doctrine is not mine, but his that sent me.**

Read the Bible Through Yearly

We have to know God's doctrine to know and do God's will for our lives. That is why we encourage everyone of those in our congregation to read the Words of God each day and their entire Bible each year. This can be done at eighty-five-verses per day, following our YEARLY BIBLE READING schedule. This is available upon request at the Bible For Today, or on the Internet by requesting BFT #0179.

- Acts 2:42
  And **they continued stedfastly in the apostles' doctrine** and fellowship, and in breaking of bread, and in prayers.

The "*apostle's doctrine*" is that which has been given to us in the Scriptures.

- Romans 6:17
  But God be thanked, that ye were the servants of sin, but **ye have obeyed from the heart that form of doctrine which was delivered you.**

- Romans 16:17
  Now I beseech you, brethren, **mark them** which cause **divisions and offences contrary to the doctrine which ye have learned; and avoid them**.

When you "*mark*" somebody, that person becomes visible or noticed. That means the pastor and other believers are commanded to name their names, pointing them out, and exposing them for their false doctrines that they are teaching.

- Ephesians 4:14
  That we *henceforth* be no more children, tossed to and fro, and **carried about with every wind of doctrine**, by the sleight of men, *and* cunning craftiness, whereby they lie in wait to deceive;

Harold Camping, President of the Family Radio Network is a good illustration of that verse. We are not to follow such false teachers as he.

- 1 Timothy 1:10
  For whoremongers, for them that defile themselves with mankind, for menstealers, for liars, for perjured persons, and **if there be any other thing that is contrary to sound doctrine;**

God wants everyone to hear "*sound*"and healthy "*doctrine*," not sick and false doctrine.

- **1 Timothy 4:1**
Now the Spirit speaketh expressly, that in the latter times some shall depart from the faith, giving heed to seducing spirits, and **doctrines of devils**;

The "*devils*" and demons are all around us. There are false and demonic doctrines such as the false doctrine that everybody in the world is saved and going to Heaven. That is not true.

Who Are Truly Saved?

Only those who genuinely trust in the Lord Jesus Christ are saved.

- **1 Timothy 4:6**
If thou put the brethren in remembrance of these things, thou shalt be a good minister of Jesus Christ, nourished up in the words of faith and of **good doctrine**, whereunto thou hast attained.
- **1 Timothy 4:13**
Till I come, **give attendance** to reading, to exhortation, **to doctrine**.
- **1 Timothy 4:16**
Take heed unto thyself, and unto the doctrine; continue in them: for in doing this thou shalt both save thyself, and them that hear thee.

Both Doctrine & Pure Life Needed

Like Pastor Timothy, every pastor, as well as every Christian, must have a good personal life as well as sound and Biblical "*doctrine*."

- **1 Timothy 5:17**
Let the elders that rule well be counted worthy of double honour, **especially they who labour in the Word and doctrine**.

That word "*labour*" means to work hard.

- **1 Timothy 6:1**
  Let as many servants as are under the yoke count their own masters worthy of all honour, **that the name of God and** *his* **doctrine be not blasphemed**.

When Christians work for somebody, they need to do a good job so that God's "doctrine" is not "*blasphemed*."

- **1 Timothy 6:3**
  If any man teach otherwise, and consent not to wholesome words, *even* the words of our Lord Jesus Christ, and **to the doctrine which is according to godliness**;

- **2 Timothy 3:10**
  But **thou hast fully known my doctrine**, manner of life, purpose, faith, longsuffering, charity, patience,

- **2 Timothy 3:16**
  All scripture *is* **given** by inspiration of God, and *is* profitable **for doctrine**, for reproof, for correction, for instruction in righteousness:

- **2 Timothy 4:2**
  Preach the word; be instant in season, out of season; reprove, rebuke, exhort **with all longsuffering and doctrine**.

Direct Orders to Preach Doctrine

Preachers and pastors have been given direct orders from the Lord to preach and teach "*doctrine*." The fact is that many, if not most, of them are not doing this. They might take one or two verses and then tell jokes, funny stories, review the current news, or major on psychological problems of life.

- **Titus 1:9**
  Holding fast the faithful word as he hath been taught, that he may be able **by sound doctrine** both to exhort and to convince the gainsayers.

- **Titus 2:1**
  But speak thou the things which become **sound doctrine**:

- **Titus 2:7**
  In all things shewing thyself a pattern of good works: **in doctrine** *shewing* **uncorruptness**, gravity, sincerity,

Paul told Titus, the Pastor of the church in Crete, that he must study the "*doctrine*" found in the Bible, showing "*uncorruptness*" in that "*doctrine*."

- **Hebrews 13:9**
  Be not carried about with divers and strange doctrines.
  For *it is* a good thing that the heart be established with grace; not with meats, which have not profited them that have been occupied therein.

If you hear a "*strange*" and foreign "*doctrine,*" it might be unscriptural. If so, avoid it and do not be "*carried about*" with it.

- **2 John 9**
  Whosoever transgresseth, and abideth not in **the doctrine of Christ**, hath not God. He that abideth **in the doctrine of Christ,** he hath both the Father and the Son.

- **2 John 10**
  If there come any unto you, and bring not this doctrine, receive him not into *your* house, neither bid him God speed:

Close False Doctrine Out

Some Jehovah Witnesses came to our house recently. We did not "*receive them into our house*" because they do not have the proper "*doctrine of Christ.*" They have many false doctrines.

---

1 Timothy 1:4

"Neither give heed to fables and endless genealogies, which minister questions, rather than godly edifying which is in faith: *so do.*"

Here again is what I call a "*stop sign.*" It is the Greek present tense which means, as I explained before, to stop an action already in progress. In the preceding verse (1:3) Paul told Timothy to "*stop*" those who are teaching false doctrines. In this verse, Paul told him to "*stop giving heed to fables and endless genealogies.*" Apparently Timothy and others around him were "*giving heed to fables and endless genealogies.*"

Beware of the Myths of Liberals

The word for *"fable"* is MYTHOIS. We get our English word *"myth"* from this Greek word. The liberals, modernists, and apostates think that the Bible is a *"myth."* That is false. A *"myth"* or a *"fable"* is an invention or a falsehood. Paul says to *"stop giving heed"* to these. A *"genealogy"* is the study of where people came from. There is no end to it. It just raises more questions. There are many warnings against *"fables"* and foolish questions in the Scripture.

- 1 Timothy 4:7
  But **refuse profane and old wives' fables**, and exercise thyself rather unto godliness.

I wonder if these people who say there are hidden codes in the words of the Hebrew Old Testament are not dealing with *"fables."* If God wants us to know something, He will give it plain and clear to us in His Words. People get all enthralled with these *"hidden codes."*

- 2 Timothy 4:4
  And they shall turn away their ears from the truth, and **shall be turned unto fables**.

If people do not believe the Words of God and the Truth of God, they turn to *"fables"* and believe them.

- Titus 1:14
  Not giving heed to Jewish fables, and commandments of men, that turn from the truth.

- 2 Peter 1:16
  For we have not followed cunningly devised fables, when we made known unto you the power and coming of our Lord Jesus Christ, but were eyewitnesses of his majesty.

- Titus 3:9
  But **avoid foolish questions, and genealogies, and contentions**, and strivings about the law; for they are unprofitable and vain.

We are to avoid all these things which are not needful and useful.

- 1 Timothy 6:4
  He is proud, knowing nothing, but **doting about questions and strifes of words**, whereof cometh envy, strife, railings, evil surmisings,

I do not believe Paul is forbidding Timothy to ask questions, but he is to avoid the wrong kinds of questions that lead to evil behavior mentioned in this verse.

- **2 Timothy 2:23**
  But foolish and unlearned questions avoid, knowing that they do gender strifes.

In the middle ages, the big burning question was how many angels could dance on the point of a pin. There were lengthy theological debates about this foolish question.

- **Titus 3:9**
  But **avoid foolish questions, and genealogies, and contentions, and strivings about the law**; for they are unprofitable and vain.

1 Timothy 1:5

"Now the end of the commandment is charity out of a pure heart, and of a good conscience, and of faith unfeigned:"

The following are verses which speak about a "*pure heart*."

- **2 Timothy 2:22**
  Flee also youthful lusts: but follow righteousness, faith, charity, peace, with them that call on the Lord out of a **pure heart.**
- **1 Peter 1:22**
  Seeing ye have purified your souls in obeying the truth through the Spirit unto unfeigned love of the brethren, see that ye love one another with a **pure heart** fervently:

Paul also spoke about "*a good conscience.*"

What Should a Conscience Do?

"Conscience" is defined as *"the soul as distinguishing between what is morally good and bad, prompting to do the former and shun the latter, commending one, condemning the other."*

The consciences of unbelievers are "*seared with a hot iron*" (1 Timothy 4:2). If the conscience is "*seared,*" it cannot be trusted.

- **Acts 23:1**
  And Paul, earnestly beholding the council, said, Men and brethren, **I have lived in all good conscience before God** until this day.

Is your "*conscience*" clear? Is my "*conscience*" clear? Paul's was.

- 1 Timothy 1:19
  Holding faith, and a good conscience; which some having
  put away concerning faith have made shipwreck:
  If people rightly accuse you, then you do not have a *"good conscience."*
  Paul also speaks of *"faith unfeigned."* To have faith that is *"unfeigned"*
  would mean a person was not a *"hypocrite."* The Greek word for *"unfeigned"*
  is ANUPOCRITOS, from which we get the term *"not hypocritical."* It has been
  variously translated in the King James Bible as: *"unfeigned, without
  dissimulation, or without hypocrisy."* It occurs only six times in the New
  Testament. It means *"unfeigned, undisguised, or sincere."*

Sincere Faith Is Needed

It is very important that we have unfeigned faith. Is your faith and your
love *"unfeigned"*? Is it *"sincere"*? Only you and the Lord know the real
answer to these questions.

- 2 Timothy 1:5
  When I call to remembrance the **unfeigned faith that is in
  thee**, which dwelt first in thy grandmother Lois, and thy mother
  Eunice; and I am persuaded that in thee also.
- 1 Peter 1:22
  Seeing ye have purified your souls in obeying the truth through
  the Spirit unto **unfeigned love of the brethren**, see that ye
  love one another with a pure heart fervently:

Some people say they have faith in the Lord Jesus Christ as their Saviour and
then seem to live for the Devil. Is their faith *"feigned"* or *"unfeigned"*?

1 Timothy 1:6

"From which some having swerved have turned aside unto vain jangling;"

- Exodus 32:8
  They have turned aside quickly out of the way which I
  commanded them: they have made them a molten calf, and
  have worshipped it, and have sacrificed thereunto, and said,
  These *be* thy gods, O Israel, which have brought thee up out
  of the land of Egypt.

Some people have *"swerved"* from the faith. False teachers have *"swerved"*
from the faith from our Bibles today. They have *"turned aside unto vain
jangling."*

- Deuteronomy 9:16
  And I looked, and, behold, ye had sinned against the LORD your God, *and* had made you a molten calf: **ye had turned aside quickly out of the way which the LORD had commanded you**.
- 1 Samuel 8:3
  And his sons walked not in his ways, but **turned aside after lucre, and took bribes, and perverted judgment.**
- 1 Timothy 5:15
  For some are already **turned aside** after Satan.

What is *"vain jangling"*? It is *"vain talking or empty talk."* When I was attending Purdue University working on my Ph.D. in the field of Speech, I had a teacher named Dr. Alan H. Monroe. He was the Chairman of the Department of Speech who wrote a textbook on Public Speaking. He would refer to this phrase *"vain jangling"* as *"phatic communion."* The word *"phatic"* comes from the Greek word PHEMI which means *"to speak."* This nonsensical talk does not mean anything. It is when people just chatter about nothing or next to nothing.

1 Timothy 1:7

"Desiring to be teachers of the law; understanding neither what they say, nor whereof they affirm."

- John 1:17
  For **the law was given by Moses**, *but* grace and truth came by Jesus Christ.
- Romans 6:14
  For sin shall not have dominion over you: for **ye are not under the law,** but under grace.

These false teachers of the *"law"* neither understand what they *"say"* (a weak term) or what they *"affirm."* This means *"to affirm strongly, or to assert confidently."* They do not even have confidence in what they are teaching. They are insincere and fake teachers.

1 Timothy 1:8

"But we know that the law *is* good, if a man use it lawfully;"

There is nothing wrong with the law. I have called this section of the book *"Fifteen Reasons for Laws."* There is nothing wrong with laws as long as they are proper.

- **2 Timothy 2:5**

  And if a man also strive for masteries, *yet* is he not crowned, **except he strive lawfully**.

Do not use the law to beat somebody over the head with it. We have many people who deal with laws. We call them lawyers. Some lawyers are better than others, that is certain. You must use the law *"lawfully"* and not twist it.

1 Timothy 1:9

"Knowing this, that the law is not made for a righteous man, but for the lawless and disobedient, for the ungodly and for sinners, for unholy and profane, for murderers of fathers and murderers of mothers, for manslayers,"

Here are nine different things about the law in this verse and six more in the next verse. There are a total of fifteen reasons given in this section for laws. Some people say we cannot make a law against this or against that because it is against our United States Constitution's First Amendment which is a document that governs (or should govern) the United States of America. Regardless of man's ideas, God says there are proper places for laws, even in this dispensation of God's Grace.

(1) The first reason for laws is for *"lawless"* people. This would include people who have no laws or rules that they go by.

(2) The second reason for laws is for "disobedient" people. This would include people who have laws, but who do not obey them.

- **Nehemiah 9:26**

  Nevertheless **they were disobedient, and rebelled against thee,** and cast thy law behind their backs, and slew thy prophets which testified against them to turn them to thee, and they wrought great provocations.

- **Romans 10:21**

  But to Israel he saith, All day long I have stretched forth my hands unto **a disobedient and gainsaying people**.

- **Titus 1:16**

  They profess that they know God; but in works they deny *him*, being abominable, and **disobedient**, and unto every good work reprobate.

This is the situation of many people today. Unfortunately, this even applies to some who name the name of Christ. Am I right? They profess to know the Lord, but they are *"disobedient."* It is an empty profession.

- Titus 3:3
  For **we ourselves also were sometimes foolish, disobedient,** deceived, serving divers lusts and pleasures, living in malice and envy, hateful, *and* hating one another.

"*Disobedient*" people need to have laws that will govern them so that the righteous people don't get stomped upon. That's why we should not just have laws on the books but those laws must be enforced.

(3) A third reason for laws is for "*ungodly*" people.

- 2 Chronicles 19:2
  And Jehu the son of Hanani the seer went out to meet him, and said to king Jehoshaphat, **Shouldest thou help the ungodly, and love them that hate the LORD?** therefore *is* wrath upon thee from before the LORD.

- Psalm 1:1
  Blessed *is* the man that walketh not in the counsel of the ungodly, nor standeth in the way of sinners, nor sitteth in the seat of the scornful.

- Psalm 1:6
  For the LORD knoweth the way of the righteous: but **the way of the ungodly shall perish**.

- Romans 4:5
  But to him that worketh not, but **believeth on him that justifieth the ungodly,** his faith is counted for righteousness.

God justifies ungodly people by faith in Christ.

- Romans 5:6
  For when we were yet without strength, **in due time Christ died for the ungodly.**

- 2 Peter 2:5
  And spared not the old world, but saved Noah the eighth *person*, a preacher of righteousness, **bringing in the flood upon the world of the ungodly;**

The whole world was "*ungodly,*" and because of this the flood came and took them all away except eight people.

- Jude 15
  To execute judgment upon all, and to convince all that are **ungodly** among them of all their **ungodly** deeds which they have **ungodly** committed, and of all their hard *speeches* which **ungodly** sinners have spoken against him.

God says when you have some "*ungodly*" people, laws are proper.

(4) A fourth reason for laws is for *"sinners."* That includes all of us. You cannot have a decent righteous society unless you have laws against these fifteen categories of sins.

- **Matthew 9:13**
  But go ye and learn what *that* meaneth, I will have mercy, and not sacrifice: for **I am not come to call the righteous, but sinners to repentance**.

That means that unless you realize you are a *"sinner,"* the Lord Jesus Christ did not come to call you and you cannot be saved. He died for *"sinners."*

- **Romans 5:8**
  But God commendeth his love toward us, in that, **while we were yet sinners, Christ died for us.**

- **Romans 5:19**
  For as by one man's disobedience **many were made sinners**, so by the obedience of one shall many be made righteous.

That *"one man"* was Adam. Because of *"one man's"* sin, the whole universe of people from that time onward are all considered by the God of the Bible to be *"sinners."* The only way we can get out of our sin was for God the Father to have God the Son come to die in the place of all the sinners of the world, taking our sins in His own body on the cross (1 Peter 2:24) and being a Saviour to those who receive Him and genuinely trust Him as their Redeemer.

- **1 Timothy 1:15**
  This *is* a faithful saying, and worthy of all acceptation, that **Christ Jesus came into the world to save sinners**; of whom I am chief.

Christ Came to Save "Sinners"

Christ Jesus came *"to save sinners."* He did not come to have a good moral influence on people. He did not come to have an example for people to follow. He did not come for religious exercises, but *"to save sinners."*

If you and I have been saved by faith in the Lord Jesus Christ we had to realize we were *"sinners"* before we could be saved. The other day Mrs. Waite and I visited someone in the hospital. There was a man in there who thought he was Jesus Christ. He said that he was the one who was on the cross. The first question I asked him was "Sir; do you realize you are a *"sinner"*? He was upset that I was implying he was a *"sinner."* I told him that all of us are *"sinners."* The Lord Jesus Christ came to die for *"sinners."* Laws were made for *"sinners."* If we did not have laws for *"sinners"* they would run rough-shod over every righteous person in this world.

(5) A fifth purpose for laws is for *"unholy"* people.

• **Leviticus 10:10**
And that ye may put **difference between holy and unholy**, and between unclean and clean;

• **2 Timothy 3:2**
For men shall be lovers of their own selves, covetous, boasters, proud, blasphemers, disobedient to parents, unthankful, **unholy,**

If we do not have laws for *"unholy"* people to bind them down, they are going to be all over us with filth. We have enough of it on TV, and on radio, and everywhere else.

(6) The sixth purpose for laws is for *"profane"* people.

• **1 Timothy 6:20**
O Timothy, keep that which is committed to thy trust, avoiding **profane** *and* vain babblings, and oppositions of science falsely so called:

These people have nothing to do with the Lord. *"Profanity"* includes swearing and cursing.

• **2 Timothy 2:16**
But **shun profane** *and* vain babblings: for they will increase unto more ungodliness.

Recently we were at one of our son's houses visiting. We were watching TV One of the programs was on and every other word was bleeped out. It was terrible profanity. I did not stay long on that program. For five years I was a Naval Chaplain on active duty listening to talk from Navy personnel and Marines. There is nothing so vile as a vile Marine or a vile sailor.

(7) A seventh purpose for laws is for *"murderers of fathers."*

• **Acts 7:52**
Which of the prophets have not your fathers persecuted? and they have slain them which shewed before of the coming of the Just One; of whom ye have been now the **betrayers and murderers:**

The Lord Jesus was murdered by the Jewish leaders who hated him.

• **Revelation 21:8**
But the fearful, and unbelieving, and the abominable, and **murderers**, and whoremongers, and sorcerers, and idolaters, and all liars, shall have their part in the lake which burneth with fire and brimstone: which is the second death.

"Murderers" are those who continue to *"murder"* time and time again. They are unrepentant *"murderers."* Remember these two sons recently who were

convicted of killing their father. It is a horrible thing. Laws are made for "*murderers of fathers.*"

(8) An eighth reason for laws is for "*murderers of mothers.*" Sometimes it is the fathers who kill the mothers. It is a terrible and wicked sin.

(9) A ninth reason for laws is for "*manslayers.*" That word is used only three times in our King James Bible.

- **Numbers 35:6**
  And among the cities which ye shall give unto the Levites *there shall be* six cities for refuge, which **ye shall appoint for the manslayer, that he may flee thither:** and to them ye shall add forty and two cities.
- **Numbers 35:12**
  And they shall be unto you cities for refuge from the avenger; **that the manslayer die not**, until he stand before the congregation in judgment.

We have "*manslayers*" all over the world. According to the *Bureau of Justice Statistics*, around the year 2000 there were 3,600 prisoners on death row. Some people criticize the states that have capital punishment. I think it is proper to have capital punishment for premeditated first-degree murder. We have laws against this terrible crime, and rightly so.

1 Timothy 1:10

"For whoremongers, for them that defile themselves with mankind, for menstealers, for liars, for perjured persons, and if there be any other thing that is contrary to sound doctrine;"

In this verse God gives us six more reasons for laws.

(10) A tenth reason for laws is for "*whoremongers.*" The word for this is PORNOS. It refers to "*a man who prostitutes his body to another's lust for hire; a male prostitute; a man who indulges in unlawful sexual intercourse, a fornicator.*" Our nation and all the nations of the world are filled with such people who think they are doing nothing wrong. God says we should have laws against "*whoremongers.*"

(11) An eleventh reason for laws is for "*them that defile themselves with mankind.*" The word used here, ARSENOKOITES, is very descriptive. The Greek word COITES is the word for sexual intercourse. The word ARSENOS means males. The word combined from these two separate words is used twice in our King James Bible. It is translated once as "*abusers of themselves with mankind*" (1 Corinthians 6:9) and the other time as in this verse. The meaning is "*one who lies with a male as with a female, sodomite, homosexual.*" God says there must be laws against such wicked people. Yet, despite this need for laws against it, the homosexuals in our country are getting more powerful than ever with our politicians aiding their cause. Some United States Congressmen and Senators are seeking to pass laws which would put pastors and others in jail for even quoting Bible verses which are against homosexuality. This indeed is a serious wickedness. God wants us to have laws against homosexuality rather than laws against those who oppose it.

The NIV's Homosexual Confusion

Since the New International Version had on its consulting staff not only a male homosexual in the Old Testament division, but the female lesbian Virginia Mollenkott as one of its language consultants, it is no wonder that the NIV translated this word in 1 Corinthians 6:9 as "*homosexual offenders.*" This could either mean "*homosexuals*" who "*offend,*" or "*those who offend homosexuals.*"

I was on the Barry Farber radio program one time on a clear-channel Station. He had me on his program many times to debate different people. One time I was on the radio about not having a law concerning the homosexuals. The other side said that we should not have any laws about homosexuals. They said that the homosexuals do not harm anybody. I pointed out this particular verse of Scripture that there were laws about those who "*defile themselves against mankind.*"

- **Leviticus 18:22**
  Thou shalt not lie with mankind, as with womankind: it *is* abomination.
- **Deuteronomy 23:17**
  There shall be no whore of the daughters of Israel, **nor a sodomite** of the sons of Israel.

The word "*sodomite*" does not appear any place in the New International Version. Virginia Mollenkott is one of the members of the translating committee who is a "*homosexual.*" Most likely she was the one who took the word "*sodomite*" out.

- **1 Kings 14:24**
  And **there were also sodomites in the land**: *and* they did according to all the abominations of the nations which the LORD cast out before the children of Israel.
- **1 Kings 15:12**
  And **he took away the sodomites out of the land**, and removed all the idols that his fathers had made.

- **2 Kings 23:7**
  And **he brake down the houses of the sodomites,** that *were*
  by the house of the LORD, where the women wove hangings
  for the grove.
- **1 Corinthians 6:9**
  Know ye not that the unrighteous shall not inherit the kingdom
  of God? Be not deceived: neither fornicators, nor idolaters, nor
  adulterers, nor effeminate, **nor abusers of themselves with
  mankind,**

(12) A twelfth reason for laws is for "*menstealers.*" This Greek
word is ANDRAPODISTES which means: "*a slave-dealer, kidnapper, man-
stealer; of one who unjustly reduces free men to slavery; of one who steals the
slaves of others and sells them.*" One of the meanings of that word is a "*slave-
dealer.*" We have laws against slavery. One of the reasons for the Civil War
between the States was slavery. This word also means one who "*steals the
slaves of others and sells them.*" It also means those who are "*kidnappers.*" We
have many people in our country who have been kidnaped and who have never
been found. God says we must have laws against such people.

(13) A thirteenth reason for laws is for "*liars.*" This word is
PSEUSTES. It is used twenty-one times in our King James Bible.

- **Proverbs 30:6**
  Add thou not unto his words, lest he reprove thee, and **thou
  be found a liar**.

The Modern Versions Are "Liars"

This is what the New International Version has done. It has added to the
Words of God. This is what the New American Standard Version has
done. This is what the Revised Standard Version has done. These new
versions have added to the Words of God, and God calls them "*liars.*"

- **John 8:44**
  Ye are of *your* father **the devil,** and the lusts of your father ye
  will do. **He was a murderer from the beginning,** and abode
  not in the truth, because there is no truth in him. When he
  speaketh a lie, he speaketh of his own: **for he is a liar,** and
  the father of it.

- **Romans 3:4**
  God forbid: yea, **let God be true, but every man a liar**; as it is written, That thou mightest be justified in thy sayings, and mightest overcome when thou art judged.

  If we do not line up with the Words of God, we are liars. God is always true.

- **1 John 2:22**
  Who is a liar but he that denieth that Jesus is the Christ?
  He is Antichrist, that denieth the Father and the Son.

  My wife's mother used to tell her children never to call anybody a "*liar*." God calls people "*liars*." We should not do this without a valid reason. The word "*liar*" is in Scripture. It is a good word, but we must be careful how we use it.

- **1 John 5:10**
  He that believeth on the Son of God hath the witness in himself: he that believeth not God **hath made him a liar**; because he believeth not the record that God gave of his Son.

- **Revelation 21:8**
  But the fearful, and unbelieving, and the abominable, and murderers, and whoremongers, and sorcerers, and idolaters, **and all liars,** shall have their part in the lake which burneth with fire and brimstone: which is the second death.

  (14) A fourteenth reason for laws is for "*perjured persons*." The Greek Word here is EIPORKOS. It means "*a false swearer, or a perjurer*." It applies to those who take an oath to tell the truth and then do not tell the truth. Former President Clinton perjured himself while under oath and was impeached by the U. S. House of Representatives because of it. We need laws against those who commit perjury. Those who swear falsely and are convicted of perjury are usually given very strong sentences by judges. We should not lie when we affirm to tell the truth in a court case. If we do not tell the truth, there are strong penalties against us. This is as it should be. God demands laws against this sin.

  (15) A fifteenth reason for laws is for "*any other thing that is contrary to sound doctrine*." God is concerned about "*sound doctrine*."

- **2 Timothy 4:3**
  For the time will come when **they will not endure sound doctrine**; but after their own lusts shall they heap to themselves teachers, having itching ears;

- **Titus 1:9**
  Holding fast the faithful word as he hath been taught, that he may be able **by sound doctrine** both to exhort and to convince the gainsayers.

- **Titus 2:1**
  But speak thou the things which become **sound doctrine**:

Laws are not for the righteous people who are doing what they should be doing. On the contrary, they are for wicked people who fall under one of the above fifteen categories or others of a similar sort. If you take a civilization where bandits, and criminals, and gangsters, and thugs practice all fifteen of these sins with no laws to bridle them, it will result in chaos, murder, death, rape, and all sorts of other wickedness. You will also see great confusion.

We Must Obey Godly Laws

God says there are certain things that must be regulated by laws. We should obey good solid laws which go along with God's Words.

---

1 Timothy 1:11

"According to the glorious gospel of the blessed God, which was committed to my trust."

Paul says that he has a "*glorious gospel.*" Preaching that "*glorious gospel*" is one of the most important responsibilities of a preacher and a pastor. Paul was giving a "*charge*" (1:3, 18) to Timothy concerning that "*gospel*" which was "*committed to* [Paul's] *trust.*" The "*gospel*" is the only thing that can save us.

Bad and Good News in the Gospel

There is good news and bad news in the "*gospel.*" The bad news is every man, woman, and child is born lost and bound for Hell, the everlasting Lake of Fire (Revelation 19:20; 20:10, 14-15). That is the bad news. The good news is that if we repent of our sins, go to the Lord Jesus Christ, genuinely trust Him and receive Him, accept Him as our Saviour Who died for our sins and paid the penalty, we will receive everlasting life and go to Heaven. That is the "*good news*" of the "*gospel*" and it is what EUANGELION means.

- Acts 8:25
  And they, when they had testified and preached the word of the Lord, returned to Jerusalem, and **preached the gospel** in many villages of the Samaritans.

The "*gospel*" was preached in apostolic times. Paul says that he has a "*glorious gospel*" which is wonderful.

- **Acts 14:7**
  And there **they preached the gospel.**

This same *"gospel,"* that the Lord Jesus Christ died for our sins and rose again, was preached in Lystra.

- **Acts 14:21**
  And **when they had preached the gospel to that city,** and had taught many, they returned again to Lystra, and *to* Iconium, and Antioch,

This was what the apostles did. This is what Paul was commissioned to do. If we are saved, we are to tell others of this *"gospel."*

- **Acts 20:24**
  But none of these things move me, neither count I my life dear unto myself, so that I might finish my course with joy, and the ministry, which I have received of the Lord Jesus, **to testify the gospel of the grace of God.**

- **Romans 1:1**
  Paul, a servant of Jesus Christ, called *to be* an apostle, **separated unto the gospel of God,**

Paul was separated unto that *"gospel."* That was the thing that he wanted to do more than anything else. We cannot force people to accept the Lord Jesus Christ as their Saviour. But we can, and we must, preach the gospel and sow the seed. The results depend upon the soil (Matthew 13:3-8). Is it good ground, or is it unproductive ground?

- **Romans 1:9**
  For God is my witness, **whom I serve with my spirit in the gospel of his Son,** that without ceasing I make mention of you always in my prayers;

- **Romans 1:15-16**
  So, as much as in me is, **I am ready to preach the gospel to you that are at Rome also.** For I am not ashamed of the **gospel of Christ**: for it is the power of God unto salvation to every one that believeth; to the Jew first, and also to the Greek.

In this verse it is called the *"gospel of Christ."*

- **Romans 15:19**
  Through mighty signs and wonders, by the power of the Spirit of God; so that from Jerusalem, and round about unto Illyricum, **I have fully preached the gospel of Christ.**

Why did Paul preach the *"gospel"*? Did Paul preach the *"gospel"* because people wanted to hear him talk about the good news that Christ died for sinners? No.

- 1 Corinthians 9:16
  For **though I preach the gospel**, I have nothing to glory of: for **necessity is laid upon me**; yea, woe is unto me, if I preach not the gospel!

He had a burden for the "*gospel.*" You and I should also have a burden to tell others of the "*gospel*" of the Lord Jesus Christ. There are many false "*gospels*" going around.

Hyper-Calvinists' False "Gospel"

The so-called "*gospel*" of the hyper-Calvinists is a false "*gospel*" in my judgment. This false "*gospel*" says that you cannot believe in the Lord Jesus Christ unless you are one of the "*elect.*" They do not believe that Christ died for the sins of the entire world, only for the sins of the "*elect.*" That would mean that you could not preach the "*gospel*" and say that the Lord Jesus Christ died for the sins of your audience, because you would not know which ones were the elect and which were not. This is a false "*gospel.*"

- John 3:16
  For **God so loved the world**, that he gave his only begotten Son, that **whosoever believeth in him should not perish, but have everlasting life**.

The "*gospel*" is for everyone and not just for the elect. Paul said "*Woe is unto me if I preach not the gospel*" (1 Corinthians 9:16b). That is exactly what he did.

- 1 Corinthians 15:1-4
  Moreover, brethren, **I declare unto you the gospel** which I preached unto you, which also ye have received, and wherein ye stand; By which also ye are saved, if ye keep in memory what I preached unto you, unless ye have believed in vain. For I delivered unto you first of all that which I also received, how that Christ died for our sins according to the scriptures; And that he was buried, and that he rose again the third day according to the scriptures:

The Meaning of Repentance

(1) The first part of the gospel is that *"Christ died for our sins."* We must first realize we are sinners. Then we must repent of our sins. *"Repent"* means to *"change our mind"* concerning our sins and concerning the Saviour Who died for them.

We who formerly might have loved sins, if we're truly repentant, we must now hate them. We must also have a *"change of mind"* regarding the Lord Jesus Christ. We must turn to Him as our Saviour who died for our sins. We must realize that He took our place. He died for the sins of the whole world.

Christ Was Buried for Three Days

(2) The second part of the gospel is that *"He was buried."* Christ did not swoon as the modernists teach. He died and was buried for three literal, twenty-four-hour days and three literal, twenty-four-hour nights (Matthew 12:40).

We believe those are literal days. We believe these seventy-two-hours began Wednesday around 6:00 p.m. (the end of Wednesday by Jewish time) and ended around 6:00 a.m. (the beginning of Sunday by Jewish time). It is impossible to have *"three days and three nights"* (Matthew 12:40) or anywhere near that if the Lord Jesus Christ's crucifixion and burial was on Friday.

Christ Arose the Third Day

(3) The third part of the gospel is that *"He rose again the third day according to the Scriptures."* That resurrection is not just spiritual. It is bodily. These are the three points of the gospel. People must accept the Lord Jesus Christ as their Saviour and receive this *"gospel."*

- John 1:12
  But as many as received him, to them gave he power to become the sons of God, *even to them that believe on his name:*

- **2 Corinthians 4:3-4**
  But **if our gospel be hid,** it is hid to them that are lost: In whom the god of this world hath blinded the minds of them which believe not, **lest the light of the glorious gospel of Christ, who is the image of God, should shine unto them.**
- **Galatians 1:6**
  I marvel that ye are so soon removed from him that called you into the grace of Christ **unto another gospel:**

Some people believe in salvation by their good works. Some people believe that salvation is evidenced through their speaking in tongues. Some people believe joining a church can save you. Some people believe that mere water baptism, either by sprinkling, by pouring, or by immersion will bring a person salvation. These are false *"gospels."*

The Gospel of the Bible

The gospel of the Bible is that all of us are sinners and there is not a single righteous person in the whole world. All of us are sinners and bound for Hell. The *"gospel"* says that all are lost. The *"gospel"* says that the Lord Jesus came to save everyone who is lost. If they would accept and genuinely receive Him by personal faith, they will be saved. If people reject the Lord Jesus Christ, they will stay in their lost condition and end up in the Lake of Fire for all eternity.

- **Philippians 1:7**
  Even as it is meet for me to think this of you all, because I have you in my heart; inasmuch as both in my bonds, and in the **defence and confirmation of the gospel**, ye all are partakers of my grace.

Notice Paul says that he is interested both in the *"defence and confirmation of the gospel."* We today must be interested in doing both of these aspects of the *"gospel."*

- **Philippians 1:17**
  But the other of love, knowing that **I am set for the defence of the gospel.**

Even as Paul, we must *"defend the gospel"* against all perverted gospels. Paul was defending it. That is a needful task for us today as well.

- **1 Thessalonians 2:4**
  But as **we were allowed of God to be put in trust with the gospel,** even so we speak; not as pleasing men, but God,

which trieth our hearts.

Have you been put in trust with the "*gospel*"? If you are saved, God has put you also, as Paul, "*in trust with the gospel.*" In this area of the "*gospel*," are you trustworthy? Do you know your Bible well enough to know the Biblical "*gospel*"? Are you using this "*gospel*" to lead others to Christ? We must seek to please the Lord when we speak the "*gospel*" clearly and forcefully.

- **1 Timothy 6:20**
  O Timothy, **keep that which is committed to thy trust**, avoiding profane *and* vain babblings, and oppositions of science falsely so called:

God's Preserved OT & NT Words

This "*gospel*" which was committed to Paul's "trust" must be kept clearly by us today. That is why we have our King James Bible. We believe that's the Bible that God has put in our trust. The Hebrew and Aramaic Masoretic Words which underlie the Old Testament and the Textus Receptus Greek Words that underlie the New Testament are God's Words. We must defend those Words.

1 Timothy 1:12

"And I thank Christ Jesus our Lord, who hath enabled me, for that he counted me faithful, putting me into the ministry;"

Paul is thankful to the Lord Jesus Christ. The word "*Lord*" is a very descriptive word. The Greek word is KURIOS. It is found 748 times in the Greek Words underlying the King James Bible. It means:

"*he to whom a person or thing belongs, about which he has power of deciding; master, lord; the possessor and disposer of a thing; the owner; one who has control of the person, the master.*"

Does Christ Have Control of You?

If you are saved, do you treat the Lord Jesus Christ as "*One Who has control*" of you? Does He have the "*power of deciding*" what you do?

Paul said that the Lord Jesus Christ "*enabled*" him. The word for "enable" is ENDUNAMOO. It means: "*to be strong, endue with strength, strengthen; to*" *receive strength, be strengthened, increase in strength."* If anybody is going to be *"enabled"* as he is preaching the gospel, the Lord Jesus Christ must *"enable"* him. He has to *"endue you with strength"* and give you the proper words to say.

The reason the Lord Jesus Christ saved Paul and put him into the *"ministry"* was that *"He counted him faithful."* I would wish that all saved people would be also *"counted faithful."* That word for ministry is DIAKONIA. It has various meanings:

> *"service, ministering, esp. of those who execute the commands of others; of those who by the command of God proclaim and promote religion among men . . . the ministration of those who render to others the offices of Christian affection esp. those who help meet need by either collecting or distributing of charities . . . the service of those who prepare and present food"*

If you are in the ministry of the Lord Jesus Christ, you are to be faithfully *"executing the commands of others."* The Lord Jesus Himself is the One Whose commands we should be executing. There are a number of verses on faithfulness.

Faithful to Biblical Principles

We must be sure we are *"faithful"* to the Biblical principles.

- **Psalm 119:138**
  Thy testimonies *that* thou hast commanded *are* righteous and **very faithful**.
- **Luke 16:10**
  He that is faithful in that which is least is faithful also in much: and he that is unjust in the least is unjust also in much.

We must be faithful in how we deal with the little things as well as the big things.

- **1 Corinthians 1:9**
  God *is* **faithful**, by whom ye were called unto the fellowship of his Son Jesus Christ our Lord.

The Lord will never let you down if you are trusting in His Word. He truly is faithful. That is part of His character and attributes.

- **1 Corinthians 4:2**
  Moreover **it is required in stewards, that a man be found faithful.**

Everyone of us who has been given the gospel of our Saviour has a *"stewardship."* That means we have to care of and give an account for what we have been given; just like Uncle Sam makes us account for all our money that

comes in.   We have to give the government a certain percentage of it.
Sometimes our taxes are very high.   We must be faithful "*stewards*" in what God
has given to those whom He has redeemed.   God has given us His Word.   He has
given us His gospel and we have to be faithful in our accounting for these things.

- **1 Corinthians 10:13**
  There hath no temptation taken you but such as is common to
  man: but **God *is* faithful**, who will not suffer you to be tempted
  above that ye are able; but will with the temptation also make
  a way to escape, that ye may be able to bear *it*.

God is "*faithful*" even in testing and temptations.   My mother-in-law wrote a
book called *Able to Bear It*.   This book is about her daughter, Beverly, who was
brain damaged due to a birth injury.   This was her verse.   God has made us "*able
to bear*" any testing, no matter what it may be.   Mom Sanborn did a good job
taking care of Beverly, and she was "*faithful.*"   Because she had to stay home
taking care of Beverly she wrote over 400 Christian poems, many of which are
found in the book *With Tears In My Heart* **(BFT #3196 for a GIFT to BFT of
$25.00 + $5.00 S&H).**   These poems were written from the heart of a woman
who was trusting and depending upon the Lord Jesus Christ.   You can see this
in her poetry.

- **Colossians 1:2**
  To the saints and **faithful brethren in Christ** which are at
  Colosse: Grace *be* unto you, and peace, from God our Father
  and the Lord Jesus Christ.

Are You A Not-"Faithful" Person?

This implies that some Christian people might not be "*faithful.*"   Are you
one of the brothers or sisters in Christ who are not "*faithful*"?   This is very
important.

- **Colossians 1:7**
  As ye also learned of Epaphras our dear fellowservant, who is
  for you a **faithful minister of Christ;**

What Is A "Faithful Minister"?

What is a *"faithful minister"*? I believe a *"faithful minister"* is one who ministers the Words of God faithfully. He is one who does not compromise his message just because of his audience.

"Faithful ministers" are scarce these days. If you do not believe me, just look around at some of the churches. What do the ministers do who are unfaithful? I'll tell you what they do. They look out and see who is in the crowd. If they see a Mason there, they do not preach against Masonry. If they see people who have been divorced and remarried, they do not preach against divorce and remarriage. They might have people who use the New International Version or some other perverted version so they do not defend the King James Bible and refute the other perversions. They are not faithful to the Lord. Furthermore, they might look and see the ones who have money and are careful not to offend those people. Epaphras was a *"faithful minister."*

- **1 Timothy 1:15**

    This *is* a **faithful saying**, and worthy of all acceptation, that Christ Jesus came into the world to save sinners; of whom I am chief.

- **1 Timothy 3:11**

    Even so *must their* wives *be* grave, not slanderers, sober, **faithful in all things**.

It is important not only to have faithful pastors and deacons, but also for them to have faithful wives.

- **2 Timothy 2:2**

    And the things that thou hast heard of me among many witnesses, **the same commit thou to faithful men**, who shall be able to teach others also.

That is what I am seeking to do here in our 𝔅𝔦𝔟𝔩𝔢 𝔉𝔬𝔯 𝔗𝔬𝔡𝔞𝔶 𝔅𝔞𝔭𝔱𝔦𝔰𝔱 𝔠𝔥𝔲𝔯𝔠𝔥. The *"things"* that have been committed to me in the Bible I am preaching and teaching to *"faithful"* people who hopefully will be able *"to teach others also."* The things of God's Words and of the Lord Jesus Christ must go on. I will die just like Paul and Timothy died. But what about our children?

Sound Generational Teaching Needed

This teaching ministry must go on from generation to generation. That is the trouble with many of our churches. They start one way, and then in the next generation they slip a little, and soon they are a compromising church. We must teach our generations to come. That is my burden.

That is why I am glad that Mrs. Waite puts these messages on video. I am glad that these videos on VHS and/or DVD are being sent each month to many families who want to hear them and study the Bible with us. I am glad Dan Waite has made it possible for us to put these streaming videos on the Internet to be heard all over the world 24-hours a day, seven days a week. I am glad I can put them on audio cassettes and publish them on the Internet through **SermonAudio.Com**. I am glad that faithful giving by our friends like you can enable us to put these messages in book form as well. That is why we put these messages in book form to be used for the glory of our Saviour.

- **Hebrews 2:17**
  Wherefore in all things it behoved him to be made like unto *his* brethren, that he might be a merciful and **faithful high priest** in things *pertaining* to God, to make reconciliation for the sins of the people.

The Lord Jesus Christ is a "*faithful high priest*" at the Father's right hand. When we who are saved have burdens, we can take them to Him.

- **1 John 1:9**
  If we confess our sins, **He is faithful** and just to forgive us *our* sins, and to cleanse us from all unrighteousness.

Cleansing the Believers' Sins

The beautiful thing about Christians is that, when we get dirty with sin, God says if we confess our sins He will forgive our sins. The word for "*confess*" is HOMOLOGEO. It comes from two Greek words, HOMO ("*same*") + LOGEO ("*to say*"). It means that in true and Biblical confession, we must "*say the same thing about our sins that God says.*" We must agree with God that our sins of thought, word, or deed are wrong. The Lord does not want His born-again children to be unrighteous. He wants us to be pure and clean. The Lord cannot use unrighteous and unfaithful people for His cause any more than a skilled surgeon must not use unclean gloves during his surgery.

1 Timothy 1:13

"Who was before a blasphemer, and a persecutor, and injurious: but I obtained mercy, because I did *it* ignorantly in unbelief."

God gave Paul grace and "*mercy.*" Before Paul was saved by God's grace, he was a "*blasphemer, and a persecutor, and injurious.*" That word "*injurious*" is an interesting word. The word is HUBRISTOS. It means: "*an insolent man; one who, uplifted with pride, either heaps insulting language upon others or does them some shameful act of wrong.*"

In Acts Chapter 9, Paul gives his own testimony about his conversion. He was breathing out threatenings and slaughter against the disciples of the Lord. Paul was a very wicked man before the Lord Jesus Christ saved him.

- **Acts 22:3-5**

  I am verily a man *which am* a Jew, born in Tarsus, *a city* in Cilicia, yet brought up in this city at the feet of Gamaliel, *and* taught according to the perfect manner of the law of the fathers, and was zealous toward God, as ye all are this day. And **I persecuted this way unto the death, binding and delivering into prisons both men and women.** As also the high priest doth bear me witness, and all the estate of the elders: from whom also I received letters unto the brethren, and went to Damascus, to bring them which were there bound unto Jerusalem, for to be punished.

- **Acts 26:9-11**

  I verily thought with myself, that I ought to do many things contrary to the name of Jesus of Nazareth. Which thing I also did in Jerusalem: and many of the saints did I shut up in prison, having received authority from the chief priests; and when they were put to death, I gave my voice against *them.* And **I punished them oft in every synagogue, and compelled *them* to blaspheme; and being exceedingly mad against them, I persecuted *them* even unto strange cities.**

Paul did these things "*ignorantly.*" For this reason he "*obtained mercy.*" "*Mercy*" has been defined as "*not getting something that we deserve.*" Certainly Paul deserved severe judgment from the Lord, but God withheld it.

1 Timothy 1:14

"And the grace of our Lord was exceeding abundant with faith and love which is in Christ Jesus."

A person who was so terrible as Paul needed *"exceeding abundant"* grace. If you are lost, God can save you just as he saved Paul. *"Exceeding abundant"* sin calls for *"exceeding abundant"* grace. That is exactly what Paul got. He received this grace *"with faith and love which is in Christ Jesus."* This is the *"love"* that sent the Lord Jesus Christ to the cross on Calvary. This is the *"love"* that first sent the Lord Jesus Christ from Heaven to earth in the first place.

- John 3:16

  For **God so loved the world**, that he gave his only begotten Son, that whosoever believeth in him should not perish, but have everlasting life.

That is the love that motivated God the Father to send His Son. That is the *"love"* that Paul received.

1 Timothy 1:15

"This *is* a faithful saying, and worthy of all acceptation, that Christ Jesus came into the world to save sinners; of whom I am chief."

The purpose for which the Lord Jesus Christ *"came into the world"* should be accepted by everyone in the world. Notice what Paul is saying in this verse.

(1) First, the Lord Jesus Christ was in Heaven with God the Father and God the Holy Spirit.

(2) Second, He *"came into the world."* This involved the Incarnation, that is God becoming Flesh (1 Timothy 3:16). It took the Virgin birth of the Lord Jesus Christ for Him to become perfect Man as well as perfect God in one Person with two distinct natures.

(3) Third, the purpose for which the Lord Jesus Christ *"came into the world"* was *"to save sinners."* That is what this verse is teaching.

"Sinners" Not Limited to the "Elect"

There is no reason to doubt that *"sinners"* means all *"sinners"* who ever lived or whoever will live. It cannot be limited only to *"elect"* sinners as taught by the hyper-Calvinists. This does not teach universalism that all *"sinners"* will be saved, but this was God's purpose for sending His Son into the world. The choice is up to all the *"sinners"* in the world to accept God's Son as their Saviour. This is an open and valid invitation to *"whosoever will"* to come to the Saviour by genuine faith in Him.

Paul's humility led him to say that he was the *"chief"* of the *"sinners."* Paul was not a puffed-up toad. He was not filled with pride. He acknowledged that he was a sinner. Paul wanted Timothy also to realize that he was a sinner. Those who are saved have both the old nature that sins and the new nature, which is God the Holy Spirit indwelling them. Only by the power of the indwelling Spirit of God can that old nature be controlled (Galatians 5:16). There are a few verses on saving sinners.

* **Matthew 18:11**
  For **the Son of man is come to save that which was lost**.

NIV Drops Out This Vital Verse

If you are reading a New International Version, you will not find that verse. It was removed from the Gnostic manuscripts Vatican ("B") and Sinai ("Aleph") and therefore Westcott and Hort removed it also. The NIV followed these false leaders and took the verse out as well. The Gnostics did not believe that Christ was necessary to be saved. This verse has been removed in most of the modern English versions. This verse shows why the Lord Jesus Christ came to this earth. He came to save the lost.

* **Luke 9:56**
  For **the Son of man is not come to destroy men's lives, but to save** *them*. And they went to another village.

The first part of this verse also gives the purpose of the Lord Jesus Christ's coming to earth. Yet it has been removed by the Gnostic Vatican ("B") and the Sinai ("Aleph") manuscripts, and from the NIV, the NASV, and almost all the modern English versions.

- Luke 19:10
  For the Son of man is come to seek and to save that which was lost.
- Romans 5:6
  For when we were yet without strength, in due time Christ died for the ungodly.

That is why Paul could say that Christ came into the world to save all the "*sinners*" of the world if they would receive Him by faith. Christ "*died for the ungodly.*" Again, this is not merely the "*elect*" ungodly, but all the "*ungodly*" people in the world, bar none.

- Romans 5:8
  But God commendeth his love toward us, in that, while we were yet sinners, Christ died for us.
- 1 Corinthians 1:21
  For after that in the wisdom of God the world by wisdom knew not God, it pleased God by the foolishness of preaching to save them that believe.
- Hebrews 7:25
  Wherefore he is able also to save them to the uttermost that come unto God by him, seeing he ever liveth to make intercession for them.
- James 5:20
  Let him know, that he which converteth the sinner from the error of his way shall save a soul from death, and shall hide a multitude of sins.

This is why the Lord Jesus Christ came to earth.

1 Timothy 1:16

"Howbeit for this cause I obtained mercy, that in me first Jesus Christ might shew forth all longsuffering, for a pattern to them which should hereafter believe on him to life everlasting."

Paul "*obtained mercy*" of the Lord so that he could be a "*pattern*" for those who afterward would believe on the Lord Jesus Christ. God's "*mercy*" is found throughout the Scripture.

- Psalm 23:6
  Surely goodness and mercy shall follow me all the days of my life: and I will dwell in the house of the LORD for ever.

If the Lord Jesus Christ is your Shepherd, this promise can be true for you.

- **Psalm 85:10**
  Mercy and truth are met together; righteousness and peace have kissed *each other*.

At the cross of Calvary God's "*mercy*" and God's "*truth*" met.

- **Psalm 86:5**
  For thou, Lord, *art* good, and ready to forgive; and **plenteous in mercy unto all them that call upon thee**.

- **Psalm 86:15**
  But thou, O Lord, *art* a God full of compassion, and gracious, longsuffering, and **plenteous in mercy** and truth.

- **Luke 18:13**
  And the publican, standing afar off, would not lift up so much as *his* eyes unto heaven, but smote upon his breast, saying, **God be merciful to me a sinner**.

- **Ephesians 2:4**
  But **God, who is rich in mercy**, for his great love wherewith he loved us,

- **Titus 3:5**
  Not by works of righteousness which we have done, but **according to his mercy he saved us**, by the washing of regeneration, and renewing of the Holy Ghost;

- **Hebrews 4:16**
  Let us therefore come boldly unto the throne of grace, **that we may obtain mercy**, and find grace to help in time of need.

Our Saviour Is Seated in Heaven

We who are born-again ought to come in prayer in the Name of the Lord Jesus Christ Who is seated at the Father's right hand.

---

1 Timothy 1:17

"Now unto the King eternal, immortal, invisible, the only wise God, *be* honour and glory for ever and ever. Amen."

The God of the Bible as a "*King*" possesses all six of these Divine attributes.

- **Deuteronomy 33:27**
  The eternal God *is thy* refuge, and **underneath** *are* **the everlasting arms**: and he shall thrust out the enemy from before thee; and shall say, Destroy *them*.

There is no beginning and no end with the God of the Bible. God the Father is eternal. God the Son, the Lord Jesus Christ, is "*eternal.*" God the Holy Spirit is "*eternal.*" All three Persons of the Godhead are also "*immortal,*" "*invisible,*" "*wise,*" honourable and glorious.

- **Colossians 1:15**
  Who is the image of **the invisible God**, the firstborn of every creature:

The Lord Jesus Christ became incarnate. He was "*God manifest in the flesh*" (1 Timothy 3:16). That made God "*visible.*" That is the only way God could be made "*visible.*"

- **Hebrews 11:27**
  By faith he forsook Egypt, not fearing the wrath of the king: for he endured, as **seeing him who is invisible**.

How can you see Someone Who is "*invisible*"? You cannot do it. But Moses did it by faith.

Our God is also "*wise.*" You cannot outsmart the Lord. Do not try it. If you try it, you will fall flat on your face. You cannot do it. Preachers have tried to do that for years. Any other ideas, other than what the Bible says, are crackpot ideas. They are foolish ideas. We must follow the Words of God. God is "*wise.*"

- **Romans 16:27**
  To God only wise, *be* glory through Jesus Christ for ever. Amen. *Written to the Romans from Corinthus, and sent by Phebe servant of the church at Cenchrea.*

- **Jude 25**
  To the only wise God our Saviour, *be* glory and majesty, dominion and power, both now and ever. Amen.

It was God's "*wisdom*" that sent His Son to the cross and into this world to die for sinners such as we. It is God's "*wisdom*" that gives us eternal life, and prepares a place for us in Heaven. That's all of God's wisdom.

1 Timothy 1:18

"This charge I commit unto thee, son Timothy, according to the prophecies which went before on thee, that thou by them mightest war a good warfare;"

Paul told Pastor Timothy that he was to "*war a good warfare.*" That verb for "*war*" is STRATEUOMAI. It means: "*to make a military expedition, to lead soldiers to war or to battle,* [spoken of a commander]*; to do military duty, be on active service, be a soldier; to fight."* The verb is in the Greek present tense. As such, Paul is telling Timothy to continue to *"war a good warfare"* without letting up for one minute. This is not a physical battle, but a spiritual battle for the things of the Lord Jesus Christ and standing up faithfully for the Lord. We who are saved today must be faithful also.

Some Christians have no fight in them. They just give in to the devil and give in to the world. They are like dead fish who float downstream. When you look at some of these so-called Christians on Television and see the way they are dressed and the way they talk, you do not know if they are genuine Christians. We have to war against that wickedness and sin.

The word for *"warfare"* is STRATEIA. It means: *"an expedition, campaign, military service, warfare; metaph. Paul likens his contest with the difficulties that oppose him in the discharge of his apostolic duties, as warfare."* Paul tells Timothy to continue to *"war a good warfare."*

- **2 Corinthians 10:3**
  For though we walk in the flesh, **we do not war after the flesh**:

Don't *"War After the Flesh"*

Every living person is said to *"walk in the flesh,"* but must not *"war after the flesh."* We must not use the *"flesh"* to fight the Lord's battles. They are spiritual battles.

- **2 Corinthians 10:4**
  (For **the weapons of our warfare *are* not carnal, but mighty** through God to the pulling down of strong holds;)

God's weaponry will pull down spiritual *"strong holds."* Every born-again Christian is fighting a spiritual battle against at least three enemies.

(1) The Flesh. The first enemy for the Christian is the flesh. He or she has two natures, the flesh and the new nature received by regeneration. Because of this every believer has a battle with his flesh. The Holy Spirit of God can help him defeat the power of the flesh.

(2) The World. A second enemy of the Christian is the world all around us.

(3) The Devil. A third enemy that every Christian has is the Devil. He is a person, not merely an influence. He is not omnipotent or eternal. He is invisible, but he is not God. He is not all-powerful. When we go to battle with spiritual forces, we must have spiritual weapons. If you go to battle against the Devil, you must have the power of God. The flesh will not do it.

- **1 John 4:4**
  Ye are of God, little children, and have overcome them: because **greater is he that is in you, than he that is in the world**.

1 Timothy 1:19

"Holding faith, and a good conscience; which some having put away concerning faith have made shipwreck:"

This verb *"holding"* is in the present tense which implies a continuous action. Paul is saying, *"Timothy <u>continue</u> to hold on to faith and a good conscience."* The reason Paul is so insistent that Pastor Timothy *"continue"* to hold on to *"the faith"* and a *"good conscience"* is that some have *"put away"* *"the faith"* and have made *"shipwreck."* That word for *"put away"* is APOTHEOMAI. It is translated as follows in our King James Bible: *"cast away"* (two times); *"thrust away"* (one time); *"put from"* (one time); *"thrust from"* (one time); and *"put away"* (one time). It is found a total of six times in the New Testament. It means: *"to thrust away, push away, repel; to thrust away from one's self, to drive away from one's self; repudiate, reject, refuse."*

Multitudes Reject "The Faith"

Some people in Timothy's day had (and many in our day have) rejected *"the faith."* The Greek words for *"the faith"* are TEN PISTIN.

TEN is an article. When the article precedes PISTIN (*"faith"*) it refers to the body of doctrine found in the Bible rather than personal *"faith."* Paul is telling Timothy not to *"put away"* the sound doctrine he had been taught. He was to *"hold"* on to it.

The word for *"conscience"* is SUNEIDESIN. It means:

"the consciousness of anything; the soul as distinguishing between what is morally good and bad, prompting to do the former and shun the latter, commending one, condemning the other; the conscience."

Paul wanted Pastor Timothy to have a *"good conscience."* Many people have a *"conscience,"* which is *"seared with a hot iron"* (1 Timothy 4:2).

Christians With "Seared" Consciences

Someone asked me recently if Christians could have a seared conscience. I believe that they can if they do not follow the things of the Lord.

These people who have "*put away*" from them "*the faith*" have made "*shipwreck*" of that body of doctrine and of themselves as well. That is what he is saying. Paul was in a shipwreck as recorded in Acts 27:14-41. The ship was a total loss because of the tempestuous storm.

- **2 Corinthians 11:25**
  Thrice was I beaten with rods, once was I stoned, **thrice I suffered shipwreck, a night and a day I have been in the deep**;

Paul was shipwrecked three times, so he knew what it was like to be shipwrecked. God wants His saved ones to have a "*good conscience*" as they live their lives on this earth.

- **Acts 24:16**
  And herein do I exercise myself, **to have always a conscience void of offence toward God, and** *toward* men.

- **1 Timothy 1:5**
  Now the end of the commandment is charity out of a pure heart, and **of a good conscience**, and *of* faith unfeigned:

1 Timothy 1:20

"Of whom is Hymenaeus and Alexander; whom I have delivered unto Satan, that they may learn not to blaspheme."

Here in this verse we see that Paul names two people, "*Hymenaeus and Alexander,*" who have "*put away*" sound doctrine and "*the faith*" of the Bible. Paul names various names to warn his readers about their false doctrines.

- **2 Timothy 2:17**
  And their word will eat as doth a canker: **of whom is Hymenaeus and Philetus;**

Paul names the names of those who are not being true to the doctrine of the Bible, and we should do so as well. When I talk about the hyper-Calvinists who are preaching error, I name Harold Camping of Family Radio which is heard in our area and all around the world. I name Billy Graham and Jack Hyles when I talk about things where they have departed from sound doctrine. Paul named some names in his day as well, setting an example for those of us today.

- **2 Timothy 4:14**
  Alexander the coppersmith did me much evil: the Lord reward him according to his works:

Here is a man Paul talked about. He also wanted Timothy to beware of Alexander. We also must warn the saints against false teachers.

- **1 Corinthians 5:5**
  To deliver such an one unto Satan for the destruction of the flesh, that the spirit may be saved in the day of the Lord Jesus.

I suppose he means to let Satan take charge of judging that person because of his evil. Who is Satan? Some have written this concerning the meaning of Satan and what he does:

> "*adversary (one who opposes another in purpose or act),* [1] *the name given to the prince of evil spirits,* [2] *the inveterate adversary of God and Christ;* [3] *he incites apostasy from God and to sin;* [4] *circumventing men by his wiles;* [5] *the worshippers of idols are said to be under his control by his demons he is able to take possession of men and inflict them with diseases;* [6] *by God's assistance he is overcome;* [7] *on Christ's return from heaven he will be bound with chains for a thousand years,* [8] *but when the thousand years are finished he will walk the earth in yet greater power,* [9] *but shortly after will be given over to eternal punishment; a Satan-like man.*"

Be Aware of Satan's Devices & Wiles

He is God's enemy, and we who are saved must be aware of Satan and of his devious "*devices*" and "*wiles.*"

- **2 Corinthians 2:11**
  Lest Satan should get an advantage of us: for **we are not ignorant of his devices.**
- **Ephesians 6:11**
  Put on the whole armour of God, **that ye may be able to stand against the wiles of the devil.**

The judgment of Satan against these two men was to have them "*learn not to blaspheme*" the Name of the Lord Jesus Christ and God the Father.

First Timothy
Chapter Two

1 Timothy 2:1

"I exhort therefore, that, first of all, supplications, prayers, intercessions, *and* giving of thanks, be made for all men;"

Paul is writing to Timothy who is a Pastor in Ephesus. This was one of the largest cities in Asia Minor (now Turkey). Paul instructed Timothy about various prayers to the Lord. There was to be made **(1)** *"supplications,"* **(2)** *"prayers,"* **(3)** *"intercessions,"* and **(4)** *"giving of thanks."*

Four Kinds of Prayers

(1) *"Supplications"* are requests. In prayer meetings it seems that there are more *"supplications"* or requests than any other sort of prayer. People have requests for many things: for sickness, for jobs, for spiritual uplifting, for family problems, for the salvation of others, for government, and for many other things. Paul encourages people to make these *"supplications."*

(2) *"Prayers"* should also be made. *"Prayer"* is talking and communicating with the Lord. If you are saved you can talk to the Lord and He will hear you. If you are unsaved the Lord does not hear your *"prayers."*

(3) *"Intercessions"* are to be made because people need to have *prayers"* made by other people on their behalf. Maybe they cannot pray for themselves, but the Lord can touch them and help them if born-again Christians are faithful in interceding for them.

(4) *"Giving of thanks"* should take place. Christians should be especially thankful for all the Lord Jesus Christ has done for them.

- **Luke 18:1**
  And he spake a parable unto them to this end, that **men
  ought always to pray, and not to faint;**

Prayer is to be made at all times and always. In our church, we have our prayer meetings every Thursday night, and we urge those who can come to be with us and to pray with us.

- **Ephesians 6:19**
  And for me, that utterance may be given unto me, that I
  may open my mouth boldly, to make known the mystery of the
  gospel,

A part of the Christian's armour is prayer (Ephesians 6:13-18).

- **1 Thessalonians 5:17**
  Pray without ceasing.

This verse tells us how long and when we should pray. We do not have to speak our "*prayer*" out loud. We can think it and pray silently. We have to be in touch with the Lord. We have to stay in contact with the Lord. We need prayer. We need to pray for ourselves and for others. We all have "*problems*" even though today people call them "*issues.*"

"Intercession"

The Father knows your heartache;
He hears your faintest cry;
And all the while you're anxious,
He's guarding with His eye.

The Spirit knows your problem;
He whispers in my ear,
"A saint is sad and crying,
Is overcome by fear."

I raise my heart to Heaven,
I tell Father there
That one He loves is anxious,
And needs His loving care.

Then the loving Saviour
Takes my humble plea,
And places it with your prayer
Which has preceded me.

Then He sends His warm compassion,
And sweet peace upon your soul
As you learn to lean on Jesus,
And to let Him take control.

By Gertrude G. Sanborn
With Tears In My Heart

1 Timothy 2:2

"For kings, and *for* all that are in authority; that we may lead a quiet and peaceable life in all godliness and honesty."

In addition to praying for "*all men*," we who are saved are instructed to pray also for two more classes of people.

For Whom Should We Pray?

(1) we are to pray "*for kings.*" They are the ones who are ruling. We do not have kings in the United States. Presently there is a queen in England. There are kings and queens in other countries. English people had a king at that time our King James Bible was translated in England. Those translated Words are Scripture . Our Old Testament speaks about kings. Kings are those who are ruling.

(2) We should also pray for "*all that are in authority.*" You might not like those who are "*in authority*," but you should "*pray*" for them anyway. We must pray for our president, our governors, our mayors, and all those who are in authority even if we do not agree with the people in authority. Many of them are wicked sinners who are "*in authority.*" That is why we must vote for the right people.

Sinners should make right decisions even if they are sinners. This verse does not say we have to agree with them. I do not agree with our mayor or with some of the articles in our town's newspaper. The **Bible For Today Baptist Church** has an advertisement in that paper every single week for our church. In that paper, a while ago, there was a picture of eight homosexuals right there in the paper, and their sexual orientation was given. I do not like that at all.

Our mayor is encouraging the homosexual lifestyle right here in our town. I am opposed to that lifestyle and believe it to be sinful and an "*abomination*" in the sight of God as the Bible calls it (Leviticus 18:22; 20:13). But, according to this verse (1 Timothy 2:2), I am to pray for my mayor. A friend of mine wrote a letter to the editor about that picture and asked when the paper was going to have a picture of straight people with their names included. They have had no such pictures to date.

The Purpose of Prayer For Leaders

The purpose of *"prayer"* for the leaders *"in authority"* is that Bible believing Christians *"may lead a quiet and peaceable life in all godliness and honesty."*

Both Paul and Timothy were under terrific persecution. They wanted to *"lead a quiet and peaceable life."* They wanted to live it *"in all godliness and honesty."* Many people with governments that are wicked and evil need our prayers. We also must pray that we will continue to *"lead a quiet and peaceable life"* in our church and that we may continue to preach the Words of God without fear or favor. We must pray that our Internet ministry and shortwave radio ministry might continue to cover potentially every nation of the world. You can hear and see our video and audio Internet ministry on our Website at **www.BibleForToday.org**. In the last two months (at the time of writing), there were 6,200 and 7,100 downloads of our 1,656 messages. There were a total of 1,057,346 views of that site. There were over 60 foreign countries and every one of our 50 states that downloaded at least one of our messages during these months. Please pray that this outreach might continue!

We must pray that nobody will storm the church and close us down. I got a letter two weeks ago from the zoning board. There is a person across the street that wants to build an extension on their property and since we live close by we had to give our okay. I thought that this letter was going to be about our church. I was glad that it was not about our church.

I met with that zoning man about our signs. We had to withdraw our signs, but we could still continue with our Bible studies and weekly church services. Some states are closing down *"home"* churches. We have heard about it. Yes, home Bible studies and churches are being stopped. I am glad that we have a *"quiet and peaceable life"* so far. That word for honesty is SEMNOTES. It means: *"the characteristic of a thing or person which entitles to reverence and respect, dignity, majesty, sanctity; honour, purity."* May we live Godly lives worthy of respect. We should be praying for that.

1 Timothy 2:3

"For this *is* good and acceptable in the sight of God our Saviour;"

This praying for those who are *"in authority"* and for all men is *"good and acceptable in the sight of God our Saviour."* This is not a reference to Christ our *"Saviour."* It is true that He is the *"Saviour"* of those who have genuinely trusted Him. In this passage, the reference is *"God our Saviour."* This refers to God the Father. Many times in the Bible we read that the Lord Jesus Christ is a *"Saviour,"* but God is also our *"Saviour."*   Some people do not realize this.

- **Luke 1:47**
  And my spirit hath rejoiced in **God my Saviour**.
- **1 Timothy 2:3**
  For this is good and acceptable in the sight of **God our Saviour;**

The Ministry of God the Father

In what sense is *"God our Saviour"*? God the Father prepared salvation for the sinful world in which we live. He prepared salvation for sinners. Part of God's preparation for salvation was to send the Lord Jesus Christ to be the "Saviour" for those who genuinely trust Him and believe in Him. The Holy Spirit applies that salvation as people trust and believe in the Lord Jesus Christ by saving faith.

- **1 Timothy 4:10**
  For therefore we both labour and suffer reproach, because we trust in **the living God, who is the Saviour of all men, specially of those that believe**.

He is the Saviour of all the people who genuinely believe. He provides salvation for all; if they sincerely trust in Him, they can be saved.

- **Titus 1:3**
  But hath in due times manifested his word through preaching, which is committed unto me according to the commandment of **God our Saviour;**
- **Titus 2:10**
  Not purloining, but shewing all good fidelity; that they may adorn the doctrine of **God our Saviour** in all things.
- **Titus 3:4**
  But after that the kindness and love of **God our Saviour** toward man appeared,
- **Jude 25**
  To the only wise **God our Saviour**, be glory and majesty, dominion and power, both now and ever. Amen.

Never in my ministry have I referred to God the Father as my *"Saviour,"* but it says so right here in this verse.

There are other verses, which refer to God the Son as our *"Saviour."*

- **Luke 2:11**

  For unto you is born this day in the city of David **a Saviour, which is Christ the Lord.**

He is the "*Saviour*" because He fulfilled all of the Divine requirements for providing salvation to lost sinners.

- **John 4:42**

  And said unto the woman, Now we believe, not because of thy saying: for we have heard him ourselves, and know that this is indeed the **Christ, the Saviour of the world**.

He has provided salvation for the entire world **if** they will only trust and receive Him in saving faith.

- **Acts 5:31**

  Him hath **God exalted with his right hand to be a Prince and a Saviour,** for to give repentance to Israel, and forgiveness of sins.

- **Acts 13:23**

  Of this man's seed hath God according to his promise raised unto Israel **a Saviour, Jesus**:

- **Philippians 3:20**

  For our conversation is in heaven; from whence also we look for **the Saviour, the Lord Jesus Christ**:

- **2 Timothy 1:10**

  But is now made manifest by the appearing of **our Saviour Jesus Christ**, who hath abolished death, and hath brought life and immortality to light through the gospel:

- **Titus 2:13**

  Looking for that blessed hope, and the glorious appearing of **the great God and our Saviour Jesus Christ**;

Here we have the Deity of the Lord Jesus Christ taught very clearly. I believe the "*blessed hope*" is the rapture of the born-again believers in this present church age. These are those who will be caught up to be with Christ at his coming to meet Him in the clouds (1 Thessalonians 4:16-18). The "*glorious appearing*" of the Lord Jesus Christ will come after the seven years of the Tribulation period. After this Tribulation, The Lord Jesus Christ will come back to this earth to set up His thousand-year millennial reign (Revelation 20:6).

The last part of this verse speaks of "*the great God and our Saviour Jesus Christ.*" Some people have criticized the King James Bible and have said that is not saying Christ is God, but it is. The word "*and*" is the Greek word KAI which means "*and*" or "*even.*" This word identifies people. In this case it is the great God even our Saviour the Lord Jesus Christ. It is referring to the same Person. This verse clearly teaches that the Lord Jesus Christ is and ever will be perfect God as well as perfect Man.

- 1 John 4:14
  And we have seen and do testify that the Father sent **the Son to be the Saviour of the world.**

God the Father sent His Son the Lord Jesus Christ to be the "*Saviour*" of the world. That does not mean that the entire world has accepted Him as their "*Saviour.*" That was His destiny and purpose, to be the "*Saviour*" of the entire world. If the entire world would accept Him, genuinely trust in Him, and receive Him, they would then have Him as their "*Saviour*" and be saved by faith in Him. There is tremendous truth here in verse three that God is referred to as "*God our Saviour.*" Our God is a Trinity. If God the Father, God the Son, and God the Holy Spirit did not plan salvation, make salvation possible, and apply salvation to those who believe, no one would have it.

The Trinity's Work In Salvation

It is God the Father Who planned it, God the Son Who fulfilled it, and God the Holy Spirit Who applies it to those who sincerely trust in Him. The entire Trinity is involved in God's eternal salvation.

---

1 Timothy 2:4

"Who will have all men to be saved, and to come unto the knowledge of the truth."

That is another reason why "*God our Saviour*" refers to the Father. It is God the Father "*who will have all men to be saved.*"

A Serious Hyper-Calvinist Error

This verse brings to the forefront a controversy that we have with our friends, the hyper-Calvinists. In reality, they deny the clear teaching of this verse. They do not believe that God wills and wants to have "*all men to be saved.*" They do not believe that. This word "*will*" is not simply an indication of futurity such as in the sentences, "*I will come tomorrow, I will go home, I will sit in the* chair, or *I will sing.*" Each of the uses of "*will*" in these sentences is an indicator of future time. The "*will*" in this present verse, however, is the verb THELO. It means:

> "*to will, have in mind, intend; to be resolved or determined, to purpose; to desire, to wish; to love; to like to do a thing, be fond of doing; to take delight in, have pleasure.*"

All people will not be saved. The reason for this is because they do not genuinely accept and receive the Lord Jesus Christ for their salvation. This does not set aside the fact that God really "*wills*" and "*wishes*" that all people will be "*saved and come to the knowledge of the truth.*" If they come through "*the Way, the Truth and the Life,*" the Lord Jesus Christ (John 14:6), they will be "*saved*" for all eternity. Our friends the hyper-Calvinists do not believe this. They believe that God only "*wills*" and wants the elect to be saved but nobody else. They do not believe that the Lord Jesus Christ died for the sins of the whole world as the Bible clearly and repeatedly states, but that He died only and exclusively for what they term "*the elect.*" The rest of the people are unable to believe on the Lord Jesus Christ and are bound for Hell because Jesus did not die for their sins. This is one of the most false and despicable "*other gospels*" (Galatians 1:6-7) ever enunciated by mortal man!

If you are a hyper-Calvinist when you preach the gospel of the Lord Jesus Christ, you cannot say that "*Christ died for your sins*" because you only believe that to be true if the listener is one of "*the elect.*" God says in 1 Timothy 2:4 that He wants and "*wills*" for all "*to be saved and to come unto the knowledge of the truth.*" But for this salvation to be accomplished, each person must change his or her mind regarding their sins and the Saviour and genuinely believe in and receive the Lord Jesus Christ as their Saviour.

* **Matthew 11:28**
  Come unto me, all ye that labour and are heavy laden, and I will give you rest.
  There are at least three parts to this verse which was spoken by the Lord Jesus Christ Himself:

    1.   This is a universal invitation.

    2.   The Lord Jesus Christ invited all people hearing Him to come unto Him and be saved.

    3.   His invitation is still good for anyone in the whole world.

- **Matthew 23:37**

  O Jerusalem, Jerusalem, thou that killest the prophets, and stonest them which are sent unto thee, **how often would I have gathered thy children together, even as a hen gathereth her chickens under her wings, and ye would not!**

It is the will of the Lord Jesus Christ that all the people in the world would come to Him in faith and be saved. Every person in the world has been given by the Lord a free will to accept or reject the Lord Jesus Christ according to this verse. What does the Bible say about all those who genuinely accept the Lord Jesus Christ?

- **John 3:16**

  For **God so loved the world**, that he gave his only begotten Son, **that whosoever believeth in him should not perish, but have everlasting life**.

Again, our hyper-Calvinists friends say that "*world*" does not mean "*world*" but only the "world of the elect." They do not believe that God loves everybody in the "*world.*" They misinterpret this gospel verse entirely. Family Radio passes out their tract written by Harold Camping. It has been translated into many languages and is distributed all over the world. The title of the tract is "*Does God Love You?*" That tract is a hyper-Calvinist tract. In the tract, Mr. Camping very cleverly concludes that God does not love everybody in the "*world*" (though this verse shouts it out very clearly) but only the few chosen elect. God the Father and the Lord Jesus Christ do love the whole "*world.*" If people reject this "*love,*" they cannot blame either God the Father or God the Son. They have only themselves to blame and they will "*perish*" in the Lake of Fire for all eternity. If, on the other hand, they accept and genuinely receive and believe in the Lord Jesus Christ, God's Son, they will "*not perish, but have everlasting life.*" This is God's promise that He is duty-bound to keep.

- **John 3:17**

  For God sent not his Son into the world to condemn the world; but **that the world through him might be saved**.

Christ Came the First Time to Save

God did not send *"His Son into the world to condemn* [or judge] *the world"* when He came the first time in His Incarnation. It is God's will that all *"the world through Him* [His Son] *might be saved."* When the Lord Jesus Christ comes back in His second coming to earth, it will be to judge and *"condemn"* the world. His mission the first time was to die for the sins of the world so that by personal and genuine faith in Him they could be saved and have everlasting life. If a person trusts in the Lord Jesus Christ they can be saved. If they reject Him, they will be lost in Hell for all eternity. It is as simple and as plain as that.

- **2 Peter 3:9**

  The Lord is not slack concerning his promise, as some men count slackness; but is longsuffering to us-ward, **not willing that any should perish, but that all should come to repentance**.

A hyper-Calvinist called me recently. I did not argue with him, I simply quoted John 1:29b *"Behold the Lamb of God, which **taketh away the sin of the world**."* I also quoted him 2 Peter 3:9. In this verse, it is very clearly stated that God is *"not willing that any should perish, but that all should come to repentance."* Language could not be any clearer than that. God wants every one in the whole world to come to the Lord Jesus Christ in *"repentance"* and accept Him by faith. Just because God offers salvation to everyone in the world does not mean that every one in the world will accept His gracious offer. Nor does this verse teach universalism, that is, that God is going to save everyone in the world. I can offer you a million dollars, but it is not yours until you receive it. Offers do not count, reception does.

- **1 John 4:14**

  And we have seen and do testify that **the Father sent the Son to be the Saviour of the world.**

This explains the mission of the Lord Jesus Christ. It explains why God the Father sent Him into this world. There is no other Saviour other than the Lord Jesus Christ. Shinto cannot save. Mohammed cannot save. Buddha cannot save. Confucius cannot save. The Pope cannot save. Priests cannot save. Pastors cannot save. Rabbis cannot save. Only the Lord Jesus Christ was sent *"to be the Saviour of the world,"* and only He can save any sinner in the world who sincerely trusts Him.

The final "nail in the coffin," so to speak, of the hyper-Calvinists who do not believe that God wants everyone to be saved, if they genuinely trust in the

Lord Jesus Christ, is found in the last chapter of the Bible.

- **Revelation 22:17**
  And the Spirit and the bride say, Come. And let him that heareth say, Come. And let him that is athirst come. And **whosoever will, let him take the water of life freely**.

"Whosoever Will"--Not the "Elect"

This offer by *"the Spirit and the bride"* is not just for *"the elect."* It is a genuine offer for *"whosoever will."* It is for everyone in the world who ever lived, whoever lives now, or whoever will live in the future. I preach and firmly believe in a *"whosoever will"* gospel. That is the Bible's clear teaching. Let me quote again John 3:16:

- **John 3:16**
  For God so loved the world, that he gave his only begotten Son, **that whosoever believeth in him should not perish, but have everlasting life**.

1 Timothy 2:5

"For *there is* one God, and one mediator between God and men, the man Christ Jesus;"

There are not several gods, but only one God. He is not Allah as the Muslims wrongly believe. Nor is it the multitude of the gods of the heathen that Paul confronted on Mars' hill (Acts 17:22-25). The heathen do not agree with this verse. They believe there is a multiplicity of gods. That is the one thing that God clearly taught the nation of Israel, the unity of *"God."* The Bible teaches this *"unity"* as a *"Tri-unity"* or *"Trinity"* consisting of three Persons, yet one *"God"* consisting of *"God "* the Father, *"God"* the Son, and *"God"* the Holy Spirit. All the heathen round about Israel believed in more than one god. They were polytheists. Abraham came from a heathen home. All those people worshiped gods, but *"God"* showed clearly to Abraham His unity.

Not only is there but one God, there is also only *"one Mediator between God and men, the Man Christ Jesus."* Though I love Catholic people and want them to be genuinely saved, I despise most of the prominent doctrines of the Roman Catholic Church. One of the doctrines of Rome is that Mary has now become the mediatrix *"between God and men."* That is nowhere found in the Bible. It is blasphemy, and it is certainly contrary to this verse. There is only *"one Mediator between God and men"* and that one and only Mediator is *"the Man Christ Jesus"* (1 Timothy 2:5).

Christ the Only "Mediator"

The Lord Jesus Christs could be a suitable and proper "*Mediator between God and men*" because He was both perfect God and perfect Man. There is none other who could fulfill that position but He. Saints cannot do it. Preachers cannot do it. Rabbis cannot do it. Popes cannot do it. Certainly Mary cannot do it. The "*Man Christ Jesus*" is the only "*Mediator.*" The word for "*Mediator*" is MESITES. It means:

> "*one who intervenes between two, either in order to make or restore peace and friendship, or form a compact, or for ratifying a covenant; a medium of communication, arbitrator.*"

Our wonderful and faithful Lord Jesus Christ is the precious "*Mediator*" for all those who have been born-again by genuine faith in Him. This is what we who are saved need desperately, and we have Him! He intervenes between God the Father and His saved children.

We have been hearing recently about a soon-coming strike in one of the school districts. There is a state "*mediator*" who is coming to get the two sides together to hear both of their arguments and try to avoid the strike. The patriarch Job complained that he had no "*Mediator*" or "*Daysman*" to help him in his distress and sorrow.

- Job 9:32-33

  For he is not a man, as I am, that I should answer him, and we should come together in judgment. **Neither is there any daysman betwixt us, that might lay his hand upon us both.**

That is what the Lord Jesus Christ was able to do. He was the *Theanthropos*, the God-Man. He was perfect God and perfect Man. He is our "Daysman" and "*Mediator between God and men*" that Job cried out for.

- Hebrews 2:17

  Wherefore **in all things it behoved him to be made like unto his brethren, that he might be a merciful and faithful high priest** in things pertaining to God, to make reconciliation for the sins of the people.

The Lord Jesus Christ is a "*faithful High Priest*" for those He has saved. He knows our testings because He was tested. Satan tested Him in the wilderness for forty days and forty nights. He was without sin and did not yield to Satan's testings, nor could He since He was God the Son. He did not sin and He could not sin!

- Hebrews 7:28
  For the law maketh men high priests which have infirmity; but **the word of the oath, which was since the law, maketh the Son, who is consecrated for evermore**.
- Hebrews 12:24
  And to **Jesus the mediator of the new covenant**, and to the blood of sprinkling, that speaketh better things than that of Abel.
- John 14:6
  Jesus saith unto him, **I am the way, the truth, and the life: no man cometh unto the Father, but by me**.

The Lord Jesus Christ truly is the one and only "*Mediator*."

1 Timothy 2:6

"Who gave himself a ransom for all, to be testified in due time."

The Lord Jesus Christ is being referred to here. That word "*Who*" refers back to the Lord Jesus Christ, the one and only true "*Mediator between God and men*." The words "*gave Himself*" speak of His leaving Heaven to come to earth and become Incarnate God. They also, and more specifically, speak of His voluntary, substitutionary, expiatory death on Calvary's cross to suffer and die for the sins of the entire world in order that those who truly trust in Him might be saved from Hell, have everlasting life, and dwell with Him in Heaven forevermore. The words "*to be testified in due time*," no doubt, refer to how Paul intended to continue talking about the "*ransom*" of the Lord Jesus Christ in his other letters in the book of Hebrews, for instance, where Paul "*testifies*" at length concerning our Saviour's "*ransom for all*."

Hyper-Calvinism Wrong Once Again

The words "*gave Himself a ransom for all*" greatly disturbs our hyper-Calvinist friends, and rightly so. They do not believe the clear teaching of this verse that the Lord Jesus Christ is a "*ransom for all*" people of the world without a single exception. They only believe that He is only a "*ransom*" for "*the elect*." They twist and warp the words "*for all*" into their preconceived and heretical view that this means "*the elect*" only. No, the Lord Jesus Christ is "*a ransom for all*" people who ever lived whether in the past, the present, or the future. This is the clear teaching and doctrine of this verse and many others.

The word for *"ransom"* is ANTILUTRON. It means: *"what is given in exchange for another as the price of his redemption, ransom."* When a person is kidnaped, the kidnappers usually ask for a ransom in exchange for the safe return of the kidnaped person.

- **Isaiah 53:6**
  All we like sheep have gone astray; we have turned every one to his own way; and **the LORD hath laid on him the iniquity of us <u>all</u>.**

The *"all"* in that verse means *"all"* people, not just the elect. Do you remember in Acts 8:26-39 when Philip was told to go to the desert to meet a man and tell him about the Lord Jesus Christ? He met an Ethiopian Eunuch who was reading Isaiah Chapter 53. The Ethiopian Eunuch asked Phillip, *"Of whom speaketh the prophet? of himself, or of some other man?"* (v. 34) The Bible says that *"Phillip opened his mouth, and began at the same Scripture, and preached unto him Jesus"* (v. 35). Philip did not ask the man if he were one of *"the elect,"* but he told him about the Lord Jesus Christ and how He died for his sin. The man received the Lord Jesus Christ as His Saviour (v. 37), was baptized by immersion (v. 38), and *"went on his way rejoicing"* (v. 39).

NIV & Other Version Omit Acts 8:37

The New International Version and some other modern versions follow the Critical Text made popular by Bishop Westcott and Professor Hort, omit all of verse 37 in Acts 8. This verse has valid support and is rightly included in our King James Bible.

- **John 1:29**
  Behold **the Lamb of God, which taketh away the sin of the world.**

The *"sin of the world"* has been taken away by the sacrifice of the *"Lamb of God,"* the Lord Jesus Christ. It remains for every person in the *"world"* to come in faith to the Saviour who indeed has taken away *"the sin of the world."* As some Pastors have said before, *"It is now no longer the <u>sin</u> question, but the <u>Son</u> question."* There is no one in the world who needs to go to Hell for their sins, because their sins have been paid for by the Lord Jesus Christ. The thing that will send them to Hell is their rejection of that One Who paid for their sins and invites them to come unto Him by genuine faith. They must roll their sins onto the Sin-Bearer or else they must pay for them themselves and spend an eternity in Hell.

- John 3:16
  For God so loved the world, that he gave his only begotten Son, **that whosoever believeth in him should not perish, but have everlasting life.**

That is why the Lord Jesus Christ came.

- John 5:24
  Verily, verily, I say unto you, He that heareth my word, and **believeth on him that sent me, hath everlasting life**, and shall not come into condemnation; but is passed from death unto life.

The Lord Jesus Christ gave Himself *"a ransom for all"* so that the one who truly trusts in Him might *"pass from death unto life."*

- Acts 16:30-31
  And brought them out, and said, Sirs, what must I do to be saved? And they said, **Believe on the Lord Jesus Christ, and thou shalt be saved, and thy house.**

I have never found a hyper-Calvinist who could satisfactorily explain these verses.

The Jailer Was Told To "Believe"

The Philippian jailer had watched Paul and Silas' testimony. He knew that they had a strong faith in their Saviour even in the jail at Philippi. You will notice that Paul treated this jailer as though he had the ability of credence or belief. He did not ask first whether or not he was one of *"the elect."* He assumed that the Lord Jesus Christ died for his sins and that he was able to be saved if he genuinely trusted in Him. He truly *"believed on the Lord Jesus Christ"* and was saved. The people in his *"house"* also believed and were saved. Then they followed the Lord in water baptism by immersion. There is a possibility for every person to accept Jesus Christ as their Saviour. The jailer did believe and so did his family.

- Romans 5:6
  For when we were yet **without strength**, in due time **Christ died for the ungodly**.
- Romans 5:8
  But God commendeth his love toward us, in that, **while we were yet sinners, Christ died for us**.

- 1 John 2:2

  And **he is the propitiation for our sins: and not for ours only, but also <u>for the sins of the whole world</u>**.

The "*ungodly,*" and "*sinners,*" and "*the whole world*" includes everybody who ever lived, not merely "*the elect.*" That is a clear picture of the Lord Jesus Christ's unlimited atonement for all "*the sins of whole the world.*" This is in stark contrast to the hyper-Calvinists' belief in a limited atonement restricted only to "*the elect.*"

- 2 Corinthians 5:19

  To wit, that God was in Christ, **reconciling the world unto himself, not imputing their trespasses unto them**; and hath committed unto us the word of reconciliation.

He reconciled the whole world, and all the "*sins of the whole world*" were placed upon the Lord Jesus Christ. We must trust that Saviour. Here are the words of a beautiful gospel song entitled "*He Ransomed Me.*" It was written by Julia H. Johnston:

"He Ransomed Me"

"There's a sweet and blessed story
Of the Christ Who came from glory
Just to rescue me from sin and misery;
He in loving kindness sought me,
And from sin and shame hath brought me,
Hallelujah! Jesus ransomed me.
Hallelujah, what a Saviour!
Who can take a poor lost sinner,
Lift him from the miry clay and set him free;
I will ever tell the story,
Shouting glory, glory, glory,
Hallelujah! Jesus ransomed me."

By Julia H. Johnston

Our Saviour, the Lord Jesus Christ, has paid the "*ransom*" for all the sinners of the world. Now, all they must do to gain the benefits of that "*ransom*" is to genuinely receive the Saviour Who made it possible.

1 Timothy 2:7

"Whereunto I am ordained a preacher, and an apostle, (I speak the truth in Christ, *and* lie not;) a teacher of the Gentiles in faith and verity."

The word *"whereunto"* goes back to Paul's going to bear *"testimony"* of these truths *"in due time."* It includes the gospel message that he proclaimed. Paul is talking about this gospel that was preached. We have our New Testament, which testifies of this *"ransom for all."*

Paul says that he is *"ordained a preacher"* of this gospel. Paul is a *"preacher,"* an *"apostle,"* and a *"teacher"* of the gospel. The word for *"preacher"* is KERUX. It means:

"a herald or messenger vested with public authority, who conveyed the official messages of kings, magistrates, princes, military commanders, or who gave a public summons or demand, and performed various other duties. In the NT God's ambassador, and the herald or proclaimer of the divine Word."

In other words, *"preachers"* or heralds represented the king. In the New Testament, God's *"ambassadors,"* as *"heralds,"* were to be *"proclaimers of the divine Word,"* the Scriptures. As *"heralds"* we who are *"preachers"* are not to change God's Words. No *"herald"* has any right or privilege to change any of the king's messages. We are to proclaim those Words as they are.

Preachers Who Alter God's Words

The *"preachers"* and paraphrasers who alter the Words of God with their phony translations and their incorrect Hebrew, Aramaic, and Greek texts are changing what God has said. That is a very serious thing to do. *"Preachers"* must preach what God has told them to preach. They can apply it, talk about it, and explain it, but they are to *"preach the Word."*

● 2 Timothy 4:2

Preach the word; be instant in season, out of season; reprove, rebuke, exhort with all longsuffering and doctrine.

- **2 Timothy 1:8-11**
  Be not thou therefore ashamed of the testimony of our Lord, nor of me his prisoner: but be thou partaker of the afflictions of the gospel according to the power of God; Who hath saved us, and called us with an holy calling, not according to our works, but according to his own purpose and grace, which was given us in Christ Jesus before the world began, But is now made manifest by the appearing of our Saviour Jesus Christ, who hath abolished death, and hath brought life and immortality to light through the gospel: **Whereunto I am appointed a preacher, and an apostle, and a teacher of the Gentiles.**
- **2 Timothy 2:2**
  And the things that thou hast heard of me among many witnesses, **the same commit thou to faithful men, who shall be able to teach others also**.

In the book of Acts, the apostles got together and elected Mathias as the twelfth apostle after Judas died. Some people feel that Mathias was the proper one. I believe that Paul was the one who replaced Judas. He was called and chosen an "*apostle*" by the Lord Jesus Christ Himself.

I am seeking to commit to "*faithful men*" the great truths of the Bible at the **Bible For Today Baptist Church**. We do this by audio tapes, by videos of our services, by the Internet (at **www.BibleForToday.org** 24/7), by books of our Bible teaching, and in our services. The truths found in the Words of God should not stop with us. We are to be "*teachers*" and examples to others. I am glad that Paul set the example as being a "*teacher*." The Lord Jesus Christ was also a "*teacher*." Teachers are first of all to have their own life in order. After that both their teaching and life can be followed by others.

1 Timothy 2:8

"I will therefore that men pray every where, lifting up holy hands, without wrath and doubting."

Paul mentions his "*will*" here. It is God's "*will*" as well since it is in His Word here. Since it is in the present tense, it is to be a continuous action. It is a continuous desire.

Males Only To Pray in Mixed Groups

When Paul told Pastor Timothy that he desired *"that men pray everywhere"* he was teaching that in the local church meetings the males were to lead in prayer, not the females. The word for *"men"* here is ANER, which is the exclusive word for *"males."* They should *"pray"* by *"lifting up holy hands, without wrath and doubting"*

The women can pray orally in their homes, in strictly women's meetings, and always silently anywhere. But in mixed church services where men and women are present, only the *"men"* (MALES) are to lead in public prayer. This is clearly what this verse is teaching Pastor Timothy. It was to serve as a pattern for his local church in Ephesus, and by application, for every local church for all time and in all places around the world. I desire that every man in our church would be able to lead in prayer in our congregational and in our prayer meetings. I realize that this teaching is not believed or practiced in most Bible-believing churches in our days.

Praying Men Must Have *"Holy Hands"*

The prayers of Timothy's men in his local church should be from those who had *"holy hands."* They should not be hypocrites or wicked men. These men should also be free from *"wrath"* or anger and bitterness. They should be walking with the Lord and in fellowship with Him. Christian men should practice praying in public by praying orally in their homes.

- 1 Corinthians 14:34-35
  Let your women keep silence in the churches: for it is not permitted unto them to speak; but they are commanded to be under obedience, as also saith the law. And if they will learn any thing, let them ask their husbands at home: for it is a shame for women to speak in the church.

If women are not supposed *"to speak"* in public church services where both men and women are attending, then certainly they must not preach in these services or preach anywhere, for that matter. This is one verse that clearly prohibits women preachers. Every woman preacher today is in clear and certain violation of this verse of the Bible and is therefore in serious trouble with the Lord.

In the early church, there was but one main meeting and that involved the teaching and preaching of the Words of God. Women were not to take part in this preaching service in any way. They were not to be women preachers and they were not to interrupt the preacher or teacher during the church service. I believe this is the main and clear teaching of this verse.

Today, things are different. There are many things that go on within the church building. There are women's Sunday School classes where "*women speak in the church*" building and properly so. There are church dinners with women attending when "*women speak in the church*" building and properly so. There are church offices with women secretaries and in this way "*women speak in the church*" building and properly so. On church cleaning days, women come to help and then "*women speak in the church*" building and properly so. In church choirs, there are many women who, in effect by this means "*women speak in the church*" building and properly so. During the examination of women for church membership in front of the deacons and pastor, "*women speak in the church*" building and properly so. After the services are over "*women speak in the church*" building and properly so. I am sure these kinds of instances and many others that could be listed of "*women speaking in the church*" building are not what Paul had in mind in this verse.

Again, let me repeat, women should not be preachers, nor should they lead in public prayer during a church service or any other service or meeting where both men and women are present. God's order is that only the "*men*" (MALES) should lead in public prayer.

1 Timothy 2:9

"In like manner also, that women adorn themselves in modest apparel, with shamefacedness and sobriety; not with broided hair, or gold, or pearls, or costly array;"

Having talked about how the "*men*" were to be the ones who lead in public prayer in the church services, Paul now speaks of seven areas of importance for the Christian "*women*" in the congregation:

(1) First, Paul instructed Pastor Timothy to tell the "*women*" in his church to "*adorn themselves in modest apparel.*" The word for "*adorn*" is KOSMEO. Its principal meaning is: "*to put in order, arrange, make ready, prepare; to ornament.*"

Women, Watch What You Wear!

The word for "*modest*" is KOSMIOS. It means: "*well arranged, seemly, modest.*" The world today, even, sad to say, some among born-again Christian women do not practice this. God wants them to be "*modest*" in their "*apparel.*" This should apply not only on the street, but also in all other places, including the work place and the beach. Christian women should not expose or draw attention to their bodies. Men should not be tempted to look with lust after these women because of their improper and immodest attire, nor should other women who are lesbians be thus tempted. This type of attire is certainly not "*modest.*"

The word for "*apparel*" is KATASTOLE. It means literally: "*a lowering, letting down; a garment let down, dress, attire.*" As those who attend our church know, I do not preach about women's "*apparel*" from the pulpit until we come to it in the Bible. Then I talk about it and write about it. Part of this Greek word KATASTOLE is STOLE. A "*stole*" has been defined as "*a loose outer garment worn by kings and persons of rank.*" This describes a long, flowing robe-type garment. Another definition of "*stole*" is "*a long, robelike outer garment worn by matrons in ancient Rome.*" This is the only time KATASTOLE is used in the New Testament. It is used describing how a woman is to dress. It is a verse that is specifically addressing modesty. It describes a "*LONG, FLOWING, LOOSE, outer garment.*" I was surprised to find out that this Greek Word KATASTOLE is on my computer search-engine where many articles are found about its meaning and use for today. Why not look it up on your computer.

Many of our ladies have asked me about wearing trousers. I do not make a big issue about it because people have to come to their own conclusion. We try to set a good example and preach the Word straight when we come to it. This word "*apparel*" implies a flowing garment such as a dress, a gown, or a robe. That is the Bible's standard.

I was talking to a lady about this one time, and I asked her what the symbol was of a woman and a man in the men's and women's bathrooms in airports and other public places. For men, it is a figure with trousers. For women, it is a figure with a skirt.

(2) Second, Paul instructed Pastor Timothy to tell the "*women*" in his church to "*adorn themselves*" "*with shamefacedness.*" The word for this is AIDOS. It means: "*a sense of shame or honour, modesty, bashfulness, reverence, regard for others, respect.*" It is only used here in the New Testament. Instead of being the center of attention, "*shamefacedness*" is acting with humility, respect, and regard for others. It seems that many women today (Christian and non-Christian alike) have no *"regard for others"* by their immodest dress.

(3) Third, Paul instructed Pastor Timothy to tell the *"women"* in his church to *"adorn themselves"* with *"sobriety."* The word for this is SOPHROSUNE. It means: *"soundness of mind; self-control, sobriety."* which means self-control over their actions and their words.

(4) Fourth, Paul instructed Pastor Timothy to tell the *"women"* in his church not to *"adorn themselves"* with *"broided hair."* The word for this is PLAGMA. It means: *"what is woven, plaited, or twisted together; a web, plait, braid; of a net; of a basket, in which the infant Moses was laid; of braided hair."* As someone has written concerning this term, *"If this prohibition is taken literally, it would preclude any braiding of the hair."*

Some of the *Webster's New World Dictionary* definitions of *"braiding"* is: *"to interweave three or more strands of (hair, straw, etc.); to make by such interweaving [to braid a rug]; to arrange (the hair) in a braid or braids."*

(5) Fifth, Paul instructed Pastor Timothy to tell the *"women"* in his church not to *"adorn themselves"* with *"gold."* The word for "gold" is KRUSTOS. It means: *"precious things made of gold, golden ornaments; an image made of gold; stamped gold, gold coin."* This would certainly set apart the rich women from the poor women in a church. James 2:2-5 speaks about the contests between the *"rich"* (v. 6) in *"gay clothing"* with *"gold rings,"* and the *"poor"* in *"vile clothing."* James speaks out against this practice of having *"respect of persons."*

(6) Sixth, Paul instructed Pastor Timothy to tell the *"women"* in his church not to *"adorn themselves"* with *"pearls."* As in the case of wearing *"gold,"* this might put the rich against the poor in the church and cause *"respect of persons"* which is not proper.

(7) Seventh, Paul instructed Pastor Timothy to tell the *"women"* in his church not to *"adorn themselves"* with *"costly array."* The two words for this are POLUTELES HIMATISMOS. The first word, *"costly,"* in this phrase means: *"precious, requiring very great outlay, very costly; excellent, of surpassing value."* The second word in this phrase, *"array,"* means simply: *"clothing, or apparel."* This is yet one more caution that Paul tells Pastor Timothy that he should teach the women who attend his church. They should not come to church with the absolute highest-priced dress or costume that they could possibly buy. They should be neat, yet wear ordinary kinds of clothing.

Timothy may have lost some of his people by preaching this, and I may lose some of our people by preaching this, but this is what the Scripture says. I am just a herald who is trying to set forth what God tells us in His Words.

How Should Women Be Adorned?

1. With modest apparel
2. With shamefacedness
3. With sobriety
4. Not with broided hair
5. Not with gold
6. Not with pearls
7. Not with costly array
8. With good works

1 Timothy 2:10

"But (which becometh women professing godliness) with good works."

By way of contrast in the preceding verse with outward adorning, God wants the "*women professing godliness*" to be adorned inwardly "*with good works*."

* 1 Timothy 2:2
  For kings, and for all that are in authority; that **we may lead a quiet and peaceable life in all godliness and honesty**.

God's emphasis is "*godliness*" all through the Scripture.

* 1 Timothy 4:7
  But refuse profane and old wives' fables, and **exercise thyself rather unto godliness**.

* 1 Timothy 6:3
  If any man teach otherwise, and consent not to wholesome words, even the words of our Lord Jesus Christ, and to the **doctrine which is according to godliness**;

Defective Walk--Defective Doctrine

If we do not have "*godliness*" in our walk and in our life, then our doctrine is defective to that extent. Our lives must measure up.

- 1 Timothy 6:5-6
  Perverse disputings of men of corrupt minds, and destitute of the truth, **supposing that gain is godliness**: from such withdraw thyself. **But godliness with contentment is great gain**.

Some people think that "*gain*" is godliness, but they are in serious error.

- 1 Timothy 6:7-11
  For we brought nothing into this world, and it is certain we can carry nothing out. And having food and raiment let us be therewith content. But they that will be rich fall into temptation and a snare, and into many foolish and hurtful lusts, which drown men in destruction and perdition. For the love of money is the root of all evil: which while some coveted after, they have erred from the faith, and pierced themselves through with many sorrows. **But thou, O man of God, flee these things; and follow after righteousness, godliness**, faith, love, patience, meekness.

Ungodliness = An Unfit Pastor

"*Godliness*" is one of the first requirements for a pastor. Ungodliness renders the pastor unfit for the ministry.

- 2 Timothy 3:1
  This know also, that **in the last days perilous times shall come**.
- 2 Timothy 3:5
  Having a form of godliness, but denying the power thereof: from such turn away.

A "*form of godliness*" could include a pastor wearing robes, with large churches and big organs, but if they are not saved they do not have the real thing. We should not attend churches that have only a "*form of godliness*" without holding to all of the doctrines of the Bible. Modernism, Roman Catholicism, Christian Science, all the world religions, and all the cults have a mere "*form of godliness*," but deny God's power.

- **2 Peter 1:2-3**
  Grace and peace be multiplied unto you through the knowledge of God, and of Jesus our Lord, According as his divine power **hath given unto us all things that pertain unto life and godliness**, through the knowledge of him that hath called us to glory and virtue:

God has given us many things in His Words that pertain to godliness. God is interested in godliness.

- **2 Peter 1:5-7**
  And beside this, giving all diligence, add to your faith virtue; and to virtue knowledge; And to knowledge temperance; and to temperance patience; **and to patience godliness**; And to godliness brotherly kindness; and to brotherly kindness charity.

Godliness--An Important Virtue

Godliness is one of the many and important virtues of the Christian faith.

- **2 Peter 3:11**
  Seeing then that all these things shall be dissolved, **what manner of persons ought ye to be in all holy conversation and godliness,**

One day this earth and the heavens will be dissolved and changed, but we should not change in our "*holy*" lives and in our "*godliness*."

The last part of this verse 10 speaks of the adornment and attire of these "*women professing godliness*." That adornment is to be "*good works*." The phrase "*good works*" is only used sixteen times in the New Testament.

- **Matthew 5:16**
  Let your light so shine before men, **that they may see your good works,** and glorify your Father which is in heaven.

Good works are not supposed to glorify you, they are to glorify your Father.

- **Acts 9:36**
  Now there was at Joppa a certain disciple named Tabitha, which by interpretation is called Dorcas: **this woman was full of good works** and almsdeeds which she did.

- **Ephesians 2:8-9**
  For by grace are ye saved through faith; and that not of yourselves: it is the gift of God: **Not of works**, lest any man should boast.

Saved Should Have Good Works

We are not saved by "*works,*" but by God's grace through genuine faith in the Lord Jesus Christ. We are saved in order that we might walk in "*good works.*" God wants all the His born-again Christians to have "*good works*" which are found in the Bible.

- 1 Timothy 5:9-10
  Let not a widow be taken into the number under threescore years old, having been the wife of one man, Well reported of for **good works**; if she have brought up children, if she have lodged strangers, if she have washed the saints' feet, if she have relieved the afflicted, **if she have diligently followed every good work.**

The widows were not to be taken into the company and supported by the church unless they were at least sixty. They also had to be the wife of only one man and well reported of "*good works.*" The churches were told to take care of the widows, but these guidelines had to be followed.

- 2 Timothy 3:16-17
  All scripture is given by inspiration of God, and is profitable for doctrine, for reproof, for correction, for instruction in righteousness: **That the man of God may be perfect, throughly furnished unto all good works**.

Our Bible gives us all the "*good works*" saved people need to have in order to please our God. That is why we need to read God's Words to find out what we should do to please the Lord.

Read the Whole Bible Every Year

I encourage you to read eighty-five verses each day which completes the entire King James Bible in one year. You can follow the YEARLY BIBLE READING SCHEDULE which is available from the Bible For Today upon request or on the Internet as BFT #0179. It is also in our *Defined King James Bible.*

- Titus 2:7
In all things shewing thyself a pattern of good works: in doctrine shewing uncorruptness, gravity, sincerity,

Paul wrote these words to Titus who was a pastor in Crete. Crete is an island in the Mediterranean Sea. This should apply to all pastors today as well. Though pastors are not perfect, they should seek to show themselves before their people and before all others to be a "*pattern of good works.*"

- Titus 2:14
Who gave himself for us, that he might redeem us from all iniquity, and **purify unto himself a peculiar people, zealous of good works.**

We who are saved are "*peculiar*" because we should be "*zealous of good works.*" That makes us "*peculiar*" in a world of wickedness. The world is not "*zealous of good works.*" They are zealous of wicked works.

- Titus 3:8
This is a faithful saying, and these things I will that thou affirm constantly, **that they which have believed in God might be careful to maintain good works**. These things are good and profitable unto men.

Christians Need *"Good Works"*

"*Good works*" must be maintained after we are saved.

- Hebrews 10:24
And let us consider one another to **provoke unto love and to good works:**

Provoke To *"Good Works"*

If we are going to "*provoke*" somebody, let us "*provoke*" them to love one another as Christians and to do "*good works*" whenever possible.

- 1 Peter 2:12
Having your conversation honest among the Gentiles: that, whereas they speak against you as **evildoers**, they may **by your good works, which they shall behold, glorify God** in the day of visitation.

The heathen people around you do not believe that the Lord Jesus Christ was sent into this world to be the Saviour of the world. They do not believe anything about the Bible. This verse says that the unsaved world will call you *"evildoers,"* but when they *"behold"* your *"good works,"* they will "glorify God."

When I was a teacher in the Philadelphia public schools, I had a principal who was on my case almost the whole eighteen years that I taught in his Junior High School. My job as a Christian was to maintain *"good works."* When I was at the Franklin Learning Center, a Senior High School, another boss was on me every chance he could get. He was a homosexual, and so he was against what I believed. I still had to maintain *"good works"* no matter what. We need to *"glorify God"* in all things so that the people around us can see Him.

1 Timothy 2:11

"Let the woman learn in silence with all subjection."

Here is another verse which shows that the Bible opposes women preachers. According to this verse *"women"* are to *"learn in silence with all subjection."* The word for *"learn"* is MANTHANO. It means:

"to learn, be appraised; to increase one's knowledge, to be increased in knowledge; to hear, be informed; to learn by use and practice; to be in the habit of, accustomed to."

Women Must Be Learners

Women in Timothy's local church, and by application in present-day churches, were to be *"learners,"* not teachers of men and certainly not preachers. They should *"learn"* with *"all subjection."* They should not dominate in the church.

The word for *"silence"* is HESUKIA. It means: *"quietness; description of the life of one who stays at home doing his own work, and <u>does not officiously meddle with the affairs of others</u>; silence."* This is the atmosphere in which the *"women"* are to *"learn"* in the church.

- 1 Corinthians 14:34
  Let your women keep silence in the churches: for it is not permitted unto them to speak; but they are commanded to be under obedience, as also saith the law.

In this chapter 14 of 1 Corinthians, Paul is talking about speaking in tongues. The women were not to speak in tongues publicly. This *"silence"* should prevail in the main church service. **IF** they are humble and respectful at all times, I do not believe this would prevent "*women*" to take part in Bible classes held in the church building by asking questions and taking part in their "*learning*" process.

The "*women*" were to "*learn . . . with all subjection.*" The trouble with our world today is that there is very little "*subjection*" by anyone in any area. The Bible speaks about various kinds of "*subjection.*"

● **Psalm 106:42**
Their enemies also oppressed them, and **they were brought into subjection** under their hand.

● **Luke 2:51**
And he went down with them, and **came to Nazareth, and was subject unto them**: but his mother kept all these sayings in her heart.

The Lord Jesus Christ Himself was in "*subjection*" to His earthly parents.

● **Luke 10:17**
And the seventy returned again with joy, saying, Lord, even **the devils are subject unto us through thy name.**

The Meaning of "Subjection"

"*Subjection*" means to be under the authority of another.

● **Romans 8:7**
Because the carnal mind *is* enmity against God: **for it is not subject to the law of God**, neither indeed can be.

● **Romans 13:1**
Let every soul be subject unto the higher powers. For there is no power but of God: the powers that be are ordained of God.

Paul is describing true Biblical government. Biblical government is defined in the following verses:

● **Romans 13:1-3**
Let every soul be subject unto the higher powers. For there is no power but of God: the powers that be are ordained of God. Whosoever therefore resisteth the power, resisteth the ordinance of God: and they that resist shall receive to themselves damnation. **For rulers are not a terror to good works, but to the evil.** Wilt thou then not be afraid of the power? do that which is good, and thou shalt have praise of the same:

"Obey God Rather Than Men"

When there are evil governments that ask Christians to do evil, we "*ought to obey God rather than men*" (Acts 5:29b) to resist the evil commands.

- 1 Corinthians 9:27
  But I keep under my body, and bring *it* into subjection: lest that by any means, when I have preached to others, I myself should be a castaway.

Paul kept his body under "*subjection*" and control, and so should all born-again Christians.

- Ephesians 5:24
  Therefore **as the church is subject unto Christ**, so *let* the wives *be* to their own husbands in every thing.
- 1 Timothy 3:4
  One that ruleth well his own house, **having his children in subjection with all gravity;**

Children Must Be In "Subjection"

The children of pastors and all other Christians should be in "*subjection*" to their parents at least as long as they live under his roof. Hopefully, after they leave home, they will still be in "*subjection*" to the will of God.

- Hebrews 12:9
  Furthermore we have had fathers of our flesh which corrected *us*, and we gave *them* reverence: **shall we not much rather be in subjection unto the Father of spirits**, and live?
- 1 Peter 2:18
  Servants, *be* subject to *your* masters with all fear; not only to the good and gentle, but also to the froward.
- 1 Peter 3:1
  Likewise, **ye wives, *be* in subjection to your own husbands**; that, if any obey not the word, they also may without the word be won by the conversation of the wives;

- **1 Peter 3:5**
  For after this manner in the old time the **holy women** also, who trusted in God, adorned themselves, **being in subjection unto their own husbands:**

We believe that *"subjection"* is a Scriptural thing.

1 Timothy 2:12

"But I suffer not a woman to teach, nor to usurp authority over the man, but to be in silence."

The word for *"suffer"* is EPITREPO. It means: *"to turn to, transfer, commit, instruct; to permit, allow, give leave."* In other words, God does not permit or allow *"women to teach, nor to usurp authority over the man."* According to the Words of God, there are to be no women preachers.

Yet, as of 1989, here are some of the numbers of women in full-time church ministry:

U.S.A. Women In Full-Time Ministry

4,743 in the United Methodist churches

4,000 in the Assemblies of God churches

2,419 in the Presbyterian Church U.S.A. churches

1,803 in the United Church of Christ churches

1,358 in the Evangelical Lutheran churches

1,225 in the Southern Baptist churches

84 of 166 denominations ordain women to full-time ministry. As of 1986, there were 20,730 women in the U.S.A. who were ordained to full-time ministry. This was 7.9% of all the U.S. clergy (*National & International Religion Report*, March 13, 1989)

The Scriptures are clear about women preachers. The word used for *"usurp authority"* is AUTHENTEO. It means:

"One who with his own hands kills another or himself; one who acts on his own authority, autocratic; an absolute master; to govern, exercise dominion over one."

In other words, a *"woman"* is not allowed by God to *"exercise dominion"* or be an *"absolute master"* over the *"man"* (which is ARSEN or *"male"*). The Women's Liberation Movement does not go along with this verse at all.

When I was a student at Dallas Theological Seminary, I worked at a Baptist Mexican Mission for a year or so. A woman was my superior in that

Mission. After a while, I had to resign because I was the pastor and it was very uncomfortable for a woman to be in authority over me in the affairs of that mission church.

The first church I pastored after my five years on active duty as a Naval Chaplain was Immanuel Baptist Church in Newton, Massachusetts. One of the most outspoken women in the congregation was the wife of a powerful deacon. It was said that she made the "snowballs," and her husband threw them. She was a woman out of place. I remember one particular night I was trying to turn the lights in the church off. She did not want those lights turned off so there was a battle over the light switch. It was a very uncomfortable mess. The Lord Jesus Christ has the proper "*authority.*" There are many uses of "*authority*" in the New Testament.

- **Matthew 7:29**
  For **he taught them as *one* having authority**, and not as the scribes.
- **John 5:27**
  And hath given him authority to execute judgment also, because he is the Son of man.
- **Acts 9:14**
  And here **he hath authority from the chief priests** to bind all that call on thy name.
- **Titus 2:15**
  These things speak, and exhort, and rebuke with all authority. Let no man despise thee.

I do not believe women should teach mixed classes in Sunday School. I think doing this would be contrary to this verse (1 Timothy 2:12). Women can teach women, but men should teach men and mixed classes of men and women. One of our own woman relatives taught both men and women. She said that the pastor gave the authority for her to do it. According to this verse "*women are not to usurp authority over the man.*" In my judgment, she was violating that provision.

1 Timothy 2:13
"For Adam was first formed, then Eve."

- **Genesis 2:7**
  And the LORD God formed man *of* the dust of the ground, and breathed into his nostrils the breath of life; and man became a living soul.
- **Genesis 2:21**
  And the LORD God caused a deep sleep to fall upon Adam, and he slept: and **he took one of his ribs, and closed up the flesh instead thereof;**

Jokes have been made that if the woman had been created first she would have told God how to make man. The word "*Eve*" means "*life*."

Women's Submission Due to Creation

The reason that God has given for submission of women in the churches is because of the order of creation. Evolution does not care anything about creation. By and large, people do not believe in God's creation.

Many people practice evolutionary thinking. So if you do not believe in the creation by God of both man and woman, there is not any proper procedure in the family and church body.

- **Genesis 3:1-4**
  Now the serpent was more subtil than any beast of the field which the LORD God had made. **And he said unto the woman, Yea, hath God said, Ye shall not eat of every tree of the garden?** And the woman said unto the serpent, We may eat of the fruit of the trees of the garden: But of the fruit of the tree which *is* in the midst of the garden, God hath said, Ye shall not eat of it, neither shall ye touch it, lest ye die. And the serpent said unto the woman, Ye shall not surely die:
Satan misquoted Scripture. He always does!

- **Genesis 3:5**
  For God doth know that in the day ye eat thereof, then your eyes shall be opened, and **ye shall be as gods, knowing good and evil.**

- **Genesis 3:6**
  And when **the woman** saw that the tree *was* good for food, and that it *was* pleasant to the eyes, and a tree to be desired to make *one* wise, she took of the fruit thereof, and **did eat, and gave also unto her husband with her; and he did eat**.
From this verse we are not told that Adam knew the source of the fruit. There were fruit trees all over the Garden of Eden. God held Adam accountable for this sin even though it was Eve who ate of the fruit first and then gave it to him.

- **Genesis 3:14**
  And the LORD God said unto the serpent, **Because thou hast done this, thou *art* cursed above all cattle,** and above every beast of the field; upon thy belly shalt thou go, and dust shalt thou eat all the days of thy life:

It is possible that Adam did not know where the fruit came from. He just ate it.

* **Genesis 3:11**
  And he said, Who told thee that thou *wast* naked? **Hast thou eaten of the tree**, whereof I commanded thee that thou shouldest not eat?

Adam and Eve now knew they were naked.

1 Timothy 2:14

"And Adam was not deceived, but the woman being deceived was in the transgression."

When God asked Adam and Eve why they took the forbidden fruit, Adam complained and blamed the woman. Eve was beguiled or deceived by the serpent, but Adam listened to his wife and ate of the fruit of the tree.

* **Romans 5:12**
  Wherefore, as by one man sin entered into the world, and death by sin; and so death passed upon all men, for that all have sinned:

God Blamed Adam, Eve's Head

Even though Eve was the first one to take of this forbidden fruit, God considered Adam, the head of his household, to be the guilty one. His sin was passed on to the whole human race. The sin of mankind was placed upon Adam. *"As by one man, sin entered into the world"* (Romans 5:12). Every human being is born a sinner because he or she inherited their sin nature from Adam, not from Eve.

1 Timothy 2:15

"Notwithstanding she shall be saved in childbearing, if they continue in faith and charity and holiness with sobriety."

This is an interesting verse that some interpret one way and some another way. I believe this verse is harking back to Genesis chapters 3 and 4. *"She shall be saved in childbearing."* Eve was under sin the same as Adam was under sin. She needed deliverance. Her deliverance and final salvation was to be found in *"childbearing"* which would one day lead to the virgin birth of the Lord Jesus Christ her Saviour.

- **Genesis 3:15**
  And I will put enmity between thee and the woman, and between thy seed and her seed; **it shall bruise thy head, and thou shalt bruise his heel**.

Calvary's Defeat of Satan

This is called the PROTOEUANGELION or the *"first gospel."* In this verse, the Lord was talking to the serpent who was Satan in disguise. The promised *"Seed"* was the Lord Jesus Christ who would be the Deliverer. Though Satan *"bruised"* the *"heel"* of the Lord Jesus Christ at Calvary, the Lord Jesus Christ will one day *"bruise"* or *"crush"* the head of the serpent when He sends him to the Lake of Fire forever and ever. *"Bruising"* a *"heel"* is far less severe than *"bruising"* or *"crushing"* a head.

- **Acts 2:23**
  Him, being delivered by the determinate counsel and foreknowledge of God, ye have taken, and **by wicked hands have crucified and slain:**

Satan was happy about that. But the Lord Jesus Christ arose bodily from the grave, victorious over it. All was not lost because of Calvary. This was the means of *"bringing many sons unto glory"* (Hebrews 2:10).

- **Genesis 4:1**
  And Adam knew Eve his wife; and she conceived, and bare Cain, and said, **I have gotten a man from the LORD**.

Eve thought this was the "seed" through which the Saviour would come, but he was not. Cain was not the one.

- **Genesis 4:2**
  And she again bare his brother Abel. And Abel was a keeper of sheep, but Cain was a tiller of the ground.

- **Genesis 4:8**
  And Cain talked with Abel his brother: and it came to pass, when they were in the field, **that Cain rose up against Abel his brother, and slew him.**

It was neither Cain nor Abel through whom the Lord Jesus Christ would one day come.

- **Genesis 4:25**
  And Adam knew his wife again; and she bare a son, and called his name Seth: **For God, *said she*, hath appointed me another seed instead of Abel, whom Cain slew**.

Through the line of Seth, the line of the Lord Jesus Christ was begun. I believe that was the Seed referred to in 1 Timothy 2:15.

- **1 Timothy 2:15**

  Notwithstanding **she shall be saved in childbearing**, if they continue in faith and charity and holiness with sobriety.

We ought to be thankful to the Lord Jesus Christ, Who was the Seed of the woman, and Who was the one Who was born of the Virgin Mary, conceived by the Holy Spirit of God, that He was the Seed Who could deliver from sin those who genuinely trusted in Him for salvation. Our deliverance is made perfect if we *"continue in faith and charity and holiness with sobriety."*

First Timothy
Chapter Three

1 Timothy 3:1

"This *is* a true saying, If a man desire the office of a bishop, he desireth a good work."

Paul here states that the *"desire"* to be a *"bishop"* would put a man in a *"good work."* There is nothing wrong with the *"desire"* and nothing wrong with the *"work"* of a *"bishop."*

Pastor-Bishop-Elder--One Office

Before getting into the *"desire"* here, let us determine what a Biblical *"bishop"* is. I believe *"bishop"* is one of three names for the same person. A man who is a *"bishop"* of a local church is also a *"pastor"* and an *"elder."* The pastor-bishop-elder as referring to one man is taught in two Bible passages.

In Acts 20:17, Paul called for the *"elders of the church"* (PRESBUTEROS) at Ephesus. In Acts 20:28, he spoke of these same men as being *"overseers"* (EPISKOPOS), or *"bishops"* of the *"flock."* Then Paul told these same men to *"feed"* or *"shepherd"* or *"pastor"* (POIMAINO) the *"church of God."*

In 1 Peter 5:1-2, Peter writes to the *"elders"* (PRESBUTEROS) that they are to *"feed"* or *"shepherd"* or *"pastor"* (POIMAINO) the *"flock of God."* In doing this, these same men are to *"take the oversight"* or *"be bishops"* (EPISKOPEO) of the *"flock."*

Pastors-Bishops-Elders--Only Males

It is to be noted that every one of these words, *"pastor,"* *"bishop,"* and *"elder"* is masculine in gender, not feminine. God wants His pastors-bishops-elders to be men, not women.

The word for *"desire"* is OREGOMAI. It means: *"to stretch one's self out in order to touch or to grasp something, to reach after or desire something; to give one's self up to the love of money."* The man must be certain that the Lord is calling him to be a pastor-bishop-elder. If the Lord does not call a man, then he should stay out of the ministry.

- Titus 1:7
  For a bishop must be blameless, as the steward of God; not selfwilled, not soon angry, not given to wine, no striker, not given to filthy lucre;
- 1 Peter 2:25
  For ye were as sheep going astray; but are now returned unto **the Shepherd and Bishop of your souls**.

As mentioned above, this word *"bishop"* is a word used also referring to *"elder"* and *"pastor."* The same word is used for all three offices.

- Acts 20:17
  And from Miletus he sent to Ephesus, and **called the elders of the church.**

These are *"elders"* which mean they are mature in the faith, and should also be mature in their age. They should know the Scriptures and the things of the Lord.

- Acts 20:28
  Take heed therefore unto yourselves, and **to all the flock, over the which the Holy Ghost hath made you <u>overseers</u>, <u>to feed</u> the church of God,** which he hath purchased with his own blood.

Here is the word *"bishop"* or *"overseer"* (EPISKOPOS). This is the one who looks over things or manages things. These same people are to *"feed"* or *"shepherd"* or *"pastor"* those in the *"flock."*

- 1 Peter 5:1-3
  The elders which are among you I exhort, who am also an elder, and a witness of the sufferings of Christ, and also a partaker of the glory that shall be revealed: **Feed the flock of God** which is among you, **taking the oversight** *thereof*, not by constraint, but willingly; not for filthy lucre, but of a ready mind; Neither as being lords over *God's* heritage, but being ensamples to the flock.

As mentioned above, Peter used the same three terms for one-and-the-same person. As the "*pastor*" of the local church, he is to be feeding and shepherding the flock. As the "*bishop*" of the local church, he is to be overseeing the flock. As the "*elder*" of the local church, he is to be mature in the faith and also mature in age.

Pastors Should Be Mature

I do not think pastors should be young men right out of college, or even right out of seminary. By this term "*elder*," I believe God indicates that they should have some maturity in years and experience behind them. As mentioned before, every local church should have only males as their pastors-bishops-elders.

---

1 Timothy 3:2

"A bishop then must be blameless, the husband of one wife, vigilant, sober, of good behaviour, given to hospitality, apt to teach;"

In 1 Timothy 3:2-7, Paul gives to Pastor Timothy a total of sixteen qualifications for any of the pastors that Timothy's local church might ordain for the ministry of the Lord Jesus Christ. Seven of the sixteen qualifications for pastors are found in this verse two. Before listing any of the sixteen qualifications for the pastor-bishop-elder let me explain something about these qualifications in general.

Pastors Must Constantly Qualify

Paul says that "*a bishop then must*" be qualified in all these areas. The verb for "*must*" is DEI. It is in the present tense indicating that it is a continuous requirement that must never be struck down for any reason for any man in the ministry. Should the pastor cease to qualify in any one of these sixteen areas, he must forfeit his pastorate.

"*Must*" (DEI) means various things:

"*it is necessary, there is need of, it behooves, is right and proper; necessity lying in the nature of the case; necessity brought on by circumstances or by the conduct of others toward us; necessity in reference to what is required to attain some end; a necessity of law and command, of duty, equity; necessity established by the counsel and decree of God; concerning what Christ was destined finally to undergo, his sufferings, death, resurrection, ascension.*"

There are sixteen requirements for a Scripturally qualified pastor/bishop/elder of a local church. Seven of the requirements are found in this present verse.

Pastors Must Be Blameless

#1 The first requirement for the pastor-bishop-elder of a local church is this: He must be "*blameless.*"

The word for "*blameless*" is ANEPILEPTOS. It means: "*not apprehended, that cannot be laid hold of; that cannot be reprehended, not open to censure, irreproachable.*" The parts of that word break down as follows; AN means "*no.*" EPI means "*upon.*" LEPTOS is from LEIPO which is from LAMBANO and means "to take." The resultant meaning is someone that no one can rightly and justly lay hold upon for committing any crime.

In other words he may be charged with a crime, as some pastors are, but he musts not be guilty of that crime. Nobody should be able to lay a hand on him for guilt of that crime. He must not be convicted justly of any crime. That is the meaning of a "*blameless*" pastor. God demands "*blameless*" pastors. So should our local churches. It does not mean he is sinlessly perfect. The word "*Blameless*" is used many times in Scripture.

- Luke 1:6
  And they were both righteous before God, walking in all the commandments and ordinances of the Lord **blameless.**
- 1 Corinthians 1:8
  Who shall also confirm you unto the end, *that ye may be* **blameless** in the day of our Lord Jesus Christ.
- Philippians 2:15
  That ye may be blameless and harmless, the sons of God, without rebuke, in the midst of a crooked and perverse nation, among whom ye shine as lights in the world;
- Philippians 3:6
  Concerning zeal, persecuting the church; **touching the righteousness which is in the law, blameless.**
- 1 Thessalonians 5:23
  And the very God of peace sanctify you wholly; and *I pray God* your whole spirit and soul and body be preserved **blameless unto the coming of our Lord Jesus Christ.**

God wants all saved people to be *"blameless."*

- Titus 1:6
  If any be blameless, the husband of one wife, having faithful children not accused of riot or unruly.
- Titus 1:7
  For a bishop must be blameless, as the steward of God; not selfwilled, not soon angry, not given to wine, no striker, not given to filthy lucre;
- 2 Peter 3:14
  Wherefore, beloved, seeing that ye look for such things, **be diligent that ye may be found of him in peace, without spot, and blameless.**

Pastors Must Be Husbands of One Wife

#2 The second requirement for the pastor-bishop-elder of a local church is this: He must be *"the husband of one wife."*

To be qualified under this restriction the pastor cannot be divorced and remarried, regardless of the circumstances, and regardless of whether the marriage happened before he was saved. If the pastor's wife dies, the Scripture permits him to marry again. This wife must be saved. She must reject divorce as an option in marriage. She must not be divorced and have a living husband.

She must love the Lord Jesus Christ and be dedicated to His cause. Should this pastor-widower re-marry, the pastor would still be considered to be "*the husband of one wife.*" Notice he is the "*husband*" of a "*wife.*"

No Female Pastors Are Permitted!

The word for "*husband*" is ANER. This word is exclusively a male. This requirement clearly and strongly prohibits any woman from being a pastor. The word for "*wife*" is GUNE. It is the word for a female. It is not a male with a male. It is a male with a female. Neither a homosexual male nor a homosexual female (a lesbian) is qualified to be a pastor, not only because they are not "*blameless,*" but also because they have no "*wife.*"

There is one more part of this requirement that many do not agree with me. This verse demands that a pastor be married. Otherwise, how could he be the "*husband of one wife*"? He is to be the "*husband*" (a male) with only one living "*wife*" (a female). I know that many pastors are single, and they do not agree with me in my interpretation of this verse. I do not believe single men should be in the pastoral ministry. It is clearly taught here, and in other places in the Bible, that a pastor should be married.

Pastors Must Be Vigilant

#3 The third requirement for the pastor-bishop-elder of a local church is this: He must be "*vigilant.*"

The word for "*vigilant*" is NEPHALEOS. It means: "*sober, temperate; abstaining from wine, either entirely or at least from its immoderate use; of things free from all wine, as vessels, offerings.*" The pastor must totally abstain from alcohol in any form. Recently a very prominent Fundamentalist pastor had to resign his pastorate and all the rest of his leadership positions because he had been drinking wine for over seven years. He had several tickets for drunken driving. Why did it take so long for him to step down? There was a cover-up. He was not Biblically "*vigilant*" in the literal sense of that word.

No Alcohol For Any Christian

This total absence of alcohol is not only for the pastors, but it applies to every born-again Christian of any age or sex.

There are six other verses in the New Testament that use either NEPHALEOS or NEPHO and take in all saved people. Here are the references and the words translating these Greek terms which mean the ones mentioned should abstain from alcohol. Again, the list is not limited to either pastors or deacons, but applies to all born-again Christians. I have indicated the words in our King James Bible that translate either NEPHALEOS or NEPHO.

Seven Verses Against Any Alcohol

1 Thessalonians 5:6 *"sober"*
1 Thessalonians 5:8 *"sober"*
1 Timothy 3:2 *"vigilant"*
1 Timothy 3:11 *"sober'*
2 Timothy 4:5 *"watch"*
Titus 2:2 *"sober"*
1 Peter 1:13 *"sober."*

Here are the various Scriptures where either NEPHALEOS or NEPHO are used, indicating total abstinence from alcohol for various groups of saved people.

- **1 Thessalonians 5:6**
  Therefore let us not sleep, as *do* others; but let us watch and **be sober**.

This is for all Christians.

- **1 Thessalonians 5:8**
  But let us, who are of the day, **be sober**, putting on the breastplate of faith and love; and for an helmet, the hope of salvation.

- **1 Timothy 3:2**
  A bishop then must be blameless, the husband of one wife, **vigilant**, sober, of good behaviour, given to hospitality, apt to teach;

The word *"vigilant"* in this verse is NEPHALEOS.

- **1 Timothy 3:11**
  Even so *must their* wives *be* grave, not slanderers, **sober**, faithful in all things.
- **2 Timothy 4:5**
  But **watch** thou in all things, endure afflictions, do the work of an evangelist, make full proof of thy ministry.

The word is translated *"watch,"* but it is still NEPHALEOS. How can you watch if you are drunk? You cannot do it.

- **Titus 2:2**
  That the aged men **be sober**, grave, temperate, sound in faith, in charity, in patience.

Aged Men Must Also Totally Abstain

God says in this verse that even when you are older you must totally abstain from alcoholic beverages.

- **1 Peter 1:13**
  Wherefore gird up the loins of your mind, **be sober**, and hope to the end for the grace that is to be brought unto you at the revelation of Jesus Christ;

I was a Navy Chaplain on active duty for five years. I was overseas in Okinawa without my family for one of those years. I was stationed with the Third Marine Division, Third Regiment, Third Battalion. I worked under a Regimental senior chaplain who graduated from Wheaton College. He was angry with me because I refused to drink alcoholic beverages of any kind. He told me that all the other chaplains in the Regiment drink.

At the time, I was endorsed by the General Association of Regular Baptist Churches (GARBC). I have since separated from any connection with the GARBC because of its drift from its founding principles and practices. Back in those years (1956 through 1961) the GARBC had in their Bylaws for their churches that each member of the GARBC churches would *"abstain from alcoholic drink as a beverage."* Sad to say, however, that phrase has been replaced for their present suggested Bylaws for their churches. At that time I could say to my senior chaplain that not only did I *"abstain from alcoholic drink as a beverage,"* but so did all the members in our GARBC churches that endorsed me as a chaplain.

Pastors Must Be Sober

#4 The fourth requirement for the pastor-bishop-elder of a local church is this: He must be *"sober."*

The word for *"sober"* is SOPHRON. It is not the same as the word above translated *"vigilant"* even though the King James Bible uses *"sober"* for both words. It is a good translation. In English, "sober" means both things. This *"sober"* word means: *"of a sound mind, sane, in one's senses; curbing one's desires and impulses, self-controlled, temperate."* These characteristics must be part and parcel of a pastor's life and practice.

Pastors Must Be Of Good Behaviour

#5 The fifth requirement for the pastor-bishop-elder of a local church is this: He must be *"of good behaviour."*

The word for this is KOSMIOS. It means: *"well arranged, seemly, modest."* It is the same word that was used in 1 Timothy 2:9 for the way Christian women should dress. The pastor also must be robed in *"seemly and modest"* behavior for the glory of the Lord Jesus Christ Whom he serves. His deportment must be exemplary for all the his flock.

Pastor Must Be Given to Hospitality

#6 The sixth requirement for the pastor-bishop-elder of a local church is this: He must be *"given to hospitality."*

The word for this is PHILOXENOS. It comes from PHILOS (*"love"*) and XENOS ("strangers.") It means: *"hospitable, generous to guests."* With many Christians passing through their towns in the New Testament days, pastors and their wives must be willing to entertain them and be *"given to hospitality."* There are a number of verses that speak of this good trait.
* **Romans 12:13**
  Distributing to the necessity of saints; **given to hospitality**.
All believers should be hospitable.

- Titus 1:8
  But **a lover of hospitality**, a lover of good men, sober, just, holy, temperate;
- 1 Peter 4:9
  Use hospitality one to another without grudging.

The early church did not have hotels or motels, so they took one another into their homes as they traveled from place to place. This means that the wife of the pastor has to be willing to be "*hospitable*" as well. "*Hospitality*" is important for all Christians, but especially the pastors. It is improper for a pastor and his wife not to be "*hospitable*." My wife and I are "*hospitable*." If this were not so, we would not have given up our living room and other parts of our home to be used by our church.

Pastors Must Be Apt To Teach

#7 The seventh requirement for the pastor-bishop-elder of a local church is this: He must be "*apt to teach*."

The word for this is DIDAKTIKOS. We get our English word "*didactic*" from this Greek word. It means: "*apt and skillful in teaching*." The pastor must know the Words of God and be "*apt to teach*" them to his people. It seems like many pastors have no burden or desire to "*teach*" their people all the truths of the Bible. No wonder that many of their people are so ignorant of the things of the Lord and how to live to please Him. Shame on non-teaching pastors! They are not qualified and should either become "*apt to teach*," or get out of the ministry.

- 2 Timothy 2:24
  And the servant of the Lord must not strive; but be gentle unto all *men*, **apt to teach**, patient,
- 2 Timothy 4:2
  Preach the word; be instant in season, out of season; reprove, rebuke, **exhort with all longsuffering and doctrine.**

"*Doctrine*" (DIDACHE) is that which is taught. That is what a pastor must do. Many churches do not teach "*doctrine*." They do not like it. If a pastor does not teach "*doctrine*" it leads to spiritual weakness in his church. Pastors must be "*apt to teach*" the Words of God. This requires diligent study on the pastor's part as well as skill in presenting the teaching.

1 Timothy 3:3

"Not given to wine, no striker, not greedy of filthy lucre; but patient, not a brawler, not covetous;"

Here are six more qualifications for a pastor in addition to the seven in the previous verse.

Pastors Must Not Be Given to Wine

#8 The eighth requirement for the pastor-bishop-elder of a local church is this: He must be *"Not given to wine."*

The Greek word here is PAROINOS. It means: *"given to wine, drunken."* I have covered the abstaining from alcohol above in verse two under NEPHALEOS or NEPHO. The best way not to be *"given to wine"* or to be *"drunken"* is to totally abstain from alcohol as a beverage.

- **Proverbs 20:1**
  Wine *is* a mocker, strong drink *is* raging: and whosoever is deceived thereby is not wise.

We have many drunks all around us. The pastors should not be one of them.

Pastors Must Not Be Strikers

#9 The ninth requirement for the pastor-bishop-elder of a local church is this: He must be *"no striker."*

The word for that is PLEKTES. It means: *"bruiser, ready for a blow; a pugnacious, contentious, quarrelsome person."*

- **Titus 1:7**
  For **a bishop must be** blameless, as the steward of God; not selfwilled, not soon angry, not given to wine, **no striker**, not given to filthy lucre;

Pastors cannot be "ready for a blow" to deliver to someone. They must watch their mouth, their heart, and their hands, regardless of how provoked they might be. The Holy Spirit of God can give you this needed control.

Pastors Must Not Be Greedy of Money

#10 The tenth requirement for the pastor-bishop-elder of a local church is this: He must be *"not greedy of filthy lucre."*

The word is AISCHROKERDES. It means: " *eager for base gain, greedy for money.*" Samuel's sons sinned along these lines.

- **1 Samuel 8:3**
  And his sons walked not in his ways, but **turned aside after lucre, and took bribes**, and perverted judgment.
- **Titus 1:7**
  For a **bishop must be** blameless, as the steward of God; not selfwilled, not soon angry, not given to wine, no striker, **not given to filthy lucre;**
- **1 Peter 5:2**
  Feed the flock of God which is among you, taking the oversight *thereof*, not by constraint, but willingly; **not for filthy lucre**, but of a ready mind;

Some pastors seem to desire more and more and more *"filthy lucre"* or money. There is nothing wrong with having money. We need money to buy food, to take care of our families, to take care of the heat, light, and rent. The word used here does not mean merely taking care of *"needs."* It speaks of *"greediness"* for more and more money.

Some pastors have as their motivation to climb to a bigger church for more money. In order to do that, they trim their sails, trim their message, and they do not talk straight from the Scriptures because some things offend people. In order to be *"all things to all men,"* these pastors bend over backwards just to get more people into their church which leads to more money for their salaries.

Many pastors do have a love for filthy lucre. In order to get more, you have to have more people so you can get more money. As you know, I preach without any salary or gifts. The Lord has provided for our family, so the offerings go to our missionaries, radio ministries, books, advertising, and various other things, but not to this preacher. In fact we take care of the heat, the air conditioning, the electricity, the taxes, the lawn, and all other expenses for the home. The church does not have to pay for any of that. Yet there are financial needs for the various ministries of the church.

Pastors Must Be Patient

#11 The eleventh requirement for the pastor-bishop-elder of a local church is this: He must be "*patient*."

The word for this is EPIEIKES. It means: "*seemingly, suitable; equitable, fair, mild, gentle.*" It is often hard to be "*patient*" and "*mild,*" but God commands all of us who are saved to be "*patient,*" but especially pastors.

- **Romans 12:12**
  Rejoicing in hope; **patient in tribulation**; continuing instant in prayer;
- **1 Thessalonians 5:14**
  Now we exhort you, brethren, warn them that are unruly, comfort the feebleminded, support the weak, **be patient toward all** *men.*
- **2 Thessalonians 3:5**
  And the Lord direct your hearts into the love of God, and into the **patient waiting for Christ**.

We do not know when the Lord will return. We have to be waiting "*patiently.*"

- **2 Timothy 2:24**
  And the servant of the Lord must not strive; but be gentle unto all *men*, apt to teach, **patient,**
- **James 5:7**
  Be patient therefore, brethren, unto the coming of the Lord. Behold, the husbandman waiteth for the precious fruit of the earth, and hath long patience for it, until he receive the early and latter rain.
- **James 5:8**
  Be ye also patient; stablish your hearts: for the coming of the Lord draweth nigh.

Pastors Must Not Be Brawlers

#12 The twelfth requirement for the pastor-bishop-elder of a local church is this: He must be "*not a brawler*."

The word for this is ANARCHOS. We get our English word *"anarchy"* from it. It is made up of two Greek words, AN (*"not"*) and ARCHO (*"to rule"*). It means: *"not to be withstood, invincible; not contentious; abstaining from fighting."* The word *"brawler"* is only used a few times in Scripture, and these other times the Bible is speaking about women.

- **Proverbs 21:9**
  It is better to dwell in a corner of the housetop, than with a **brawling woman** in a wide house.

Apparently some women *"brawl."* The Scriptures say so.

- **Proverbs 25:24**
  It is better to dwell in the corner of the housetop, than with a **brawling woman** and in a wide house.

Preachers should not be in fist fights and *"brawling."* That disqualifies a pastor for the ministry.

Pastors Must Not Be Covetous

#13 The thirteenth requirement for the pastor-bishop-elder of a local church is this: He must be *"not covetous."*

The word for this is APHILARGUROS. It is made up of three words: (1) A (*"not"*)+PHILOS (*"loving"*)+ARGUREOS (*"silver"*). It means therefore: *"not loving money, not avaricious."* This carries with it a strong *"avarice"* or *"desire"* for anything that you do not yet have. Covetousness has been defined as *"the itch for more."* The pastor *cannot love silver"* or money. Our United States government took us off both the gold and the silver standard. There is very little *"silver"* in any of our money, including the coins. So it is almost impossible to love *"silver"* these days (unless you buy real silver coins or silver bullion). It means money and what money can buy. This sin cannot be a part of a pastor's life. There are many references to covetousness in the Bible.

- **Exodus 18:21**
  Moreover thou shalt provide out of all the people able men, such as fear God, men of truth, **hating covetousness;** and place *such* over them, *to be* rulers of thousands, *and* rulers of hundreds, rulers of fifties, and rulers of tens:

- **Exodus 20:17**
  Thou shalt not covet thy neighbour's house, thou shalt not covet thy neighbour's wife, nor his manservant, nor his maidservant, nor his ox, nor his ass, nor any thing that *is* thy neighbour's.

Do not covet your neighbor's wife, your neighbor's house, or anything else your neighbor has.

- **Psalm 119:36**
  Incline my heart unto thy testimonies, and **not to covetousness.**

Covetousness is a heart sin.

- **Mark 7:21-23**
  For **from within, out of the heart of men, proceed** evil thoughts, adulteries, fornications, murders, Thefts, **covetousness**, wickedness, deceit, lasciviousness, an evil eye, blasphemy, pride, foolishness: All these evil things come from within, and defile the man.

All these evil things come from the heart, and God's man is not to be defiled.

- **Luke 12:15**
  And he said unto them, Take heed, and beware of **covetousness**: for a man's life consisteth not in the abundance of the things which he possesseth.

Our Life Is Not Possessions

Our life is not about the things we possess. Paul said: *"For me to live is Christ to die is gain"* (Philippians 1:21). Paul's life was about the Lord Jesus Christ and not about loving money or having covetousness.

- Acts 20:31-35
  Therefore watch, and remember, that by the space of three years I ceased not to warn every one night and day with tears. And now, brethren, I commend you to God, and to the word of his grace, which is able to build you up, and to give you an inheritance among all them which are sanctified. **I have coveted no man's silver, or gold, or apparel.** Yea, ye yourselves know, that these hands have ministered unto my necessities, and to them that were with me. I have shewed you all things, how that so labouring ye ought to support the weak, and to remember the words of the Lord Jesus, how he said, It is more blessed to give than to receive.

By saying what he did, this means that it may have been a temptation for Paul to covet various things. Paul worked hard and gave of his funds to those who needed them more than he. He was generous.

- 1 Corinthians 5:11
  But now **I have written unto you not to keep company, if any man that is called a brother be a fornicator, or covetous**, or an idolater, or a railer, or a drunkard, or an extortioner; with such an one no not to eat.
- Ephesians 5:3
  But fornication, and all uncleanness, or **covetousness, let it not be once named among you, as becometh saints;**
- Colossians 3:5
  Mortify therefore your members which are upon the earth; fornication, uncleanness, inordinate affection, evil concupiscence, and **covetousness, which is idolatry**:

Right in the midst of all these other sins is *"covetousness."*

- 1 Timothy 6:10
  For **the love of money** is the root of all evil: **which while some coveted after**, they have erred from the faith, and pierced themselves through with many sorrows.
- Hebrews 13:5
  Let your **conversation** *be* **without covetousness**; *and be* content with such things as ye have: for he hath said, I will never leave thee, nor forsake thee.

If we have the Lord Jesus Christ as our Saviour, we have everything that is important. We should be content with the things that we have.

1 Timothy 3:4

"One that ruleth well his own house, having his children in subjection with all gravity;"

Pastors Must Rule Their Own Houses

#14 The fourteenth requirement for the pastor-bishop-elder of a local church is this: He must *"rule his own house."*

The verb for *"rule"* is PROHISTEMI. It breaks down into two Greek words, PRO (*"before"*) and HISTEMI (*"to stand"*). Therefore it means literally *"to stand before or over."* The various meanings are:

"to set or place before; to set over; to be over, to superintend, preside over; to be a protector or guardian; to give aid; to care for, give attention to; profess honest occupations."

Since this verb is in the present tense, it means that this *"ruling"* of his own house by the pastor should be continuous. He must be in charge of his home and his family. That word "*house*" (OIKOS) includes among other things, "*the inmates of a house, all the persons forming one family, a household.*" The pastors, just like all husbands are to "*rule*" well their own homes.

The next clause in this verse is very important also. It says: "*having his children in subjection with all gravity.*" I realize that there are others who do not agree with me on this point, but the clear implication to me is that the pastor is to have children, either his own or those he might adopt. We have seen already that a pastor is to be the "*husband of one wife,*" so he is to be married. Now we see that the pastor is to have "*children*" and to have them "*under subjection with all gravity.*" How can you have your "*children under subjection*" if you do not have any "*children*"? It certainly is implied that the pastor should have "*children.*"

I believe that pastors should have children. If you can not have children, then adopt some. I think God wants us to know, as pastors, what children are like and how they grow so that we can help the people in our churches with their children. God wants a man who is married with children. In summary, I do not believe a person should be a pastor who is single or one who is married without children.

1 Timothy 3:5

"(For if a man know not how to rule his own house, how shall he take care of the church of God?)"

This verse logically follows the preceding one. The word "*rule*" is the same Greek word as in verse four and with the same meanings. The pastor is to do this in a very decided and determined way.

If he does not know how to "*rule his own house,*" it stands to reason that he is, therefore, unable to "*take care*" of the "*church of God.*" The word for "take care" is EPIMELEOMAI. It means: "*to take care of a person or thing.*" If a pastor's "*own house*" is in disorder or chaos, he should not be a pastor or in the ministry of the Lord Jesus Christ. I maintain that these children are to be managed and "*ruled*" well by the pastor as long as they are living in his "*house.*" When they move out of his "*house*" and are on their own, then that is a different story. Pastors who have children they cannot manage, and who are still living in his house as a part of his household, should leave the pastorate. They are disqualified. I do not know how else I could apply this verse.

When my children were under my roof they behaved. I remember I told my sons (I had three at the time, now I have four) and my daughter when I pastored my first church in Newton, Massachusetts, that if they acted up I am out of the ministry and can no longer be a pastor. They got that straight and they were well-behaved children. If they got out of line, I handled it.

You have to tell these young pastors about this. There are a lot of pastors

whose families are out of order. They have no business being in the ministry.
That is God's standard. If a pastor does not know how to rule well his own
house how can he function as one who has a genuine and proper "*care*" for his
church which is called here "*the house of God*"? This is reasonable. God
knows what he is talking about. The word "*rule*" is used throughout the Bible.

- **Genesis 3:16**
  Unto the woman he said, I will greatly multiply thy sorrow and
  thy conception; in sorrow thou shalt bring forth children; and
  **thy desire *shall be* to thy husband, and he shall rule over
  thee**.

Before the fall perhaps there was more of an equality in leadership (though the
Bible does not clearly say), but after the fall, any such equality was obliterated.
The husband was now to "*rule over*" the wife. He was to be the authority in the
home. He was to be responsible to God for his household.

- **Isaiah 3:12**
  As for my people, children *are* their oppressors, and **women
  rule over them**. O my people, they which lead thee cause
  thee to err, and destroy the way of thy paths.

God does not say that in a good way. Women "*rulers*" are not what God
expects.

- **Matthew 2:6**
  And thou Bethlehem, *in* the land of Juda, art not the least
  among the princes of Juda: for out of thee shall come a
  Governor, that shall rule my people Israel.

This is speaking about the Lord Jesus Christ.

- **Colossians 3:15**
  And **let the peace of God rule in your hearts**, to the which
  also ye are called in one body; and be ye thankful.

- **1 Timothy 5:17**
  Let the elders that rule well be counted worthy of double
  honour, especially they who labour in the word and doctrine.

- **Revelation 19:15**
  And out of his mouth goeth a sharp sword, that with it he
  should smite the nations: and **he shall rule them with a rod
  of iron**: and he treadeth the winepress of the fierceness and
  wrath of Almighty God.

The Lord Jesus is coming back to the earth. We do not know when He is
coming in the air to rapture the born-again Christians and take them to Heaven.
After that event takes place, we know that seven years later He is going to come
back to this earth with the saved ones after the Judgment Seat of Christ. Then
the Lord Jesus Christ is going to come down from Heaven and His feet will
touch the Mount of Olives.

After He returns to this earth, the Lord Jesus Christ is going to set up His Millennial reign for one thousand years. The Lord Jesus Christ will have peace on this earth. There will be no war between Iraq and the United States or any other nation in the world. He will "*rule*" the nations "*with a rod of iron.*" Peace will be there when the Prince of Peace "*rules*" this old wicked earth. Until He comes back, there will be no lasting peace. We were reading in our Bible reading recently that "*there will be wars and rumors of wars . . . but the end is not yet*" (Matthew 24:6).

Remember the story of the Good Samaritan? There was a man bleeding at the side of the road. Both the priest and the Levite walked by him without helping him or "*caring*" for him. Then the Good Samaritan came. He put this wounded and beaten man on his own beast and came to an inn. The Good Samaritan told the innkeeper to "*take care*" of this hurt man. He told the innkeeper that whatever it costs, he would pay it when he came back to the inn. In like manner, the Lord has given pastors the responsibility and the ability to "*take care of the house of God.*" If the pastor does not know how to "*take care of his own house,*" how can he successfully and Scripturally "*take care*" of the church to which God has called him?

1 Timothy 3:6

"Not a novice, lest being lifted up with pride he fall into the condemnation of the devil."

Pastors Must Not Be Novices

#15 The fifteenth requirement for the pastor-bishop-elder of a local church is this: He must be "*not a novice.*"

A pastor should not be newly saved. The word for "*novice*" is NEOPHUTOS. We get our English word neophyte from this. It is made up of NEOS ("*new*") and PHUO ("*to spring up or plant*"). It means: "*newly planted; a new convert, neophyte (one who has recently become a Christian).*" Again, that middle word for the one office of "*pastor-elder-bishop*" is important. The word "*elder*" (PRESBUTEROS) in the literal sense means: "*elder, of age; the elder of two people; advanced in life, an elder, a senior; forefathers.*"

When I became a pastor of my first Baptist church, I was only thirty-four. This is older than many men who take their first pastorates. When I became the pastor of the **Bible For Today Baptist Church**, I was seventy-one. Obviously I did not know as much at thirty-four as I did when I was seventy-one. Maturity is a must if you are going to have a pastor who has wisdom. That does not mean that just because a pastor has maturity that they will have all the wisdom he needs, but at least it is a start.

What did Paul tell Timothy was the reason why pastors should not be a "*novice*"? "*lest being lifted up with pride he fall into the condemnation of the devil.*" "*Pride*" is a dangerous thing for a pastor to have. It is something that "*novices*" tend to have more than more mature men, though it can be had by them as well. "*Pride*" is used in many places in the Bible.

- **Proverbs 13:10**
  Only by pride cometh contention: but with the well advised *is* wisdom.

- **Proverbs 16:18**
  Pride *goeth* before destruction, and an haughty spirit before a fall.

- **Obadiah 3**
  The pride of thine heart hath deceived thee, thou that dwellest in the clefts of the rock, whose habitation *is* high; that saith in his heart, Who shall bring me down to the ground?

Pride is deceptive.

- **Mark 7:21-23**
  For from within, out of the heart of men, proceed evil thoughts, adulteries, fornications, murders, Thefts, covetousness, wickedness, deceit, lasciviousness, an evil eye, blasphemy, **pride**, foolishness: All these evil things come from within, and defile the man.

Pride is one of the things that comes out of the heart and defiles a man.

- **1 John 2:16**
  For **all that *is* in the world**, the lust of the flesh, and the lust of the eyes, and **the pride of life**, is not of the Father, but is of the world.

We are not to love the things of the world, and one of them is "*the pride of life.*" What is "*pride*"? The word for it is TUPHOO. It means:

> "*to raise a smoke, to wrap in a mist; metaph. to make proud, puff up with pride, render insolent; to be puffed up with haughtiness or pride; to blind with pride or conceit, to render foolish or stupid; beclouded, besotted.*"

If any of these things in the definition occur in the life of a pastor, he has fallen into the "*condemnation of the devil.*" Someone has listed some of the things the "*devil*" (DIABOLOS) does:

> "*Satan the prince of the demons, the author of evil, persecuting good men, estranging mankind from God and enticing them to sin, afflicting them with diseases by means of demons who take possession of their bodies at his bidding.*"

Pastors Should Be Mature Christians

No one, especially pastors, should want to fall under the "*condemnation of the devil.*" To avoid this, the pastor should not be a "*novice,*" but should be saved for a number of years and have become a seasoned and mature Christian.

---

1 Timothy 3:7

"Moreover he must have a good report of them which are without; lest he fall into reproach and the snare of the devil."

Pastors Must Have a Good Report

#16 The sixteenth requirement for the pastor-bishop-elder of a local church is this: He must have "*a good report of them which are without.*"

Let us look at both of these words, "*good*" and "*report.*" "*Good*" is KALOS which means many important things. Look at this definition.

"*beautiful, handsome, excellent, eminent, choice, surpassing, precious, useful, suitable, commendable, admirable; beautiful to look at, shapely, magnificent; good, excellent in its nature and characteristics, and therefore well adapted to its ends; genuine, approved; precious; joined to names of men designated by their office, competent, able, such as one ought to be; praiseworthy, noble; beautiful by reason of purity of heart and life, and hence praiseworthy; morally good, noble; honourable, conferring honour; affecting the mind agreeably, comforting and confirming.*"

As you can see, this standard #16 is extremely high for any prospective pastor of a local church.

The word "*report*" is MARTURIA which means: "*a testifying; the office committed to the prophets of testifying concerning future events; what one testifies, testimony, i.e. before a judge.*" Notice that this "*good report*" is before "*them that are without,*" that is, the unsaved watching world. The unbelievers must know this pastor to be of a "*good report.*" That phrase is used in different ways in the Bible.

- **Acts 10:22**
  And they said, Cornelius the centurion, a just man, and one that feareth God, and **of good report among all the nation of the Jews,** was warned from God by an holy angel to send for thee into his house, and to hear words of thee.
- **Acts 22:12**
  And one Ananias, a devout man according to the law, **having a good report of all the Jews** which dwelt *there,*
- **2 Corinthians 6:8**
  By honour and dishonour, **by evil report and good report**: as deceivers, and *yet* true;
- **Philippians 4:8**
  Finally, brethren, whatsoever things are true, whatsoever things *are* honest, whatsoever things *are* just, whatsoever things *are* pure, whatsoever things *are* lovely, **whatsoever things *are* of good report**; if *there be* any virtue, and if *there be* any praise, think on these things.
- **Hebrews 11:2**
  For **by it the elders obtained a good report**.
- **3 John 12**
  Demetrius hath good report of all *men*, and of the truth itself: yea, and we *also* bear record; and ye know that our record is true.

We must have pastors with "*good reports*" from the lost of this world, "*those without*." If the pastor does not have a "*good report*," two things might happen: (1) he might fall into "*reproach*" and/or (2) he might fall into the "*snare of the devil*." The word for "*reproach*" is ONEIDISMOS. It means: "*a reproach; such as Christ suffered, for the cause of God, from his enemies.*" The word for "*snare*" is PAGIS. It has many meanings. Notice them:

"*snare, trap, noose; of snares in which birds are entangled and caught; implies unexpectedly, suddenly, because birds and beasts are caught unawares; a snare, i.e. whatever brings peril, loss, destruction; of a sudden and unexpected deadly peril; of the allurements and seductions of sin; the allurements to sin by which the devil holds one bound; the snares of love.*"

The devil has all kinds of traps for pastors, and pastors have to be careful lest they fall into these traps. Sad to say, many of these traps are of the pastors' own making. That is why pastors must have a "*good report*" from those who are "*without*."

All these sixteen qualifications for pastors have been a message to me. I hope that you have made note of these things. All pastors should meet these qualifications, or they should not be pastors.

1 Timothy 3:8

"Likewise _must_ the deacons _be_ grave, not doubletongued, not given to much wine, not greedy of filthy lucre;"

As for the pastors, so for the deacons.

Sixteen Standards for Deacons

Paul tells pastor Timothy that there are sixteen standards to be observed for deacons in a local church. The first four standards are in this verse.

The word for "_deacon_" is DIAKONOS. It means:
"_one who executes the commands of another, esp. of a master, a servant, attendant, minister; the servant of a king; a deacon, one who, by virtue of the office assigned to him by the church, cares for the poor and has charge of and distributes the money collected for their use; a waiter, one who serves food and drink._"

It is in the masculine gender. Like the pastor-bishop-elder, only males are to be "_deacons._" There is no Biblical support for women "_deacons._" Therefore, I believe that "_deaconesses_" are unscriptural.

Deacons Must Be Grave

#1 The first requirement for a "_deacon_" of a local church is this: He must be "_grave._"

The word for this is SEMNOS. It means: "_August, venerable, reverend; to be venerated for character, honourable; of persons; of deeds._"

- **1 Timothy 3:11**
  Even **so _must their_ wives _be_ grave**, not slanderers, sober, faithful in all things.
- **Titus 2:2**
  That **the aged men be** sober, **grave**, temperate, sound in faith, in charity, in patience.

Deacons Must Not Be Doubletongued

#2 The second requirement for a "*deacon*" of a local church is this: He must be "*not doubletongued.*"

The word for this is DILOGOS. It means: "*saying the same thing twice, repeating; double tongued, double in speech, saying one thing with one person, another with another (with the intent to deceive).*"

Deacons Must Not Be Given to Wine

#3 The third requirement for a "*deacon*" of a local church is this: He must be "*not given to much wine.*"

We have verses in Scripture that tell us we are not to have any alcohol of any kind.

I am going to repeat these verses here as I mentioned them earlier for the qualifications of the pastors in verse three above. There are six other verses in the New Testament that use either NEPHALEOS or NEPHO and take in all saved people.

Seven Uses of NEPHO or NEPHALEOS

Here are the references and the words translating these Greek terms which mean the ones mentioned should abstain from alcohol. The list is not limited to either pastors or deacons, but applies to all born-again Christians. I have indicated the words in our King James Bible that translate either NEPHALEOS or NEPHO.

> 1 Thessalonians 5:6 "*sober*"
> 1 Thessalonians 5:8 "*sober*"
> 1 Timothy 3:2 "*vigilant*"
> 1 Timothy 3:11 "*sober*'
> 2 Timothy 4:5 "*watch*"
> Titus 2:2 "*sober*"
> 1 Peter 1:13 "*sober.*"

Here are the various Scriptures where either NEPHALEOS or NEPHO are used, indicating total abstinence from alcohol for various groups of saved people.

- **1 Thessalonians 5:6**
Therefore let us not sleep, as *do* others; but let us watch and **be sober**.

This is for all Christians.

- **1 Thessalonians 5:8**
But let us, who are of the day, **be sober**, putting on the breastplate of faith and love; and for an helmet, the hope of salvation.
- **1 Timothy 3:2**
A bishop then must be blameless, the husband of one wife, **vigilant**, sober, of good behaviour, given to hospitality, apt to teach;

The word *"vigilant"* in this verse is NEPHALEOS.

- **1 Timothy 3:11**
Even so *must their* wives *be* grave, not slanderers, **sober**, faithful in all things.
- **2 Timothy 4:5**
But **watch** thou in all things, endure afflictions, do the work of an evangelist, make full proof of thy ministry.

The word is translated *"watch,"* but it is still NEPHALEOS. How can you watch if you are drunk? You cannot do it.

- **Titus 2:2**
That the aged men **be sober**, grave, temperate, sound in faith, in charity, in patience.

God says in this verse that even when you are older you must totally abstain from alcoholic beverages.

- **1 Peter 1:13**
Wherefore gird up the loins of your mind, **be sober**, and hope to the end for the grace that is to be brought unto you at the revelation of Jesus Christ;

Deacons Must Not Love Filthy Lucre

#4 The fourth requirement for a *"deacon"* of a local church is this: He must be *"not greedy of filthy lucre."*

The word for this is AISCHROKERDES. It means: *"eager for base gain, greedy for money."* Though a "deacon" can have money, he must not be *"greedy for money"* and make it the center and circumference of his life.

- **1 Samuel 8:3**
  And his sons walked not in his ways, but **turned aside after lucre, and took bribes**, and perverted judgment.

Samuel's sons took bribes. They *"turned aside"* from the right path after money. God does not want deacons or pastors to be greedy of money.

- **Proverbs 15:27**
  He that is greedy of gain troubleth his own house; but he that hateth gifts shall live.

- **1 Timothy 3:3**
  Not given to wine, no striker, **not greedy of filthy lucre**; but patient, not a brawler, not covetous;

- **Titus 1:7**
  For a bishop must be blameless, as the steward of God; not selfwilled, not soon angry, not given to wine, no striker, **not given to filthy lucre;**

- **1 Peter 5:2**
  Feed the flock of God which is among you, taking the oversight *thereof*, not by constraint, but willingly; **not for filthy lucre,** but of a ready mind;

In a normal church situation a pastor is paid, but a *"deacon"* is not usually paid. Whether they are paid or not paid they are not to be *"greedy of filthy lucre."* This does not say that you should not have enough money to feed, house, and clothe your family. The greediness is manifested in what some have called *"the itch for more."* You want more of this and more of that.

What does someone do if he is *"greedy of filthy lucre"*? He might not sleep as much as they should because he must put in long hours to make more money. He cannot limit his work to only five-or six-days a week, but quite often work all seven days of the week in order to make more money. He has no time for the Lord or for church attendance because he is *"greedy of filthy lucre."* God says this is not for *"deacons."*

1 Timothy 3:9

"Holding the mystery of the faith in a pure conscience."

Deacons Must Hold to the Faith

#5 The fifth requirement for a *"deacon"* of a local church is this: He must be *"Holding the mystery of the faith."*

The word used for *"holding"* is ECHO. It means many things:

> *"to have, i.e. to hold; to have (hold) in the hand, in the sense of wearing, to have (hold) possession of the mind (refers to alarm, agitating emotions, etc.), **to hold fast, keep**, to have or comprise or involve, to regard or consider or hold as; to have i.e. own, possess; external things such as pertain to property or riches or furniture or utensils or goods or food etc.; used of those joined to any one by the bonds of natural blood or marriage or friendship or duty or law etc, of attendance or companionship; to hold one's self or find one's self so and so, to be in such or such a condition; to hold one's self to a thing, **to lay hold of a thing, to adhere or cling to**; to be closely joined to a person or a thing."*

This verb is in the present tense which implies a continuous *"holding"* to the *"mystery of the faith."* A *"deacon"* cannot drift from that faith or he disqualifies himself for that office. The *"mystery"* is a secret or hidden thing. Some of the doctrines of the Bible need to be searched out in order to bring out the truth. This takes study. *"The faith"* has the definite article in the Greek phrase. It is TES PISTEOS. Whenever the definite article is used with *"faith"* it means the body of doctrine taught in the Bible. The *"deacon"* cannot hold to any false doctrine not taught in the Bible. There are a number of verses that speak of *"the faith."*

- Acts 6:7
  And the word of God increased; and the number of the disciples multiplied in Jerusalem greatly; and **a great company of the priests were obedient to the faith**.
- Acts 14:22
  Confirming the souls of the disciples, *and* **exhorting them to continue in the faith**, and that we must through much tribulation enter into the kingdom of God.

All of us who are born-again Christians should *"continue in the faith"* of the Bible. Our church should be exhorting people to *"continue in the faith"* that we find in the Scriptures. That is why I urge all of you to read God's Words from Genesis through Revelation each year. If you read eighty-five verses per day it will accomplish that goal.

- **Acts 16:5**
  And **so were the churches established in the faith**, and increased in number daily.
- **1 Corinthians 16:13**
  Watch ye, **stand fast in the faith**, quit you like men, be strong.

Do not let anybody shake you. Stand fast. Stand permanently. Stand concretely in *"the faith."*

- **Galatians 1:23**
  But they had heard only, That he which persecuted us in times past now **preacheth the faith** which once he destroyed.

The *"deacons"* have to uphold *"the mystery of the faith."* You cannot have a deacon who is an apostate or an heretic.

- **Colossians 1:23**
  If ye continue in the faith grounded and settled, and *be* not moved away from the hope of the gospel, which ye have heard, *and* which was preached to every creature which is under heaven; whereof I Paul am made a minister;

We have to be *"grounded and settled"* in *"the faith."*

- **Colossians 2:7**
  Rooted and built up in him, and stablished in the faith, as ye have been taught, abounding therein with thanksgiving.
- **1 Timothy 4:1**
  Now the Spirit speaketh expressly, that in the latter times **some shall depart from the faith**, giving heed to seducing spirits, and doctrines of devils;

All over we see churches that are *"departing from the faith."* They have their new music, they water-down their services with stories rather than Bible teaching and preaching, they despise the King James Bible, and they no longer preach *"the faith."*

One pastor here locally said that he no longer preaches the gospel or gives any invitations to repent and receive the Lord Jesus Christ as Saviour because that might hurt somebody's feelings. That is *"departure from the faith."* God commands His pastors to *"preach the Word"* (2 Timothy 4:2). The gospel includes the fact that all people are sinners and bound for hell. To have a pastor not preaching the gospel means that pastor is *"departing from the faith."*

- **1 Timothy 6:10**
  For the love of money is the root of all evil: which while some coveted after, **they have erred from the faith,** and pierced themselves through with many sorrows.

This verse does not teach that "*money*" is "*evil*" in and of itself. It is the "*love of money that is the root of all evil.*" "*Money*" and things that are involved with it will often cause you to "*depart from the faith.*"

- **2 Timothy 3:8**
  Now as Jannes and Jambres withstood Moses, so do these also resist the truth: men of corrupt minds, **reprobate concerning the faith.**

- **2 Timothy 4:7**
  I have fought a good fight, I have finished *my* course, **I have kept the faith:**

That "*faith*" which Paul "*kept*" was "*the faith*" found in the Bible. That is what I seek to do in our church ministry.

- **Titus 3:15**
  All that are with me salute thee. **Greet them that love us in the faith.** Grace *be* with you all. Amen.

- **1 Peter 5:9**
  Whom resist stedfast in the faith, knowing that the same afflictions are accomplished in your brethren that are in the world.

The Devil Hates The Faith

The devil does not like "*the faith.*" For this reason, every born-again Christian should resist him. One of most important doctrines of the devil is to get Christians to "*depart from the faith.*" We must "*resist*" the devil and "*stand fast in the faith.*"

- **Jude 3**
  Beloved, when I gave all diligence to write unto you of the common salvation, it was needful for me to write unto you, and **exhort *you* that ye should earnestly contend for the faith which was once delivered unto the saints.**

That is the body of doctrine. You may not want a battle or to be a contender, but the Bible says we must be a contender for "*the faith.*" We do not battle for our opinions, but for the doctrine of "*the faith.*"

Deacons Must Have Pure Consciences

#6 The sixth requirement for a *"deacon"* of a local church is this: He must have a *"pure conscience."*

That is important. That word for *"pure"* is KATHAIROS which means: *"clean, pure; physically; purified by fire; in a similitude, like a vine cleansed by pruning and so fitted to bear fruit; in a levitical sense; clean, the use of which is not forbidden, imparts no uncleanness; ethically; free from corrupt desire, from sin and guilt; free from every admixture of what is false, sincere genuine; blameless, innocent; unstained with the guilt of anything."*

It is important to see some of the various uses of the *"conscience"* which must be *"pure"* to qualify as a *"deacon."* The word for *"conscience"* is SUNEIDESIS which means: *"the consciousness of anything; the soul as distinguishing between what is morally good and bad, prompting to do the former and shun the latter, commending one, condemning the other; the conscience."*

- **Acts 24:16**
  And herein do I exercise myself, **to have always a conscience void of offence toward God, and** *toward* **men**.

- **1 Timothy 4:2**
  Speaking lies in hypocrisy; **having their conscience seared with a hot iron;**

Seared Consciences Do Not Work

If your conscience is *"seared"* you are not controlled by it. It does not register. It is like a thermostat that does not work to regulate the heat in a home. A conscience that is *"seared with a hot iron"* is as good as dead or cauterized. It does not work as it should.

- **2 Timothy 1:3**
  I thank God, whom **I serve from** *my* **forefathers with pure conscience**, that without ceasing I have remembrance of thee in my prayers night and day;

- Titus 1:15
  Unto the pure all things *are* pure: but unto them that are defiled and unbelieving *is* nothing pure; but **even their mind and conscience is defiled.**

We do not need deacons who have their consciences defiled.

1 Timothy 3:10

"And let these also first be proved; then let them use the office of a deacon, being *found* blameless."

Deacons Must First Be Proved

#7 The seventh requirement for a *"deacon"* of a local church is this: He must *"first be proved."*

The word for *"proved"* is DOKIMAZO. This means: *"to test, examine, prove, scrutinise (to see whether a thing is genuine or not), as metals; to recognise as genuine after examination, to approve, deem worthy."* You do not lay hands on a *"deacon"* too quickly. You must *"test, examine, prove, and scrutinise"* the candidates to make sure they are *"blameless."*

Deacons Must Be Found Blameless

#8 The eighth requirement for a *"deacon"* of a local church is this: He must be *"found blameless."*

Remember, this qualification was listed for the pastor as well. The word for *"blameless"* is ANENGLETOS. It means: *"that cannot be called into account, unreproveable, unaccused, blameless."* This does not mean that they are sinlessly perfect, but they are not to be called into an account and proved guilty for that for which they are accused.

1 Timothy 3:11

"Even so *must their* wives *be* grave, not slanderers, sober, faithful in all things."

It must be said here that *"wives"* is the correct translation of GUNE in this context. Its usual meaning is: *"a woman of any age, whether a virgin, or" married, or a widow; a wife; or a betrothed woman.*" Though some churches take this word to refer to "*deaconesses*," there is no grammatical justification for this. This is a clear reference to the qualification of the "*wives*" of the deacons in a local church.

Deacons Must Be Grave

#9 The ninth requirement for "*deacons*" of a local church is this: They must have wives that are "*grave.*"

That word is SEMNOS. It means: "*August, venerable, reverend; to be venerated for character, honourable; of persons; of deeds.*" The wives of the deacons must keep private those things that are to be kept private. This is "*honourable.*"

Deacons Must Not Be Slanderers

#10 The tenth requirement for "*deacons*" of a local church is this: They must have wives that are "*not slanderers.*"

That word is DIABOLOS. It means:

> "*prone to slander, slanderous, accusing falsely; a calumniator, false accuser, slanderer; metaph. applied to a man who, by opposing the cause of God, may be said to act the part of the devil or to side with him; Satan the prince of the demons, the author of evil, persecuting good men, estranging mankind from God and enticing them to sin, afflicting them with diseases by means of demons who take possession of their bodies at his bidding.*"

There are many verses that refer to "*slander*" and "*false accusers.*" It would be good to look at a few of them.

* **Proverbs 10:18**
  He that hideth hatred *with* lying lips, and **he that uttereth a slander,** *is* **a fool.**

  Have you ever known someone who hid their hatred of you with lying lips? They do not like you. They hate you. They despise you. But they have lying lips and act like they are your friend. God says that is a "*slander*" and that the person who utters it is a "*fool.*"

- **2 Timothy 3:3**
  Without natural affection, trucebreakers, **false accusers**, incontinent, fierce, despisers of those that are good,

Qualified deacon's *"wives"* cannot fall into this category.

- **Titus 2:3**
  The aged women likewise, that *they be* in behaviour as becometh holiness, **not false accusers**, not given to much wine, teachers of good things;

Deacons Must Be Sober

#11 The eleventh requirement for *"deacons"* of a local church is this: They must have wives that are *"sober."*

The word for *"sober"* here is NEPHOLEOS. As mentioned above, this word indicates an abstaining from wine or other forms of alcohol as a beverage. In its addicting properties, by analogy, it would include drug addition as well.

- **1 Thessalonians 5:6**
  Therefore let us not sleep, as *do* others; but let us watch and **be sober**.
- **1 Thessalonians 5:8**
  But let us, who are of the day, **be sober**, putting on the breastplate of faith and love; and for an helmet, the hope of salvation.
- **Titus 2:2**
  That the aged men be sober, grave, temperate, sound in faith, in charity, in patience.
- **1 Peter 1:13**
  Wherefore gird up the loins of your mind, **be sober**, and hope to the end for the grace that is to be brought unto you at the revelation of Jesus Christ;

Deacons Must Be Faithful

#12 The twelfth requirement for *"deacons"* of a local church is this: They must have wives that are *"faithful in all things."*

The word for *"faithful"* is PISTOS. It means:

> *"trusty, faithful; of persons who show themselves faithful in the transaction of business, the execution of commands, or the discharge of official duties; one who kept his plighted faith, worthy of trust; that can be relied on; easily persuaded; believing, confiding, trusting; in the NT one who trusts in God's promises; one who is convinced that Jesus has been raised from the dead; one who has become convinced that Jesus is the Messiah and author of salvation."*

Faithfulness is found in many places of the Bible. Here are a few of the places to consider.

- **Psalm 119:138**
  Thy testimonies *that* **thou hast commanded** *are* **righteous and very faithful.**

God's commands are *"faithful"* so deacon's *"wives"* must also be *"faithful."*

- **Proverbs 14:5**
  A faithful witness will not lie: but a false witness will utter lies.

- **1 John 1:9**
  If we confess our sins, **he is faithful** and just to forgive us *our* sins, and to cleanse us from all unrighteousness.

1 Timothy 3:12

"Let the deacons be the husbands of one wife, ruling their children and their own houses well."

Deacons Must Be Husbands of One Wife

#13 The thirteenth requirement for a *"deacon"* of a local church is this: They must be *"the husbands of one wife."*

A while back in a little church there were nominations held for deacons. One person nominated a man who was not married. That person became a deacon and remained a deacon for many years. According to this verse a *"deacon"* is presumed to be and supposed to be married. After a few years, a new pastor came to that church. That new pastor believed this verse was to be taken literally. This new pastor said that all *"deacons"* had to be the *"husbands of one wife"* and therefore had to be married. The deacon who was single was upset. He left that church because he could not be a *"deacon"* anymore. The word for *"husbands"* is ANER. It means: *"with reference to sex; of a male; of a husband; of a betrothed or future husband; with reference to age, and to distinguish an adult man from a boy; any male."* This indicates that the *"deacons"* must be male and married to only one living wife. If his wife dies, he is free to re-marry (as the pastor/bishop/elder also is). They cannot be females and they cannot be single.

Deacons Must Rule Their Children

#14 The fourteenth requirement for a *"deacon"* of a local church is this: they must be *"ruling their children . . . well."*

As in the case of the pastor, so with the *"deacons."* It is assumed that they have *"children."* I believe it is a requirement of the Bible that they have children, either their own or theirs by adoption if they cannot have their own. You might wonder why would God want the pastor and the *"deacons"* to have children. I think it is because God wants them to be mature men who can handle difficult things that come along in the churches. I realize that just because you are married and have children you are not necessarily wise. A person could be married and be unwise. You could be a father and unwise as well. But being married with children, a *"deacon"* should be more prepared to help and counsel other married people with children than if he were single or were married without children. His own personal experience with his wife and his children should help him understand the problems that others might have in their marriage, and in the raising of their children.

Notice that the *"deacons"* should *"rule their children . . . well."* The same word is used for *"rule"* as for the pastor in verse 5 above. The word is PROHISTEMI. It means: *"to set or place before; to set over; to be over, to superintend, preside over; to be a protector or guardian; to give aid; to care for, give attention to; profess honest occupations."* All the aspects that go with *"ruling"* should be done *"well."* Otherwise, the *"deacon"* is disqualified to serve.

Deacons Must Rule Their Houses

#15 The fifteenth requirement for a *"deacon"* of a local church is this: They must *"rule . . . their own houses well."*

That means "*deacons*" are "*to be good protectors, to care for, give aid to, and preside over*" their "*houses*" and those who dwell within them. And they must do this "*well.*" This would imply that a "*deacon*" should not be over his head in debt. It would imply that he would pay his bills on time and keep the "*house*" running smoothly. It would also mean that he would "*preside over*" his "*house*" and be the head of his home rather than turn the headship over to his wife or children and be run by them. He must be the spiritual leader in his "*house.*"

1 Timothy 3:13

"For they that have used the office of a deacon well purchase to themselves a good degree, and great boldness in the faith which is in Christ Jesus."

Deacons Must Use the Office Well

#16 The sixteenth requirement for a "*deacon*" of a local church is this: He must be able to "*use the office of a deacon well.*"

I realize this is in the past tense, "*used,*" but it implies that after a man has become a "*deacon*" he must be able to "*use*" the "*office of a deacon well.*" A major part of this proper "*use*" of his "*office*" is to know what "*deacon*" means and what he does. Acts 6:1-4 gives some background of the duties and mission of "*deacons*" in the early church. The word is DIAKONOS. There are various meanings of this word:

"*to be a servant, attendant, domestic, to serve, wait upon; to minister to one, render ministering offices to; to be served, ministered unto; to wait at a table and offer food and drink to the guests; of women preparing food; to minister i.e. supply food and necessities of life; to relieve one's necessities (e.g. by collecting alms), to provide take care of, distribute, the things necessary to sustain life; to take care of the poor and the sick, who administer the office of a deacon; in Christian churches to serve as deacons; to minister; to attend to anything, that may serve another's interests; to minister a thing to one, to serve one or by supplying any thing.*"

As you can see, this word has a wide variety of meanings, but the one sense that goes throughout the various meanings is that of "*serving and ministering.*"

Many Deacons Are Out-of-Line Today

Some of our fundamental Baptist churches have *"deacons"* who are not servants but masters. They look on themselves as being executives on the board of a corporation or secular business. They rule over the pastor and over every one in the church. This should not be! There is not a shred of evidence in the Bible for *"deacons"* to act like that. It is a gross distortion of the truth. If you told some of these kinds of *"deacons"* in these churches that they are to be *"servants,"* they would be outraged.

If these *"deacons"* use their office well, they *"purchase"* for themselves a *"good degree"* or dignity and wholesome influence in their churches. They also will have *"great boldness in the faith."* The word for *"boldness"* is PARRHESIA. The word means:

"freedom in speaking, unreservedness in speech; openly, frankly, i.e without concealment; without ambiguity or circumlocution; without the use of figures and comparisons; free and fearless confidence, cheerful courage, boldness, assurance; the deportment by which one becomes conspicuous or secures publicity."

What a wonderful local church if they had every one of their "deacons" equipped with *"great boldness in the faith which is in Christ Jesus"*! They would not only know *"the faith"* and doctrines, but be bold in expressing them and teaching them to others. We need *"boldness"* for our Lord and Saviour.

- Acts 4:13

  Now when **they saw the boldness of Peter and John**, and perceived that they were unlearned and ignorant men, they marvelled; and they took knowledge of them, that they had been with Jesus.

The Lord Jesus gives us *"boldness"* when we are with Him in close fellowship and communion.

- Acts 4:31

  And when they had prayed, the place was shaken where they were assembled together; and they were all filled with the Holy Ghost, and **they spake the word of God with boldness**.

You should not be timid when you *"speak the Words of God."*

- Philippians 1:20

  According to my earnest expectation and *my* hope, that in nothing I shall be ashamed, but *that* **with all boldness**, as always, *so* now also **Christ shall be magnified in my body, whether** *it be* **by life, or by death.**

Paul did not care if he lived or died. He wanted the Lord Jesus Christ to make him *"bold"* as a witness for Him in prison. Even though Paul was a prisoner, he was *"bold."*

Steering a Straight Course

"Good men are sometimes afraid of a straight course of action because it may cause trouble, or appear to be too bold. In such a case we must not be silent out of respect for them, but openly oppose them. Dear is Peter, but dearer still the truth." [Comment on Galatians 2:11-14 by Charles H. Spurgeon, *Morning and Evening,* p. 701]

---

1 Timothy 3:14

"These things write I unto thee, hoping to come unto thee shortly:"

Paul thought he would see Timothy in the near future. He was not sure of it, but he *"hoped"* he could come to him at Ephesus *"shortly."* I am sure that Timothy would have been glad to have Paul come to minister to him at any time.

1 Timothy 3:15

"But if I tarry long, that thou mayest know how thou oughtest to behave thyself in the house of God, which is the church of the living God, the pillar and ground of the truth."

Paul hastened to say that if he had a delay and would *"tarry long,"* that is, wait for a long time before he came, that Paul had some expectations for Pastor Timothy. What did Paul expect of Pastor Timothy? Paul's burden for Pastor Timothy, and I am sure for all pastors of all the ages, was that he might *"know how thou oughtest to behave thyself in the house of God."* The word for *"oughtest"* is DEI. It means:

> *"it is necessary, there is need of, it behooves, is right and proper; necessity lying in the nature of the case; necessity brought on by circumstances or by the conduct of others toward us; necessity in reference to what is required to attain some end; a necessity of law and command, of duty, equity; necessity established by the counsel and decree of God."*

It is a necessary thing. Pastors must of necessity know how to *"behave themselves*" when ministering in the "*house of God*" in their local churches. The word for this is ANASTREPHO. The main meaning in this context is: "*to turn hither and thither, to turn one's self about, sojourn dwell in a place; metaph. to conduct one's self, behave one's self, live.*" Members of local churches should also, of necessity, know how to "*behave themselves*" in God's house. There is so much impropriety in God's house today. It should be stopped. This misbehavior is not limited to children. It is true of all too many adults as well. "*Behaving*" is important.

- Psalm 101:2
  I will behave myself wisely in a perfect way. O when wilt thou come unto me? I will walk within my house with a perfect heart.
- 1 Timothy 3:2
  A bishop then must be blameless, the husband of one wife, vigilant, sober, **of good behaviour**, given to hospitality, apt to teach;
- Titus 2:3
  The aged women likewise, **that they be in behaviour as becometh holiness,** not false accusers, not given to much wine, teachers of good things;

We Must Behave Ourselves Well

We have to know how to "*behave*" ourselves. It is one thing to believe, and another thing to "*behave*." I am glad that many of us have genuinely believed in and trusted the Lord Jesus Christ as our Saviour, but how do we "*behave*"? People look at us. If they are observant, they can usually tell if we are real or not by our "*behaviour.*"

Coming back from Lancaster, Pennsylvania, recently, Mrs. Waite and I stopped at a Chinese restaurant for supper. We saw a woman there who, from her dress, demeanor, and behavior, looked like she was a born-again Christian. What was it about that woman whereby we knew she was a Christian? There was something about her, that neither of us could explain, but we suspected that she knew the Lord Jesus Christ as her Saviour and Lord. When we were finished our supper, Mrs. Waite went over to her table and talked with her. Sure enough, we were right. She was a genuinely saved Christian lady. Our Lord Jesus Christ said to His disciples: "*Let your light so shine before men, that they may see your good works, and glorify your Father which is in heaven*" (Matthew 5:16) This lady's "*light*" did "*shine*" before us, and may the "*light*" of every born-again Christian "*shine*" as well.   This is good Christian "*behaviour.*"

Then Paul defines the "*church of the living God.*" He says it is "*the pillar and ground of the truth.*" "*Pillars*" go up.   The word for "pillar" is STULOS. It means: "*a pillar; a column; pillars of fire i.e. flames rising like pillars; a prop or support.*"   The church is to be a "*prop or support*" for the "*truth*" of God's Words.

- **Genesis 28:18**
  And Jacob rose up early in the morning, and **took the stone that he had put** *for* **his pillows, and set it up** *for* **a pillar,** and poured oil upon the top of it.

The "*ground*" is the basis.   The word is HEDRAIOMA meaning almost the same as "*pillar.*"   It means: "*a stay, prop, support.*"   It comes from the root of HADRAIOS which means: "*sitting, sedentary; firm, immovable, steadfast.*" For a local church to be a "*pillar and ground of the truth*" it must support that "*truth*" in a "*firm, immovable, and steadfast*" manner.   The "*truth*" is found in the Bible.   The church and all the its members must have the proper Bible in which to find all the that "*truth.*"   In English, I believe firmly you must have, use, and defend the King James Bible because of its superior Hebrew, Aramaic, and Greek texts and Words, its superior translators, its superior translation technique, and its superior theology.   I have given this in full in my book, *DEFENDING THE KING JAMES BIBLE.* (**BFT #1594**).

Local Church--Pillar & Ground of Truth

The local church is to be "*the pillar and ground of the truth.*" The Bible is the truth. Too many local churches have relinquished their authority as the "*pillar and ground of the truth*" to mission boards, to publishers, to Bible societies, to Christian schools, to Bible Institutes, to colleges, to theological seminaries, to fellowships, to associations of churches, to synods, to presbyteries, to cardinals, to Popes, or to some other entity. This should never be.

All the above things might fail and slide into error, but "*the truth*" of God's Words must prevail.   That is why I am glad that our Bible For Today ministry has produced the *DEFINED KING JAMES BIBLE* which makes the King James Bible and its "*truth*" understandable to all.   Many local churches have purchased these Bibles for their people.   We now have over 56,000 in print and distributed all around the world.   We must continue, as local churches to fight in the battle for "*truth*" as the "*pillar and ground.*"   Apostasy and compromise enter churches when the *"truth"* of the Words of God are no longer recognized by them as the *"pillar and ground."*

1 Timothy 3:16

"And without controversy great is the mystery of godliness: God was manifest in the flesh, justified in the Spirit, seen of angels, preached unto the Gentiles, believed on in the world, received up into glory."

This is a verse that is mangled by the modern versions. These versions deny the Incarnation of God the Son into sinless human flesh.

Heretical Denial of the Incarnation

In the phrase *"God was manifest in the flesh,"* the Word *"God"* has been eliminated in the modern versions because it was eliminated by the critical texts of Westcott and Hort, Nestle/Aland, and United Bible Societies. It is eliminated from these three critical texts because it is eliminated from the foundation of these texts, Egyptian Gnostic manuscripts "B" (Vatican) and "Aleph" (Sinai). The false modern versions such as the NASV, NIV, ESV, RSV, NRSV, and many others substitute "HE" for "GOD." This is serious heresy.

If you insert *"he"* (instead of *"God"*) into this verse, you do not know to whom it is referring. It was *"God manifest in the flesh,"* the Lord Jesus Christ Who was *"justified in the Spirit, seen of angels, preached unto the Gentiles, believed on in the world, received up into glory."*

If these modern versions are heretical in this Word, how can you trust their Words in the rest of their Bible?

Evidence For "God" Manifest in the Flesh

Dean John William Burgon has analyzed the Greek manuscripts in this verse. He shows how many manuscripts in his day had THEOS ("God"), how many had HOS ("who"), and how many had HO ("which").

1. The Evidence for THEOS ("God")

    The Lectionaries and Copies---------------------289

    Ancient translations or Versions---------------- 3

    Early Church Fathers quotes-------------------- 20
                                                    ====
                                                    312

2. The Evidence for WHICH ("HO")

    The Lectionaries and Copies--------------------- 1

    Ancient Translations or Versions---------------- 5

    Early Church Fathers quotes-------------------- 2
                                                    ====
                                                    8

3. The Evidence for WHO ("HOS")

    The Lectionaries and Copies--------------------- 6

    Ancient Translations or Versions---------------- 1

    Early Church Fathers quotes--------------------- 0
                                                    ====
                                                    7

With few exceptions, all these modern versions have rejected "***God*** *was manifest in the flesh*" despite the fact that there are at least 312 pieces of evidence that had THEOS ("*God*") in the Greek text.

Gnostics Corrupted the New Testament

The Gnostics, with headquarters in Alexandria, Egypt, removed THEOS ("*God*") from this verse because they did not believe that the Lord Jesus Christ was God. They also did not believe in the bodily resurrection of the Lord Jesus Christ or His virgin birth, and most of the other foundations of the Christian faith.

- John 1:14
  And **the Word was made flesh, and dwelt among us,** (and
  we beheld his glory, the glory as of the only begotten of the
  Father,) full of grace and truth.
- Philippians 2:6
  Who, **being in the form of God**, thought it not robbery to be
  equal with God:

Christ's Virgin Birth & Deity Vital

The modernists and liberals believe that the Lord Jesus Christ was just a
man. On the contrary, He was *"God manifest in the flesh."* When you say,
as the NIV does, that *"He appeared in a body"* instead of *"God was manifest
in the flesh,"* it takes away and removes the deity of the Lord Jesus Christ.
Everyone has *"appeared in a body,"* but the fact is that this verse clearly
teaches that it was <u>GOD</u> Who was *"manifest in the flesh"* by the process of
the Virgin Birth. This is very serious.

Many people take the position if the doctrine is taught in another part of
the Bible it does not matter if it is taken away in some other place. No, I want
it to be found everywhere it is supposed to be. Nowhere in the entire New
Testament is there a verse that very clearly states that *"God was manifest in the
flesh"* except right here in 1 Timothy 3:16. That makes this verse even more
important. The Lord Jesus Christ was, and is, perfect God and perfect Man.
The Bible teaches this very clearly right here in this verse.

Let me tell you another thing. The Greek words HOS and HO are both
relative pronouns. To use relative pronouns in this sentence instead of THEOS,
which is a noun, is not grammatical. It makes no grammatical sense in Greek,
and it makes no grammatical sense in English.

Let me give you an example of what it would be like. This verse says,
*"And without controversy great is the mystery of godliness: **God** was manifest
in the flesh."* *"God"* is the subject of that last clause. That defines what the
"mystery of godliness" was.

If you read it with HOS (*"who"*) which is a relative pronoun, even in
English it is not grammatically correct. Here is the translation of that: *"Great
is the mystery of godliness **who** was manifest in the flesh."* This does not make
any sense. You can not refer *"who"* back to *"godliness."* That does not make
sense in the Greek either.

If you read it with HO (*"which"*), which is also a relative pronoun, even
in English it is not grammatically correct. Here is the translation of that: *"Great*

*is the mystery of godliness **which** was manifest in the flesh.*" "*Which*" cannot refer back to "*godliness.*" That makes no sense either in English or in Greek.

First Timothy
Chapter Four

1 Timothy 4:1

"Now the Spirit speaketh expressly, that in the latter times some shall depart from the faith, giving heed to seducing spirits, and doctrines of devils;"

Here is an "*express*" revelation by God the Holy Spirit that is spelled out clearly and precisely concerning the "*latter times.*" The Spirit speaking "*expressly*" is RHETOS. It means "*expressly, in express words.*" During these "*times*" certain definite things are to take place. I believe that we in A.D. 2006, and even before and after that date are living, have been living, and will be living in these "*latter times.*" I believe that these specific prophetic predictions given by the Holy Spirit, through Paul to us in this chapter of 1 Timothy have been, are now being, and will be seen in the world.

In the Scripture we have a number of references to the "*latter times*" or the "*last days.*"

- **Acts 2:17**
  And it shall come to pass **in the last days**, saith God, I will pour out of my Spirit upon all flesh: and your sons and your daughters shall prophesy, and your young men shall see visions, and your old men shall dream dreams:

- **2 Timothy 3:1**
  This know also, that **in the last days** perilous times shall come.

- **Hebrews 1:2**
  Hath **in these last days** spoken unto us by *his* Son, whom he hath appointed heir of all things, by whom also he made the worlds;

- **James 5:3**
  Your gold and silver is cankered; and the rust of them shall be a witness against you, and shall eat your flesh as it were fire. Ye have heaped treasure together **for the last days**.

- **2 Peter 3:3**
  Knowing this first, that there shall come **in the last days** scoffers, walking after their own lusts,

In the first three verses of this chapter there are a total of seven prophetic predictions that Paul reveals to Pastor Timothy.

Departing From the Faith

#1 The first prophetic prediction is *"some shall depart from the faith."*

Notice that both in the English and the Greek there is a definite article before *"faith."* It is *"the faith"* (HE PISTIS), which means it is the entire body of Bible doctrine. This is not simply personal faith in Christ. It is *"the faith."* The verb for *"depart from"* is APHISTEMI. It carries with it a number of ideas:

"to make stand off, cause to withdraw, to remove; to excite to revolt; to stand off, to stand aloof; to go away, to depart from anyone; to desert, withdraw from one; to fall away, become faithless; to shun, flee from; to cease to vex one; to withdraw one's self from, to fall away; to keep one's self from, absent one's self from."

We have modernism, liberalism, and apostasy on every hand today both inside and outside the churches. All of those systems are outside of and contradictory to *"the faith."*

Giving Heed to Seducing Spirits

#2 The second prophetic prediction is that those who **"depart from the faith"** will be **"giving heed to seducing spirits."**

The word *"seducing"* is PLANOS. It means: *"wandering, roving; misleading, leading into error; a vagabond, 'tramp,' imposter; corrupter, deceiver."* These will lead the followers into error. Spiritism in its various forms, including the mediums who allegedly communicate with the dead, is an example of this. It includes astrology as well. These heresies are prevalent in our days.

The Astrology of the Reagans

A quote from the Internet on *"Sydney Omar, The Reagans and Astrology"* stated:

> *"As the world remembers the passing of Sydney Omar, a prominent astrologer whose column appeared in more than 300 newspapers across the country including the Washington Post, it is interesting to look back to the days of the Reagan Administration, and the use by the President and First Lady of astrology to guide in the making of important decisions in the White House."*

If the quote is true, this is *"giving heed to seducing spirits"* at the highest level of our United States of America.

There are various books on Spiritism listed on the Internet on that theme. The five *"basic books"* are listed as: (1) *The Spirits' Book*, (2) *The Book on Mediums* (3) *The Gospel According to Spiritism;* (4) *Heaven and Hell*; and (5) *The Genesis According to Spiritism.* They list three things as "precursors" of Spiritism: (1) The Fox Sisters, (2) Talking Boards, and (3) Mesmerism.

Heeding Doctrines of Devils

#3 The third prophetic prediction is that those who *"depart from the faith"* will be *"giving heed to . . . doctrines of devils."*

The word for "devils" is DAIMONION. It means: *"the divine power, deity, divinity; a spirit, a being inferior to God, superior to men; evil spirits or the messengers and ministers of the devil."* "Devils" is a good translation because it clarifies once and for all that these are evil beings, not good ones. *"Demons,"* on the other hand, are worshipped as gods in some religions and philosophies. Because of this, this word should not be transliterated into *"demons"* but translated as *"devils"* showing that they are subservient to the Devil himself. The power of the Devil is manifested in many Bible verses.

- **1 Corinthians 10:20**
  But I *say*, that **the things which the Gentiles sacrifice, they sacrifice to devils**, and not to God: and I would not that ye should have **fellowship with devils**.

Heathen who worship idols, whether in the United States or in other places throughout the world, are, in truth, sacrificing to "*devils.*" The Devil himself is behind that worship. The "*dashboard dollies*" which are carried on the automobile dashboards of some Roman Catholics is idolatry, as far as I'm concerned.

* **James 2:19**
  Thou believest that there is one God; thou doest well: **the devils also believe, and tremble.**

"Head Belief" Alone Will Not Redeem

Simple "head belief" will not save because the "*devils*" have "head belief." They know there is a God. They do not have the belief in their heart, and that is essential for people to be saved. To be saved, people must have genuine heart faith in the Lord Jesus Christ.

---

* **Revelation 9:20**
  And the rest of the men which were not killed by these plagues yet **repented not of the works of their hands, that they should not worship devils,** and idols of gold, and silver, and brass, and stone, and of wood: which neither can see, nor hear, nor walk:

God is going to send terrible plagues during the seven years of Tribulation after all the born-again Christians are snatched away from this earth in the Rapture. During this Tribulation period, the people who are on the earth will be "*worshiping devils.*"

* **Revelation 16:14**
  For **they are the spirits of devils, working miracles,** *which* go forth unto the kings of the earth and of the whole world, to gather them to the battle of that great day of God Almighty.

Special miracles will be performed by the "*devils*" during this Tribulation time. I believe that today much of the healings in the charismatic movement are done by "*devils.*"

As far as the apostasy of our day, if you look in the book *Weniger's Words of Warning* (**BFT #863**), you will see that back in 1965 the author analyzed some of the statements of the Northern Baptist Convention. The General Association of Regular Baptist Churches came out of the Northern Baptist Convention in the 1940's. Apostasy was even rampant then; but of course it is worse today. The following are some quotations from Dr. Archer Weniger which I believe illustrates some of these "*doctrines of devils.*"

The reason I call these doctrines of "*devils*" is because they come from religious leaders who are unsaved. The Lord Jesus Christ called the religious leaders of his day, the Pharisees, children of the Devil. *"Ye are of your father the Devil . . ."* (John 8:44a). The false teachings of the children of the Devil (the unsaved people) can be called *"the doctrines of devils."*

This was a professor and the head of the Religious Studies at Andover-Newton Seminary in Massachusetts. His name is Wesner Fallaw. He said, *"Jesus is not God."*

Here is another quote. Remember this is back in 1965. Do you think it is any better today? It has grown worse. He is the president of the Colorado Springs Women's College, Dr. Val Wilson. He was asked if he believed in the *"literal resurrection of Christ."* He said, *"No, I do not accept it."* Here was a Baptist minister teaching in that college over forty-two years ago. Things are not getting any better. They are getting worse.

Here is another quote from Sherwood Eddie who was, at that time, one of the speakers at the American Baptist Convention. He was talking about the Person of our Lord Jesus Christ. In answer to the *"Person of Christ,"* Eddie said *"He was limited and fallible"* That meant this man thought the Lord Jesus Christ could sin and was not and is not impeccable, or sinless.

Here is a quotation from Duncan Littlefair who was also in the American Baptist Convention leadership. In answer to the question, *"Was Jesus God?"* Littlefair said: *"There are two major approaches to this question. One of them is to make Jesus God, . . . but this is idolatry. Jesus is not and cannot be God."*

Here is a quotation from an American Baptist Convention leader, Edwin Aubrey who was a professor in one of their seminaries. In his book, *Man's search for God,* Aubrey said of Christ, *"He is not the Creator Who made heaven and earth, nor is He all of God."*

This next quotation is Nels Ferre who was a professor at Andover-Newton Seminary near Boston, Massachusetts. He wrote a book called, *Understanding of God.* In that book he said, *"But if Jesus takes the place of God, we still have idolatry. . . . Hence Jesus must have been the child of a German solider."* This is a denial of Christ's virgin birth and Deity.

Apostate World Council of Churches

The World Council of Churches is led by apostates from all over the world. The National Council of Churches, in our country, is also led by apostates. They teach *"doctrines of devils."* I do not think that all the members in these churches are lost, but the leadership of the whole World and National Councils of Churches is an apostate leadership. They deny the deity of the Lord Jesus Christ, His bodily resurrection, His miracles, His blood atonement, and salvation by grace through faith alone.   They have departed from the faith. This is a serious situation. The Lord Himself predicted this departure right here in 1 Timothy.

●   1 Timothy 4:1
Now the Spirit speaketh expressly, that in the latter times **some shall depart from the faith, giving heed to seducing spirits, and doctrines of devils;**

The Methodist Church's Apostasy

This is a fact that we cannot escape. We have this apostasy on every hand. You cannot assume because your grandmother used to go to the Methodist Church that it must be all right. No, it is not all right. My mother was born in 1900. When my mother first went to the Methodist Church, when she was a girl, it was all right. I do not agree with the doctrine of the Methodist Church, but the doctrine of salvation by grace through faith was all right in my grandmother's day. My Grandpa Peirce was saved and was so zealous in his salvation that he joined the Salvation Army and went out preaching the gospel. That was my maternal grandfather.

My grandmother was a Baptist to start with and then turned Methodist. That was how my mother got into the Methodist Church. My mother sent her children to the Methodist Church in Berea, Ohio, which was just as apostate as the day is long. I questioned the preacher when I came back from Dallas Theological Seminary one summer. I told my mom I was going to ask her pastor a few questions. He failed every question. He failed on the deity of Christ. He failed on the blood atonement of Christ. He failed on the virgin birth of Christ. He failed on the bodily resurrection of Christ. He failed on salvation by grace through faith. I told mom what he said. She told me that I must have misunderstood him. It is not safe in many of these churches today because they have *"departed from the faith"* and *"giving heed to seducing spirits and doctrines of devils."* We who know and stand for *"the faith"* must expose these apostate leaders and their *"doctrines of devils."*

1 Timothy 4:2

"Speaking lies in hypocrisy; having their conscience seared with a hot iron;"

Speaking Lies In Hypocrisy

#4 The fourth prophetic prediction is that those who *"depart from the faith"* will be *"speaking lies in hypocrisy."*

Paul is speaking of those who are apostates and false religious teachers. They have departed from the faith, and they are *"speaking lies."* It is one thing to *"depart from the faith,"* but it is another thing to lie. That is compounding the problem. It is one thing to depart from the Lord Jesus Christ as Saviour and Redeemer, but this goes beyond that. That is exactly what God says here. *"Speaking lies in hypocrisy"*" The word for *"speaking lies"* is just one Greek word, PSEUDOLOGOS. It means: *"speaking (teaching) falsely, speaking lies."*

The speaking of these *"lies"* is done *"in hypocrisy."* The word is HYPOCRISIS. It means: *"an answering; an answer; **the acting of a stage player**; dissimulation, hypocrisy."* This *"acting of a stage player"* is a very descriptive meaning of *"hypocrisy."* Actors do not necessarily mean what they are saying on the stage. They are just acting. A person could play the part of a wicked woman on the stage and be a decent woman off the stage. By the same token, it is possible for an actress to portray a godly woman on stage, but be a wicked woman in real life. That is *"hypocrisy."* This is what unsaved ministers do in their pulpits. They pretend to believe in the historic doctrines of their church, but they really do not believe them. This is an illustration of *"speaking lies in hypocrisy."*

Satan As An Angel of Light

Remember Paul's admonition that *"Satan himself is transformed into an angel of light.   Therefore it is no great thing if his ministers also be transformed as the ministers of righteousness . . ."* (**2 Corinthians 11:14-15b**).

Here are some verses to ponder both on *"lies"* and on *"hypocrisy."*

- **Psalm 58:3**
  The wicked are estranged from the womb: **they go astray as soon as they be born, speaking lies.**

- **John 8:44**
  Ye are of *your* father the devil, and the lusts of your father ye will do. He was a murderer from the beginning, and abode not in the truth, because there is no truth in him. When he speaketh a lie, he speaketh of his own: **for he is a liar, and the father of it.**

- **1 John 2:4**
  He that saith, I know him, and keepeth not his command-ments, **is a liar**, and the truth is not in him.

My mother-in-law never liked me to call anybody a *"liar."* She did not like to use such a strong word. God calls people *"liars"* who claim to know God, but they do not follow His Words. That is falsehood.

- **1 John 4:20**
  If a man say, I love God, and hateth his brother, he is a liar: for he that loveth not his brother whom he hath seen, how can he love God whom he hath not seen?

There are also many verses dealing with *"hypocrisy."*

- **Matthew 23:28**
  Even so ye also outwardly appear righteous unto men, but **within ye are full of hypocrisy and iniquity**.

The Lord Jesus Christ with His omniscience could look right into the heart of those Pharisees.

- **Mark 12:15**
  Shall we give, or shall we not give? But **he, knowing their hypocrisy**, said unto them, Why tempt ye me? bring me a penny, that I may see *it*.

- **Luke 12:1**
  In the mean time, when there were gathered together an innumerable multitude of people, insomuch that they trode one upon another, he began to say unto his disciples first of all, **Beware ye of the leaven of the Pharisees, which is hypocrisy.**
The Pharisees were the most religious people in the Lord's day.

- **James 3:17**
  But the wisdom that is from above is first pure, then peaceable, gentle, *and* easy to be intreated, full of mercy and good fruits, without partiality, and **without hypocrisy.**
"Wisdom that is from above" is *"without hypocrisy."* There should be no *"hypocrisy"* with wisdom that is from Him. The Lord gives us wisdom that we should abide by and accept. Fundamental churches are not without *"hypocrisy."* I hope that we have no *"hypocrisy"* here in our local church. As I found out later, we had some of it in our church also. I hope that what the Lord Jesus Christ said to the Pharisees cannot be applied here. There are some churches where this can be honestly applied. Outwardly they seem fine, but inwardly is a different story.

Consciences Seared With a Hot Iron

#5 The fifth prophetic prediction is that those who *"depart from the faith"* will be those *"having their conscience seared with a hot iron."*

The *"conscience"* originally was like a thermostat for the soul. If the thermostat is broken or *"seared with a hot iron,"* you cannot feel anything and you do not have any control over evil. The word for *"conscience"* is SUNEIDESIS. It means:
> *"the consciousness of anything; the soul as distinguishing between what is morally good and bad, prompting to do the former and shun the latter, commending one, condemning the other; the conscience."*
If the conscience is *"seared with a hot iron"* it does not work. It is just like a broken thermostat that does not work. The phrase *"seared with a hot iron"* is just one word: KAUTERIAZO. We get our English word *"cauterized"* from it. It means:
> *"to mark by branding, to brand, branded with their own consciences; whose souls are branded with the marks of sin; who carry about with them the perpetual consciousness of sin; seared; in a medical sense, to cauterise, remove by cautery."*

Hypocritical Lying With a Straight Face

These men who say that they believe that *"the faith,"* as taught in the Bible, is all right and then deny it are *"speaking lies in hypocrisy,"* and truly their *"conscience is seared with a hot iron."* When you lie does it hurt your conscience? I hope so, if you are saved. If you should lie, I hope it hurts your conscience so that you will repent of it. The people referred to in this verse *"lie"* and preach the *"doctrine of devils"* with a straight face.

1 Timothy 4:3

"Forbidding to marry, and commanding to abstain from meats, which hath created to be received with thanksgiving of them which believe and know the truth."

Forbidding to Marry

#6 The sixth prophetic prediction is that those who *"depart from the faith"* will be those who are *"forbidding to marry."*

Even in Paul's day there were teachings that people should forbid people *"to marry."* From the Catholic Encyclopedia we read: *"In the Spanish Council of Elvira (between 295 and 302) in canon xxxiii, it imposes celibacy upon the three higher orders of the clergy, bishops, priests, and deacons."* Celibacy is practiced today among the Roman Catholic priests and nuns. The Bible says that *"marriage is honourable in all, and the bed undefiled. . ."* (Hebrews 13:4). It is wrong to *"forbid to marry."* That is one reason for the terrible debacle of the Roman Catholic Church today. Perhaps there are pedophiles and homosexuals among the Roman Catholic priesthood because of this wicked and unscriptural position. That is a terrible thing. God wants those who are able to marry to marry and not to be forbidden from doing so.

Abstaining From Meats

#7 The seventh prophetic prediction is that those who *"depart from the faith"* will be those who are *"commanding to abstain from meats."*

The word for "*meats*" is BROMA. It means: "*that which is eaten, food.*" This refers to food of all kinds, including "*meat.*" This again could refer to some of the Roman Catholic teachings. They have an imposition of some dietary rules at certain times. Years ago Catholic people were forbidden to eat meat on Friday. Now, that has been changed.

We should thank the Lord for our food. Some of us eat better than others. Some of us eat more than others. There are some people in other parts of the world who do not have a lot of food. God has given us food that we are to eat. You may have a certain diet where you don't eat certain foods. That is good if it helps you for health reasons. But to have a church force you not to eat certain things is not right. I may not eat pork, but I don't say that you cannot eat pork. I don't eat ants either, but you can eat them if you want to.

When I was going to Dallas Theological Seminary (1948--1953), once a month I went up to Tahlequah, Oklahoma, to do some country preaching with some other students. We went to different country churches that did not have pastors. The families would feed us lunch after the Sunday morning service. One time, a hostess asked one of these students if he wanted a piece of cake. The cake had white frosting and what looked like raisins on top. Well, as he looked closer he discovered those raisins were flies. Needless to say, he politely declined her offer of the cake.

- Luke 17:27
  They did eat, they drank, they married wives, they were given in marriage, until the day that Noe entered into the ark, and the flood came, and destroyed them all.

- Hebrews 13:4
  Marriage *is* honourable in all, and the bed undefiled: but whoremongers and adulterers God will judge.

This is God's view of marriage.

- 1 Corinthians 6:13
  Meats for the belly, and the belly for meats: but God shall destroy both it and them. **Now the body *is* not for fornication, but for the Lord; and the Lord for the body**.

- 1 Corinthians 8:13
  Wherefore, **if meat make my brother to offend, I will eat no flesh while the world standeth,** lest I make my brother to offend.

- Colossians 2:16
  Let no man therefore judge you in meat, or in drink, or in respect of an holyday, or of the new moon, or of the sabbath *days*:

We should not be under the influence of those who are telling us to "*abstain*" from any kind of food as an obligation. Eating or not eating must be on a voluntary basis by each individual. Of course, there are some foods and drinks that are not good for us and should not be used by us as born-again Christians.

Thank God For Food He Gives Us

God has "*created*" foods to be "*received with thanksgiving*" by those who "*believe and know the truth.*" We should not forget to thank God for the food He has given us.

---

1 Timothy 4:4

"For every creature of God *is* good, and nothing to be refused, if it be received with thanksgiving:"

In Acts 10:11-16, the Lord showed Peter, by way of illustration, that he could minister to Gentiles. The illustration was that of a sheet being let down from Heaven containing all kinds of animals. The Lord said, "*rise, Peter; kill and eat.*" Some of the animals were unclean according to the Old Testament standards of Leviticus 11. Peter told the Lord he had never eaten anything that was unclean. The Lord told Peter "*What God hath cleansed , that call not thou unclean*" (Acts 10:15b). Peter understood that he was to preach the gospel to the Gentile Cornelius, without doubting, and so he did, and Cornelius was saved.

This present verse reminds us that when we eat our food, we must receive it "*with thanksgiving,*" whatever our food might be and what quantity or quality it might be.

- **Psalm 95:2**
  Let us come before his presence with thanksgiving, and make a joyful noise unto him with psalms.

I am glad that every Lord's Day in our church we sing, "*Thank you Jesus for all you've done.*" God wants us to have a thankful heart and a thankful spirit.

- **Philippians 4:6**
  Be careful for nothing; but in every thing by prayer and supplication with thanksgiving let your requests be made known unto God.

God wants us to be a thankful people at all times.

- **Colossians 2:7**
  Rooted and built up in him, and stablished in the faith, as ye have been taught, abounding therein with thanksgiving.

Are you thankful? For what should you be thankful? Do you have two eyes so you can see? Do you have a mouth that can speak? Do you have hands that can touch and work? Do you have feet that can walk? Do you have a heart that beats? God has given us so much. We are *"fearfully and wonderfully made"* (Psalm 139:14a). It is true that some of us are made more *"wonderfully"* than others.

- **Colossians 4:2**
  Continue in prayer, and **watch in the same with thanksgiving**;

God wants us to be thankful for all we have. Before we eat a meal we thank the Lord for our food. The Lord Jesus gave thanks before he broke the bread (Matthew 15:36; 26:27; Mark 8:6), and we need to give thanks also.

"I Thank Thee, Lord"

Dear Lord, I raise my heart in praise
As morning gives its early rays,
And thank Thee for a clean new day
To live for Thee and walk Thy way.
And Lord, I magnify Thy name
For Thou art evermore the same,
And thank Thee for Thy Word so true,
And every promise proven thru
Which is in the very mind of You.
I thank Thee for my morning meal
And for the strength and health I feel;
I thank Thee, too, for home and mate,
Protective care that compensates.
Oh, Lord, what grace that I may speak
To Thee my God--my day's complete,
That I may tell in words so plain
My hearts own praise, I will proclaim!

By Gertrude G. Sanborn

With Tears In My Heart

One of the author's latter poems found after death in her own hand writing.
Gertrude Sanborn died in June of 1988. This was probably written a year or more before her death.

1 Timothy 4:5

"For it is sanctified by the word of God and prayer."

The word for *"sanctified"* is HAGIAZO. It means:

> *"to render or acknowledge, or to be venerable or hallow; to separate from profane things and dedicate to God; consecrate things to God; dedicate people to God; to purify; to cleanse externally; to purify by expiation: free from the guilt of sin; to purify internally by renewing of the soul."*

Something is *"sanctified"* or *"purified"* because it is *"separated from profane things"* and set apart for the Lord. In this verse it says that the food we eat is *"sanctified"* by both the *"Words of God"* and by *"prayer."* This is why we should give thanks for our food at each meal.

In Paul's day there were men who offered meat to idols. They could buy this meat in a cheaper place. Some Christians were bothered by another Christian buying meat which had been offered to idols. In this verse it tells us that even if meat has been offered to idols it is *"sanctified."* Meat is meat even if it has been offered to idols, but if it offends your Christian brother, then as Paul said, we should eat no meat at all. That is showing us that some things, although they are all right in themselves, can be stumbling blocks to our Christian brothers and sisters.

The Sin of Gluttony

Can you *"sanctify"* overeating? I do not think you can do that because it is excess and not in *"moderation"* (Philippians 4:5). Though I am not in favor of either the Popes or the Roman Catholic Church, it was Pope Gregory in the 6th Century A.D. who first listed *"gluttony"* as one of the *"seven deadly sins."* It is an important list of sins from which Bible-believing Christians should abstain, regardless of who made up the list. From the Internet *Wikipedia*, here is his list *"in order of increasing severity"*:

1. Lust
2. Gluttony
3. Greed or Avarice
4. Sloth, Laziness, or Sadness
5. Wrath
6. Envy
7. Pride

The "*glutton*" pattern would be "*eat, vomit, eat, vomit, and continue that cycle.*" That was terrible. We should not be "*gluttons.*" I do not believe that kind of eating can be "*sanctified by the Word of God and prayer.*" We who are saved must be calm and "*temperate*" in all things that we do, including our eating.

1 Timothy 4:6

"If thou put the brethren in remembrance of these things, thou shalt be a good minister of Jesus Christ, nourished up in the words of faith and of good doctrine, whereunto thou hast attained."

Timothy was the pastor of the church of Ephesus, which is located in the country of Turkey. Paul was teaching Timothy on a daily basis while they went together on many missionary journeys all over the then-known world. Paul wanted Pastor Timothy to "*put the brethren in remembrance of these things*" that Paul had told him. This included the things in the previous four chapters and all other things Paul had taught him. If he did this, he would be a "*good minister of Jesus Christ.*" The word for "*minister*" is DIAKONOS. It means:

> "**_one who executes the commands of another_**, *esp. of a master, a servant, attendant, minister; the servant of a king; a deacon, one who, by virtue of the office assigned to him by the church, cares for the poor and has charge of and distributes the money collected for their use; a waiter, one who serves food and drink.*"

We get the English word "*deacon*" from this Greek word. The first part of that definition is what most "*deacons*" are not; "*one who executes the commands of another.*"

Deacons—Execute Orders, Not Give Them

All too many "*deacons*" are "*giving*" commands rather than "*executing commands.*" Paul reminded Timothy that although he was the pastor of that church, he was also to be a "*good*" servant of the Lord Jesus Christ. As a pastor, I am to be a "*good*" servant of the Lord Jesus Christ also. My duty is to execute the commands of another, the Lord Jesus Christ.

I must do the will of God as He has given it to us in His Words. The word for "*good*" is KALOS. It means many things, including:

> "*beautiful, handsome, excellent, eminent, choice, surpassing, precious, useful, suitable, commendable, admirable; beautiful to look at, shapely, magnificent; good, excellent in its nature and characteristics, and therefore well adapted to its ends; genuine,*"

approved; precious; joined to names of men designated by their office, competent, able, such as one ought to be; praiseworthy, noble; beautiful by reason of purity of heart and life, and hence praiseworthy; morally good, noble; honourable, conferring honour; affecting the mind agreeably, comforting and confirming."

May my ministry and that of all the Bible-believing pastors, measure up to this level of "*goodness*"!

If Timothy would follow this admonition, he would then be "*nourished up in the words of faith and of good doctrine, whereunto he had attained.*" The word for "*nourished up*" is ENTREPHO. It means: "*to nourish in: a person or a thing; metaph. to educate, form the mind.*" If Timothy "*put the brethren in remembrance*" of Paul's teachings, he would "*form in his mind*" more solidly "*the faith*" (used with the definite article) and "*good doctrine.*"

Nourishing Others Nourishes Us

In other words, when Pastor Timothy would teach others, he himself would be "*nourished up*" and solidified in "*the faith*" and "*good doctrine.*" It is a good thing to bring the things of the Lord to "*remembrance*" so they are not forgotten. The Holy Spirit brought to "*remembrance*" the things concerning the Lord Jesus Christ's ministry.

- **John 14:26**
  But the Comforter, *which is* the Holy Ghost, whom the Father will send in my name, **he shall teach you all things, and bring all things to your remembrance, whatsoever I have said unto you.**

- **1 Corinthians 4:17**
  For this cause have I sent unto you Timotheus, who is my beloved son, and faithful in the Lord, **who shall bring you into remembrance of my ways which be in Christ**, as I teach every where in every church.

  Paul wanted Timothy to "*bring into remembrance*" to the Corinthian believers "*his ways which be in Christ.*" Timothy knew the ways of Paul because he had been with Paul, and he knew his teachings.

- **1 Corinthians 11:24**
  And when he had given thanks, he brake *it*, and said, Take, eat: this is my body, which is broken for you: **this do in remembrance of me.**

The Purpose of the Lord's Supper

The special event we are told to remember about the Lord Jesus Christ was His shed blood and broken body on the cross of Calvary. It is not a sacrament which gives us some kind of *"grace."* It is a *"remembrance."* It is not something we do to get salvation. It is a *"remembrance"* of the atoning sacrifice the Lord Jesus Christ made because of, and to atone for, the sins of the whole world.

- **Philippians 1:3**
  I thank my God **upon every remembrance of you**,
  Paul was very thankful for the *"remembrance"* of the Christians at Philippi. I hope that our lives will be such that when our friends remember us they will thank God for that *"remembrance."* Can you think of someone who is really antagonistic and bitter toward you? What comes to your mind when you think of that particular person? Paul said that he thanked God for *"every remembrance"* of the Philippians people. I would hope that our lives would be so straight with the Lord that our friends would thank God for us also.

- **2 Peter 1:12**
  Wherefore **I will not be negligent to put you always in remembrance of these things**, though ye know *them*, and be established in the present truth.
  You may know things, but you should be reminded of these things so you will not forget them.

- **2 Peter 1:15**
  Moreover I will endeavour **that ye may be able after my decease to have these things always in remembrance**.
  The Apostle Peter knew he was going to die. He wrote the book of 2 Peter so the truths he had written would be *"in remembrance"* after his death. Do you have things that you want to be in *"remembrance"* after your decease? Are you leaving things for people to remember? That is what I am trying to do before the Lord calls me Home to Heaven. That is exactly what I believe I have been called of the Lord to do in my pulpit. In 1965, when I left the pastorate of Faith Baptist in Newton, Massachusetts, I never wanted to be a pastor again. I had had enough of churches and church people, having been the pastor of two churches in Massachusetts and saw how these church people behaved.

  However, thirty-three years later, in 1998, the Lord spoke to my heart and I was led, along with my wife, to begin our **Bible For Today Baptist Church** in our home. In addition to benefitting those who attend our church, an important reason for beginning this church was to *"preach the Words"* of God

(2 Timothy 4:2a) as I had been trained, and to leave what I believed to my four sons, one daughter, my grandchildren, and my great grandchildren.

The First Eight Years of Development

How the ministry has developed during its first eight years at the

Bible For Today Baptist Church

900 Park Avenue, Collingswood, NJ 08108

WEB: www.BibleForToday.org   E-MAIL: bft@BibleForToday.org

1. **We began with audio tapes,**
2. **then also video tapes,**
3. **then radio messages,**
4. **then Internet access to both audio and video messages,**
5. **then seven verse-by-verse preaching books (so far),**
6. **then streaming videos of our morning services preaching verse-by-verse from Romans through Revelation 24/7, and then**
7. **live worldwide video "webcasting" on SermonAudio.com each Sunday morning at 10 a.m., beginning on Sunday, December 31, 2006.**

The Lord has more than enabled me to make a "*remembrance*" for my family and any others who might care to have these items. I praise the Lord for His enablement.

1 Timothy 4:7

"But refuse profane and old wives' fables, and exercise thyself *rather* unto godliness."

Paul says to "*refuse*" two things: "*profane and old wives fables.*" The word for "*refuse*" is PARAITEOMAI. It means various things:

"*to ask along side, beg to have near one; to obtain by entreaty; to beg from, to ask for, supplicate; to avert by entreaty or seek to avert, to deprecate; to entreat that ... not; **to refuse, decline; to shun, avoid;** to avert displeasure by entreaty; to beg pardon, crave indulgence, to excuse; of one excusing himself for not accepting a wedding; invitation to a feast*"

The word "*refuse*" is in the present tense and would usually convey the idea that this "*refusal*" was to be continuous and without letup.

The word for "*profane*" is BEBELOS. It means: "*accessible, lawful to be trodden; of places; profane; unhallowed, common, public place; of men, ungodly."*

Refuse Ungodly Places and People

Timothy was to *"refuse"* the *"unhallowed and ungodly"* places and people so far as close fellowship is concerned. Timothy was to *"preach the Word"* (2 Timothy 4:2). He was to give the Scriptures out and be faithful to the Lord.

The second thing Timothy was to *"refuse"* and avoid was *"old wives fables."* The word for *"fables"* is MUTHOIS. It has various meanings: *"a speech, word, saying; a narrative, story; a true narrative; <u>a fiction, a fable; an invention, a falsehood</u>."* We get our word *"myth"* from this Greek term.

Church Women--Blessing or Bane?

Sometimes *"old wives"* have some false things that they talk about. The women in churches can either be a great blessing to the pastor or a great bane. Apparently there were some older women in the Timothy's church at Ephesus who were spinning some false yarns.

Paul told Timothy to stand aside from such things, having nothing to do with these things. Paul told Timothy *"exercise thyself rather unto godliness."* The word for *"exercise"* is GUMNAZO. It means: *"to exercise vigorously, in any way, either the body or the mind."* In Timothy's case, he was to *"exercise vigorously"* his mind and spirit to the honor of the Lord Jesus Christ, leading to *"godliness."*

The word *"profane"* is also used elsewhere in Scripture.

- **1 Timothy 6:20**
  O Timothy, keep that which is committed to thy trust, **avoiding profane *and* vain babblings,** and oppositions of science falsely so called:

- **2 Timothy 2:16**
  But **shun profane *and* vain babblings**: for they will increase unto more ungodliness.

1 Timothy 4:8

"For bodily exercise profiteth little: but godliness is profitable unto all things, having promise of the life that now is, and of that which is to come."

Although this is not what Paul was talking about here, as far as dollars and cents goes, I think there is great *"profit"* in the *"exercise"* industry. You can see it on TV where advertisers are trying to sell different things to improve our ability to *"exercise."* Right in Collingswood there is a new *"exercise"* gym. As far as God is concerned the *"profit"* of *"bodily exercise"* is just *"little."*

On the other hand, *"godliness is profitable unto all things."* Notice that, though *"bodily exercise"* is good only for this life, *"godliness"* is *"profitable"* and has *"promise of the life that now is, and of that which is to come."* It has a present and a future that goes with it.

Does Your Light Shine?

A godly life on the part of a born-again Christian can be used of the Lord to get others to *"glorify our Father which is in Heaven"* (Matthew 5:16). This happens when our godly *"light so shines before men."* This life is profitable because people see the fruits of *"godliness."* A consistent godly life on the part of the saved person will bring rewards in the future at the Judgment Seat of Christ. Truly, *"godliness is profitable unto all things. "* May we who know the Lord Jesus Christ as our Saviour be godly, not ungodly.

---

1 Timothy 4:9

"This *is* a faithful saying and worthy of all acceptation."

This phrase, *"faithful saying,"* appears four times in the King James Bible's New Testament.

- **1 Timothy 1:15**
  This *is* a faithful saying, and worthy of all acceptation, that **Christ Jesus came into the world to save sinners**; of whom I am chief.

  That is why the Lord Jesus Christ *"came into the world."* It was to *"save sinners."* Though all *"sinners"* will not receive His salvation, He did come into the world to save all the those who would receive Him. The views of the hyper-

Calvinists are incorrect on this theological point. The choice is up to every *"sinner"* in the world, not just the *"elect."* It is their move.

Christ Died For All Sinners

The Lord Jesus Christ has come to die for all the *"sinners"* of the world. He wants these *"sinners"* to receive Him and be saved. If you do not consider yourself to be a "sinner," it is not likely that you will be interested in the One Who bore your sins on Calvary. You will not receive Him and trust Him and therefore will be lost in the Lake of Fire for all eternity. The choice is yours.

- **1 Timothy 4:9**
  This *is* a faithful saying and worthy of all acceptation.
  This is the verse in our text.
- **2 Timothy 2:11**
  It *is* a faithful saying: For if we be dead with *him*, we shall also live with *him*:
- **Titus 3:8**
  This *is* a faithful saying, and these things I will that thou affirm constantly, that they which have believed in God might be careful to maintain good works. These things are good and profitable unto men.
  Something that is *"faithful"* will not let you down. I hope all of us are faithful in what we say. I hope that we have *"faithful sayings."* I hope that if we say we are going to do something we will do it. We have to be faithful in what we say and what we do. This is what is *"worthy of all acceptation."*

1 Timothy 4:10

"For therefore we both labour and suffer reproach, because we trust in the living God, who is the Saviour of all men, specially of those that believe."

Because of Paul's "exercise" unto *"godliness,"* he *"labours."* The word for *"labour"* is KOPIAO. It means: *"to grow weary, tired, exhausted (with toil or burdens or grief); to labour with wearisome effort, to toil; of bodily labour."* This is *"wearisome effort"* that Paul is expending in order to maintain *"godliness"* in the face of a wicked world around him. Paul worked with his hands so that the people would not have to support him. The word *"labour"* is used many places.

- Matthew 11:28
  Come unto me, all *ye* that labour and are heavy laden, and I will give you rest.

- John 6:27
  Labour not for the meat which perisheth, but for that meat which endureth unto everlasting life, which the Son of man shall give unto you: for him hath God the Father sealed.
  We are to "*labour*" for the meat which lasts, the Words of God and eternal life.

- 1 Corinthians 4:12
  And labour, working with our own hands: being reviled, we bless; being persecuted, we suffer it:
  Paul was a pastor, minister, missionary, and apostle. He could have had the churches support him, which is proper (as he discussed in 1 Corinthians 9:6-15), but he "*laboured*" working with his hands. Some pastors have million-dollar houses and many material possessions. Paul did not want anyone to say anything about his being a lover of money, so he worked and supported himself.

- 1 Corinthians 15:58
  Therefore, my beloved brethren, be ye stedfast, unmoveable, always abounding in the work of the Lord, forasmuch as ye know that your labour is not in vain in the Lord.
  This was one of my father-in-law's favorite verses.

- 2 Corinthians 5:9
  Wherefore we labour, that, whether present or absent, we may be accepted of him.

- Galatians 4:11
  I am afraid of you, **lest I have bestowed upon you labour in vain.**
  I hope that our "*labour*" here in our **Bible For Today Baptist Church** is not "*in vain.*" I hope that the Lord is going to honor our "*labour*" and ministry. Presently, we have over twenty-eight families who have requested our monthly services by VHS, or DVD. We have many around the world who watch our live and recorded streaming videos of our services and preaching verse by verse from Romans through Revelation. Many of these families have told me they cannot find where they live a sound King James Bible church with expository preaching and good music. I trust that these families will be blessed so our "*labour*" will not be "*in vain*" and worthless.

  As of the date of publication, our church has over 1,640 messages on the **SermonAudio.Com** Internet site where they can listen to our audio and/or video services and other special messages, 24/7, by clicking on **www.BibleForToday.org**. To date ,there have been over 1,026,332 audio views of our messages and of those, there have been over 231,887 audio downloads. This means these people have put these messages on their own computers. Last month as this is written, there were 62 foreign countries and all 50 States that downloaded at least one of our messages. I trust that our *"labour"* as pastor and people is not *"in vain."* I am personally very grateful for the reception that our messages have received worldwide. Paul did not want his *"labour"* to be *"in vain,"* and I hope you do not want your *"labour"* to be *"in vain."*

- **Ephesians 4:28**
  Let him that stole steal no more: but rather **let him labour, working with *his* hands** the thing which is good, that he may have to give to him that needeth.

- **1 Thessalonians 2:9**
  For **ye remember, brethren, our labour and travail: for labouring night and day**, because we would not be chargeable unto any of you, we preached unto you the gospel of God.

- **2 Thessalonians 3:8**
  Neither did we eat any man's bread for nought; **but wrought with labour and travail night and day**, that we might not be chargeable to any of you:

The Reproach of the Gospel

Paul not only *"labours"* but also *"suffers reproach."* The word for *"suffer reproach"* is ONEIDIZO. It means: *"to reproach, upbraid, revile; of deserved reproach; of undeserved reproach, to revile; to upbraid, cast (favours received) in one's teeth."* Does anybody reproach or revile you because of your faith? That's what Paul was going through when he was in the prison in Rome and in other prisons as well. There are many verses about *"reproach."*

- **Psalm 69:7**
  Because **for thy sake I have borne reproach**; shame hath covered my face.

  I hope that if you are *"reproached"* it will be for God's sake and not for your own orneriness.

- **Psalm 79:4**
  We are become a reproach to our neighbours, a scorn and derision to them that are round about us.

  I hope it is for good things and not for bad things that we are scorned by our neighbors.

- Luke 6:22

  Blessed are ye, when men shall hate you, and when they shall separate you *from their company*, and **shall reproach *you*,** and cast out your name as evil, for the Son of man's sake.

  If people hate us here at the 𝕭𝖎𝖇𝖑𝖊 𝕱𝖔𝖗 𝕿𝖔𝖉𝖆𝖞 𝕭𝖆𝖕𝖙𝖎𝖘𝖙 𝕮𝖍𝖚𝖗𝖈𝖍 because we stand for the Lord Jesus Christ and the doctrines of Christ, so be it.

Ten of Our Church Distinctives

Let me list a few of our distinctives:

1. We use and defend the King James Bible and its underlying Hebrew, Aramaic, and Greek Words;
2. We have expository verse-by-verse preaching;
3. We have traditional Christian music;
4. We do not have drums;
5. We do not have "*worship leaders*";
6. We are dispensational, pre-millennial, and believe in the pre-tribulation rapture of all born-again Christians;
7. We believe the Lord Jesus Christ died for the sins of the entire world;
8. We oppose hyper-Calvinism;
9. We oppose apostasy, modernism, liberalism, new-evangelicalism, the charismatic movement, and Rick Warrenism;
10. We oppose speaking in tongues and faith healing.

I could go on, but will stop at this point.

- Hebrews 11:26

  Esteeming the reproach of Christ greater riches than the treasures in Egypt: for he had respect unto the recompence of the reward.

  The reason we might suffer "*reproach*" is that we "*trust in the living God*" rather than in men or organizations. Notice what Paul tells Timothy about hyper-Calvinism, even before it was ever systematized into its false teaching about God's salvation. Paul wrote about "*the living God, Who is the Saviour of all men, specially of those that believe.*"

  What does this mean? It means that there is no other "*Saviour*" in the whole world. This does not mean that everyone is saved. The hyper-Calvinists wrongly teach that the Lord Jesus Christ is only the "*Saviour*" of the "*elect*" and not the "*Saviour of all men.*" Thus they deny the truth of this verse. No, the

Lord Jesus Christ is the "*Saviour of all men.*" He is the only One people can turn to in order to be saved. The words "*specially of those that believe*" shows that by genuine "*believing*" in Him, He has a "*special*" sense of being their personal "*Saviour.*" This means that anyone who genuinely trusts and believes on Him as their "*Saviour*" can be saved.

The Saviour to "Those that Believe"

Notice, Paul did not say or imply that the Lord Jesus Christ is only the "special Saviour" to the "*elect*" but to "*those that believe.*" This implies the possibility and freedom of credence or belief on the part of anyone in the world who genuinely "*believes*" and trusts in the only "*Saviour*" in the world that ever was or ever shall be.

There are many verses about the Lord Jesus Christ as a "*Saviour.*"

- **Luke 2:11**
  For **unto you is born this day in the city of David a Saviour,** which is Christ the Lord.
- **John 4:42**
  And said unto the woman, Now we believe, not because of thy saying: for we have heard *him* ourselves, and know that **this is indeed the Christ, the Saviour of the world.**

He is the only "*Saviour*" that ever was or shall be.

- **Acts 5:31**
  Him hath **God exalted with his right hand** *to be* **a Prince and a Saviour,** for to give repentance to Israel, and forgiveness of sins.

  He is a Prince, a Leader, a Ruler, and a "*Saviour.*"
- **Philippians 3:20**
  For our conversation is in heaven; from whence also **we look for the Saviour, the Lord Jesus Christ:**

  Are you looking for the "*Saviour*"? One day He is going to come. If you are saved, you should be looking for Him. He might come back again today!
- **2 Timothy 1:10**
  But is now **made manifest by the appearing of our Saviour Jesus Christ,** who hath abolished death, and hath brought life and immortality to light through the gospel:
- **1 John 4:14**
  And we have seen and do testify that the Father **sent the Son** *to be* **the Saviour of the world.**

Now let us look at some verses that read not only "*Saviour,*" but "*OUR Saviour.*" He is the personal "*Saviour*" of those who truly trust Him.

* **Titus 2:13**
  Looking for that blessed hope, and the glorious appearing of the great God and **our Saviour Jesus Christ;**

Are you looking for Him? David said, "*The Lord is MY Shepherd . . .*" (Psalm 23:1). That made it personal with David.

* **Titus 3:4**
  But after that the kindness and love of God **our Saviour** toward man appeared,

* **Titus 3:6**
  Which he shed on us abundantly through Jesus Christ **our Saviour;**

* **2 Peter 1:1**
  Simon Peter, a servant and an apostle of Jesus Christ, to them that have obtained like precious faith with us through the righteousness of God and **our Saviour** Jesus Christ:

* **2 Peter 1:11**
  For so an entrance shall be ministered unto you abundantly into the everlasting kingdom of **our Lord and Saviour** Jesus Christ.

* **2 Peter 3:18**
  But grow in grace, and *in* the knowledge of **our Lord and Saviour** Jesus Christ. To him *be* glory both now and for ever. Amen.

Is Jesus Christ <u>Your</u> Saviour?

The most important question for you who may read these words is this: Is the Lord Jesus Christ <u>your</u> "*Saviour*"? If not, why not let Him become that for you?

---

1 Timothy 4:11
"These things command and teach."

Paul says Pastor Timothy is both to "*command*" and to "*teach.*" Both of these imperative verbs are in the present tense which usually demand a continuous action. He should never stop "*commanding*" and "*teaching*" his church the truths Paul is disclosing in this epistle. The word for "*command*" is

PARAGGELLO. It means: "*to transmit a message along from one to another, to declare, announce; to command, order, charge.*" Timothy was not to be timid or squeamish about these important doctrinal and practical matters. The word for "*teach*" is DIDASKO. It has many shades of meaning:

> "*to teach; to hold discourse with others in order to instruct them, deliver didactic discourses; to be a teacher; to discharge the office of a teacher, conduct one's self as a teacher; to teach one; to impart instruction; instill doctrine into one; the thing taught or enjoined; to explain or expound a thing; to teach one something.*"

Pastors Must <u>Teach</u> God's Words

One of the requirements of a pastor is that he is not only able to "*preach*" but also willing and able to "*teach*" the Words of God. Ephesians 4:11b uses the term "*pastors and teachers.*" Many feel these two gifts are combined. I believe many pastors have not been "*teachers*" of the Words of God, but rather have been story-tellers or having no unified "*curriculum*" of instruction for God's people they serve. Many are ill-prepared and some even copy other men's outlines and sermons. Shame on these non-teaching pastors!

There are various verses concerning "*commands.*" Here are a few of them to look at briefly.

- **John 15:14**
  Ye are my friends, if ye **do whatsoever I command you**.
- **John 15:17**
  These things I command you, that ye love one another.
  That is a command.
- **2 Thessalonians 3:6**
  Now **we command you, brethren**, in the name of our Lord Jesus Christ, that ye withdraw yourselves from every brother that walketh disorderly, and not after the tradition which he received of us.
  We are to separate even from Christians who are walking disorderly.
- **2 Thessalonians 3:12**
  Now **them that are such we command** and exhort by our Lord Jesus Christ, that with quietness they work, and eat their own bread.

Paul was commanding many things here.

In addition to verses on "*commands,*" there are also various verses on the *"teaching"* need of pastors and other believers in Christ.

- **1 Timothy 3:2**
A bishop then must be blameless, the husband of one wife, vigilant, sober, of good behaviour, given to hospitality, **apt to teach;**
  A *"bishop"* is both a pastor and an elder. All three titles, as used in the New Testament, apply to the same man. He is a *"pastor-bishop-elder."*

- **2 Timothy 2:2**
And the things that thou hast heard of me among many witnesses, the same commit thou to **faithful men, who shall be able to teach others also.**

- **2 Timothy 2:24**
And the servant of the Lord must not strive; but be gentle unto all *men*, **apt to teach**, patient,

---

All Can Be "Servants" of the Lord"

You can be a *"servant of the Lord."* You do not have to be a pastor to be a *"servant of the Lord."* Every Christian should be able to *"teach"* the Words of God. That is what God wants all born-again Christians to do.

---

1 Timothy 4:12

"Let no man despise thy youth; but be thou an example of the believers, in word, in conversation, in charity, in spirit, in faith, in purity. "

Before Paul outlines six things that Timothy should exemplify. He gives him a direct order. He wrote: *"Let no man despise thy youth."* This is a present imperative in the negative mood. It is a negative prohibition. Being a negative prohibition, in the present tense it means to stop an action already going on. He is telling Pastor Timothy to *"stop letting anyone despise thy youth."* He was permitting them to do this. The word for *"despise"* is KATAPHRONEO. It means: *"to contemn, despise, disdain, think little or nothing of."* This is what his people in Ephesus were doing. If the negative command were in the aorist tense, it would mean *"do not even begin to let anyone despise thy youth."* But this structure implies that people were *"despising"* Timothy's *"youth."* We do not know how old he was, but he was no doubt younger than some, or many, of those in his church. How can a pastor *"stop having people despise him"*?

Keep Being An Example of Believers

Paul tells him how this be done in this verse. He was to be an *"example"* of the *"believers,"* or saved ones, in six areas of his life. The verb *"be thou"* is an imperative in the present tense and implies that these six areas of exemplification were to be continuously followed. The pastor must not let down being an *"example"* for one minute! He is always on display.

The word for *"example"* is TUPOS. It has various meanings:

*"the mark of a stroke or blow, print; a figure formed by a blow or impression; of a figure or image; of the image of the gods; form; the teaching which embodies the sum and substance of religion and represents it to the mind, manner of writing, the contents and form of a letter; an example; in the technical sense, the pattern in conformity to which a thing must be made; in an ethical sense, a dissuasive example, a pattern of warning; of ruinous events which serve as admonitions or warnings to others; **an example to be imitated; of men worthy of imitation**; in a doctrinal sense; of a type i.e. a person or thing prefiguring a future; (Messianic) person or thing."*

"An example to be imitated" is the only way a pastor, young or old, can answer those who *"despise"* him. What is demanded of Pastor Timothy should also be demanded for every Bible-believing pastor of today as well.

Example #1--in Word

[1] To avoid anyone *"despising"* him, the first area in which Pastor Timothy was to be an *"example of the believers"* was *"in word."*

Timothy was to be careful about his *"words,"* that is, what he says to his people and to others. He was to be able to speak, to preach, and to teach in clear *"words"* so people could understand the *Words* and will of God. He had to use right and proper *"words."*

What About Your Words?

What about your *"words"*? Do you swear? Do you say *"Oh my God"*? Do you use dirty *"words"*? Are your *"words"* clean and proper? Do you tell *"off-color"* jokes or stories?   Is your language *"suggestive"* or *"provocative"*? Do you use *"minced oaths"* like *"heck," "gee," "golly," "darn," "heck,"* and many others of a similar nature? Paul told Pastor Timothy that he had to be an *"example of the believers"* in his *"words."*

Example #2--In Conversation

[2] To avoid anyone *"despising"* him, the second area in which Pastor Timothy was to be an *"example of the believers"* was *"in conversation."*

The word for *"conversation"* is ANASTROPHE. In 1611, *"conversation"* meant more than it means today. The Greek words means: *"manner of life, conduct, behaviour, deportment."* In addition to *"words,"* Pastor Timothy had to be an *"example of the believers"* in his *"conduct, behaviour and deportment."* All believers, and especially pastors, must live their lives in such a way that it is pleasing to the Lord. We need to be examples where we go, where we spend our time, what we watch on TV, and what we read, and in many other ways.

Example #3--In Charity

[3] To avoid anyone *"despising"* him, the third area in which Pastor Timothy was to be an *"example of the believers,"* was *"in charity."*

The word for this is AGAPE. It means: *"brotherly love, affection, good will, love, benevolence."* Pastor Timothy and all pastors today must have and must show love and holy affection toward all their people, even for those who are unlovely. With some, this task is more difficult than with others, but it must be done. The Lord Jesus told the saved people to love one another as He has loved us (John 13:34; 15:12, 17). This is a difficult yet vitally important pastoral duty as an *"example of the believers."*

Example #4--In Spirit

[4] To avoid anyone *"despising"* him, the fourth area in which Pastor Timothy was to be an *"example of the believers,"* was *"in spirit."*

This word is PNEUMA. It has many shades of meaning, including:
"a movement of air (a gentle blast of the wind, hence the wind itself; breath of nostrils or mouth; the spirit, i.e. the vital principal by which the body is animated; the rational spirit, the power by which the human being feels, thinks, decides; the soul; a spirit, i.e. a simple essence, devoid of all or at least; all grosser matter, and possessed of the power of knowing, desiring, deciding, and acting; a life giving spirit; a human soul that has left the body; a spirit higher than man but lower than God, i.e. an angel; used of demons, or evil spirits, who were conceived as inhabiting the bodies of men; the spiritual nature of Christ, higher than the highest angels and equal to God, the divine nature of Christ; of God; God's power and agency distinguishable in thought from his essence in itself considered; manifest in the course of affairs; by its influence upon the souls productive in the theocratic body (the church) of all the higher spiritual gifts and blessings; the third person of the trinity, the God the Holy Spirit; <u>the disposition or influence which fills and governs the soul of any one; the efficient source of any power, affection, emotion, desire, etc.</u>"
It is this last sense in which this word is used here. It is the *"disposition or influence which fills and governs the soul of any one."* You have heard of *"spirited"* people and *"spirited"* horses. They are lively, but they must be *"governed"* as well. I used to have a horse named Babe. She was a spirited horse. She had five gates and was very frisky. She had to be *"governed"* by the rider. Pastor Timothy was to be an *"example of the believers"* in his *"spirit"* which should be lively, yet governed and controlled. He was to be on fire for the things of the Lord.

Example #5--In Faith

[5] To avoid anyone *"despising"* him, the fifth area in which Pastor Timothy was to be an *"example of the believers,"* was *"in faith."*

The word is PISTIS. It has various meanings:

> "*conviction of the truth of anything, belief; in the NT of a conviction or belief respecting man's relationship to God and divine things, generally with the included idea of trust and holy fervour born of faith and joined with it; relating to God; the conviction that God exists and is the creator and ruler of all things, the provider and bestower of eternal salvation through Christ; relating to Christ; a strong and welcome conviction or belief that Jesus is the Messiah, through whom we obtain eternal salvation in the kingdom of God; the religious beliefs of Christians; belief with the predominate idea of trust (or confidence) whether in God or in Christ, springing from faith in the same; fidelity, faithfulness; the character of one who can be relied on.*"

Faith in All the Promises of God

Pastor Timothy was to have "*conviction*" and "*confidence*" in the things of the Lord and in His Words. He was to have "*faith*" in the promises of God. What He promised, He will fulfill. For example, God has promised to preserve His Hebrew, Aramaic, and Greek Words. Pastors must take the lead in "*faith*" in such promises. Such "*faith*" is absent in even many Fundamentalist quarters today.

- **Matthew 5:18**
  For verily I say unto you, Till heaven and earth pass, **one jot or one tittle shall in no wise pass from the law, till all be fulfilled**.

"*Heaven and earth*" have not "*passed*." Until then, the Lord Jesus Christ has promised that not even the smallest letter or the smallest DOT or Hebrew accent will "*pass*" until "*all be fulfilled*." Pastors must exemplify "*faith*" in such promises by the Lord.

- **Proverbs 3:5**
  Trust in the LORD with all thine heart; and lean not unto thine own understanding.

There are many areas of "*faith*" and "*trust*" that a pastor must be an "*example of the believers*." If he lacks strong and genuine "*faith*" in God and in His Words, how can he lead his people in that important area of the Christian life?

Example #6--In Purity

[6] To avoid anyone *"despising"* him, the sixth area in which Pastor Timothy was to be an *"example of the believers"* was *"in purity."*

Timothy was to be careful to be pure. The word is HAGNEIA which comes from HAGNOS which means: *"exciting reverence, venerable, sacred; pure;* **pure from carnality, chaste, modest;** *pure from every fault, immaculate; clean."* For many decades now, there have been many examples of pastors who have been impure. In recent months there were two such examples in a short space of time. One pastor was a charismatic and other a fundamentalist Baptist. Both of them are homosexuals and have been such for a number of years. They were masquerading as pastors in the pulpits of their churches, but were finally found out and resigned. I would only wish that none of these pastors would ever seek to be a pastor again, but I cannot be sure of this since many such men have re-entered the pastorate after such impurity. As far as the Bible is concerned, they have lost their qualifications in this area of *"purity"* and in many others. Shame on all such pastors for their hypocrisy!

* **1 Peter 1:15**
  But as he which hath called you is holy, so **be ye holy in all manner of conversation**;

"Holiness" is enjoined by Peter here. This involves *"purity."*

* **1 Timothy 5:2**
  "The elder women as mothers; **the younger as sisters, with all purity**."

There is a very vivid, yet horrible, example, as I write these words, concerning a pastor in Florida who has been *"impure"* for more than twenty years and just now has been arrested for being a pedophile. What a blight on the Christian faith when this happens to have a prominent Baptist pastor who is known far and wide. He was acting as someone that he was not. Pastors must be an *"example of the believers"* in *"purity"* of life and testimony.

1 Timothy 4:13

"Till I come, give attendance to reading, to exhortation, to doctrine."

Paul intended to come for a visit to Pastor Timothy at Ephesus. Until that time, he was to give special attention to at least these three things. The word for *"give attendance"* is PROSECHO. It means:

"to bring to, bring near; to bring a ship to land, and simply to touch

at, put in; *to turn the mind to, attend to be attentive; to a person or a thing: of caring for, providing for; to attend to one's self, i.e. to give heed to one's self; give attention to, take heed; to apply one's self to, attach one's self to, hold or cleave; to a person or a thing; to be given or addicted to; to devote thought and effort to.*"

Being in the present tense, this means that Pastor Timothy is to "*devote thought and effort to*" these three things.

Reading Is Important for Pastors

1. Reading is important to pastors and all born-again Christians.

- Nehemiah 8:8
So they read in the book in the law of God distinctly, and gave the sense, and caused *them* to understand the reading.

Read Your Bible Through Yearly

We urge everyone of you to read God's Words daily. If you read eighty-five-verses per day you can read through the Bible in a year. We encourage you to do that.

- Jeremiah 36:8
And Baruch the son of Neriah did according to all that Jeremiah the prophet commanded him, **reading in the book the words of the LORD in the LORD'S house**.

Exhortation Is Important For Pastors

2. Exhortation is needed on the part of the pastors and all believers.

The word for "*exhortation*" is PARAKLESIS. It means various things, including:

"*a calling near, summons, (esp. for help); importation, supplication, entreaty; exhortation, admonition, encouragement; consolation, comfort, solace; that which affords comfort or refreshment; thus of the Messianic salvation (so the Rabbis call the Messiah the consoler, the comforter); persuasive discourse, stirring address; instructive, admonitory, conciliatory, powerful hortatory discourse.*"

This word, as can be seen by the definitions, carries with it "*admonition*" as well as "*consolation, comfort, and solace.*"

- **Luke 3:18**
  And **many other things in his exhortation preached he** unto the people.
- **Acts 20:2**
  And when he had gone over those parts, and **had given them much exhortation,** he came into Greece,

---

Doctrine Is Important For Pastors

3. Doctrine is also needed on the part of the pastors and all believers as well. The word for it is **DIDASKALIA.**

It means: "*teaching, instruction; that which is taught, doctrine; teachings, precepts.*"

Many Pastors Neglect Doctrine

It seems, from reports I have read, and from listening to many Christians, that there are many churches that do not think that "*doctrine*" is important. Because of this, the pastors do not teach Bible doctrine either in a systematic form or in any other form. This leaves the believers lost in the middle of so much that is false "*doctrine,*" not knowing what to believe.

- **Acts 2:42**
  And **they continued stedfastly in the apostles' doctrine** and fellowship, and in breaking of bread, and in prayers.

The early churches "*continued steadfastly*" in the "*doctrine*" taught them by the "*apostles*" of the Lord Jesus Christ. Churches today should do no less. I try to do this in our church with each message and in each service.

- **Romans 6:17**
  But God be thanked, that ye were the servants of sin, but **ye have obeyed from the heart that form of doctrine which was delivered you.**

- Ephesians 4:14
  That we *henceforth* **be no more children, tossed to and fro, and carried about with every wind of doctrine,** by the sleight of men, *and* cunning craftiness, whereby they lie in wait to deceive;

Paul is encouraging the Christians at Ephesus not to be babies any longer in the things of "*the faith.*" They were to stand upon the "*doctrine*" found in the Bible and not let anyone move them. We must stand for what is true.

- 1 Timothy 6:3
  If any man teach otherwise, and consent not to wholesome words, *even* the words of our Lord Jesus Christ, **and to the doctrine which is according to godliness;**

We must know the true "*doctrine*" so that we know whether or not the "*doctrine*" found in magazines or books and heard on the TV and radio is Scripturally based. Only by knowing the truth are you able to detect error.

- 2 Timothy 3:10
  But **thou hast fully known my doctrine,** manner of life, purpose, faith, longsuffering, charity, patience, . . .

Timothy traveled with Paul as we see in Acts 16 and elsewhere. He had heard Paul teach "*doctrine*" everywhere they went.

- 2 Timothy 3:16
  All scripture *is* **given by inspiration of God, and** *is* **profitable for doctrine,** for reproof, for correction, for instruction in righteousness:

The formulation of proper "*doctrine*" is one of the chief purposes of the Bible.

- 2 Timothy 4:2
  Preach the word; be instant in season, out of season; reprove, rebuke, exhort **with all longsuffering and doctrine**.

This was the motto of Dallas Theological Seminary where I graduated in 1952 with the Master of Theology (Th.M.) degree and again in 1955 with the Doctor of Theology (Th.D.) degree. I suppose it is still the motto, but I am not certain. Sound "*preaching of the Words*" of God must include all these elements, including "*doctrine.*"

- Titus 1:9
  Holding fast the faithful word as he hath been taught, **that he may be able by sound doctrine both to exhort and to convince the gainsayers.**

Only by "*sound doctrine*" can any "*gainsayers*" be convinced of their errors. Even then, there is no guarantee that this will happen, but without it, it assuredly will never happen.

- Titus 2:1
  But **speak thou the things which become sound doctrine:**

- **Titus 2:7**
  In all things **shewing thyself a pattern of good works: in doctrine *shewing* uncorruptness**, gravity, sincerity,

Paul tells Pastor Titus, who was a preacher on the island of Crete, to have his *"doctrine"* show *"uncorruptness"* so that nobody can find any false *"doctrine"* in his teachings. That is why pastors must understand the *"doctrine"* of the Bible fully, so as to avoid heretical teachings both on their part and also on the part of their congregations.

- **2 John 9**
  Whosoever transgresseth, and **abideth not in the doctrine of Christ,** hath not God. **He that abideth in the doctrine of Christ,** he hath both the Father and the Son.

The key as to whether or not a born-again Christian should receive into their house a religious teacher centers around that teacher's *"doctrine of Christ."* For this reason, saved people should not receive false teachers such as the Jehovah's Witnesses and the Mormons into their houses because they do not bring the proper *"doctrine of Christ."* This *"doctrine"* includes a proper understanding of many things about the doctrines known as Christology which concern both the Person and Work of the Lord Jesus Christ:

The "Doctrines" of the Lord Jesus Christ

1. His eternal preexistence
2. His virgin birth
3. His Incarnation
4. His Deity
5. His miracles
6. His substitutionary, expiatory, vicarious death on the cross of Calvary to "*bear in His body*" the sins of the entire world.
7. His being the only "*Way, the Truth and the Life*" to Heaven
8. His acceptance and reception as personal Saviour as the only Way to Heaven
9. His preparation in Heaven of a place for all those who have repented of their sins and have genuinely received Him as their Saviour
10. His bodily resurrection
11. His bodily ascension
12. His bodily session at the right hand of God the Father
13. His intercession for believers now
14. The first phase of His second coming in the air, before the Tribulation period, to transform their bodies and to take all the born-again Christians to Heaven
15. The second phase of His second coming, after the Tribulation period, to return to earth and to reign on this earth for one thousand years
16. His judgment of the saved ones at the Judgment Seat of Christ
17. His judgment of the lost ones at the Great White Throne judgment
18. Many other vital "*doctrines*" concerning our Lord Jesus Christ.

1 Timothy 4:14

"Neglect not the gift that is in thee, which was given thee by prophecy, with the laying on of the hands of the presbytery."

We do not know for certain what "*gift*" was in Timothy given to him "*by prophecy*" and with the "*laying on of the hands of the presbytery*." The "*presbytery*" was the group of pastors-bishops-elders who "*laid hands*" on Timothy probably when he was ordained to the ministry. This custom is still practiced today by Fundamental Baptist churches and others. The special "*gift*" conferred on Timothy was without doubt a spiritual "*gift*" of great value to him as a pastor. One thing that we do know is that he was not to "*neglect*" this "*gift*."

If this were an aorist prohibition, it would mean "*do not even begin to neglect*" this "*gift*." But since it is a present tense prohibition, it means "*stop neglecting*" this "*gift*." Apparently Pastor Timothy was "*neglecting*" this valuable "*gift*," and Paul admonished him concerning this "*neglect*" by the way he stated it.

Make Use of Your Spiritual Gifts

If God has given you a "*gift*," whatever it may be, whether you are a pastor or not, by all means do not "*neglect*" it. A "*neglected gift*" is a very unfortunate thing. Though you might not be a pastor as Timothy, has the Lord given you some spiritual "*gift*"? Do you know what it is? If you know it, are you using it for the glory of the Lord Jesus Christ? If not, why not?

---

1 Timothy 4:15

Meditate upon these things; give thyself wholly to them; that thy profiting may appear to all.

Paul told Pastor Timothy to "*meditate*" on all the things he has been writing about. The word for "*meditate*" is MELETAO. It means: "*to care for, **attend to carefully, practise; to meditate** i.e. to devise, contrive; used of the Greeks of the **meditative pondering** and the practice of orators and rhetoricians.*" Timothy was not to treat Paul's teachings as of no value nor importance. He was to "*ponder*" them and "*attend to*" them "*carefully.*"

Bible Meditation Brings Benefits

The Bible's truths must not be treated lightly. Timothy was told to be continually in these truths, *"giving himself wholly to them."*   If this happens, his *"profiting"* will *"appear to all."* When a pastor *"meditates"* on and *"gives himself wholly"* to the Words of God, all who observe him can see that he is *"profiting"* by this undertaking.

The word for "appear" is PHANEROS. It means: *"apparent, manifest, evident, known; manifest, i.e to be plainly recognised or known."* The pastor's *"profiting"* should become apparent to the people who observe him and listen to him. Am I not right? If the preacher has no profit, then the people listening will have no profit. It should be crystal clear that if Timothy, or any other pastor, has been with the Lord in study and has the right doctrine, the right spirit, the right love, the right manner of life, and all the other right things Paul mentioned, the people will see them and profit by them.

• Genesis 24:63

  And **Isaac went out to meditate in the field at the eventide**: and he lifted up his eyes, and saw, and, behold, the camels *were* coming.

• Joshua 1:8

  This book of the law shall not depart out of thy mouth; but thou shalt meditate therein day and night, that thou mayest observe to do according to all that is written therein: for then thou shalt make thy way prosperous, and then thou shalt have good success.

As the Lord Himself told Joshua, so we born-again believers today must *"meditate"* on the Words of God *"day and night"* from Genesis through Revelation throughout our Christian lives. Eighty-five verses per day, as outlined on my *YEARLY BIBLE READING SCHEDULE*, will allow you to accomplish this goal on a daily basis.

Bible Reading Schedules Available

I have put a copy on our Bible For Today Web site at http://www.bible fortoday.org/reading_schedule.htm if you wish to see it. You can hear my reading these verses daily also by going to our Web site at http://www.biblefortoday.org/idx_bible_reading.htm if you wish also. It is difficult to do this on a daily basis, but it is needful for all of us. I give my brief comments on the daily readings at http://www.biblefortoday.org/ Bible Sermons/bible_comments.htm if you want to hear them.

- **Psalm 1:2**
  But his delight *is* in the law of the LORD; and **in his law doth he meditate day and night.**
- **Psalm 119:15**
  I will meditate in thy precepts, and have respect unto thy ways.
- **Numbers 32:12**
  Save **Caleb** the son of Jephunneh the Kenezite, and **Joshua** the son of Nun: for **they have wholly followed the LORD.**

Only two of the twelve spies entered into the land of Canaan because they believed God was able to kill the giants. God is still able to kill giants if we have faith and "*wholly follow the Lord.*"

- **Deuteronomy 1:36**
  Save **Caleb** the son of Jephunneh; he shall see it, and to him will I give the land that he hath trodden upon, and to his children, because **he hath wholly followed the LORD.**

Dear Caleb was eighty-five years of age and he still said, "*Give me this mountain*" (Joshua 14:10-12). God enabled him to conquer the "*mountain*" even at that old age. Certainly Caleb is an example for us Christians who are in our "bonus" years of our lives. We should follow this octogenarian's example by continuing to conquer the mountains of life whether they be personal or public challenges.

- **1 Thessalonians 5:23**
  And **the very God of peace sanctify you wholly**; and *I pray God* your whole spirit and soul and body be preserved blameless unto the coming of our Lord Jesus Christ.

God wants every born-again Christian to be "*sanctified wholly*" for service for His cause. We must give ourselves "*wholly*" to the Words and will of our God!

"Give Me This Mountain"

By Gertrude G. Sanborn

Give me this mountain,
O Lord I pray.
Give me the victory
O'er the hard things today.

Give me this mountain;
Thy promises I claim,
Give me this high place;
Thus to praise Thy Name.

Give me this mountain;
What matter my age,
Give me provision
The battle to wage.

Give me this mountain;
O Lord I pray,
Though there are giants
That stand in the way.

Grant me Thy blessing,
O Lord I long.
Give me this mountain;
I'll climb with a song.
(Joshua 14:12)
[from *With Tears in My Heart*
Published by the Bible For Today Press]

1 Timothy 4:16

"Take heed unto thyself, and unto the doctrine; continue in them: for in doing this thou shalt both save thyself, and them that hear thee."

Notice the two very important things that Pastor Timothy was to "*take heed*" of. The word for "*take heed*" is EPECHO. It means: "*to have or hold upon, apply, to observe, attend to; to give attention to; to hold towards, hold forth, present; to check; delay, stop, stay.*" It is in the present tense and signifies a constant continuous action without any letup.

A Pastor Must Give Heed to Himself

[1] Pastor Timothy was to "*take heed*" to "*himself.*"

Any pastor who does not look inward and "*take heed*" to his life, his talk, his walk, and his love for the Lord Jesus Christ is not going to be an effective pastor. The pastor's life must be in tune with the Words of God and with His Saviour. If it is not, the Lord Jesus Christ cannot bless his ministry as He wants to bless it.

A Pastor Must Give Heed to Doctrine

[2] Pastor Timothy was to "take heed" to the "*doctrine.*"

Notice, it was "*thyself*" first and "*doctrine*" second. I believe the order is important. Timothy's "*doctrine*" should be in line with the Words of the Bible and with the teachings he learned from the apostle Paul. If you are taking heed to the "*thyself*" and not to "*doctrine,*" you are not in line. In other words, Timothy life should line up with the doctrine. He should practice what he preaches.

The result of taking care of both self and "*doctrine*" is that "*thou shalt both save thyself, and them that hear thee.*" The word for "*save*" is SOZO. It has various meanings:

"*to save, keep safe and sound, to rescue from danger or destruction; one (from injury or peril); to save a suffering one (from perishing), i.e. one suffering from disease, to make well, heal, restore to health; to preserve one who is in danger of destruction, to save or rescue; to save in the technical biblical sense; negatively; to deliver from the penalties of the Messianic judgment; to save from the evils which obstruct the reception of the Messianic deliverance."*

This word applies spiritually, but also it often means to rescue from some danger. If Timothy would constantly *"take heed"* to both of the above things, he would not only rescue himself from danger, but also those who *"hear"* him. Pastor Timothy was to be a godly example for the believers to follow. If we are born-again, you and I are to be examples as well.

First Timothy Chapter Five

1 Timothy 5:1

"Rebuke not an elder, but intreat *him* as a father; *and* the younger men as brethren;"

The words, *"rebuke not an elder,"* are a prohibition, or negative command. The verb is EPIPLESSO. It means: *"to strike upon, beat upon; to chastise with words, to chide, upbraid, rebuke."* Since this is in the aorist tense, it means that Timothy was not even to begin to *"rebuke an elder."* He was not doing it, but he was not to start it. He was to respect his *"elders."* This practice is not found among the youth of today as it was in earlier years. I was taught as a young man to respect my *"elders."* I was also taught that I was to never call my elders by their first names. That was how I was brought up, and I think that is a good thing. Today I have noticed young people calling their mothers, fathers, mothers-in-law, fathers-in-law, and even grandparents by their first names. To me this is a sad development.

Respect Your Elders

On the contrary, Pastor Timothy was told regarding the elders, *"intreat him as a father."* He was to respect an older person just like he would respect his own father. We should do the same in our day.

The word for *"intreat"* is PARAKALEO. It has many meanings, but the one for this context would be: *"to address, speak to, (call to, call upon), which may be done in the way of exhortation, entreaty . . ."* That is the respect you should show to an elder.

The *"younger men"* were to be treated as *"brethren."* In all too many cases, there is fighting among siblings. That is not what Paul is telling Timothy. He was to treat the *"younger men"* with the same respect that you **should** treat your brothers in Christ. We all should have respect one for another.

1 Timothy 5:2

"The elder women as mothers; the younger as sisters, with all purity."

Notice that Pastor Timothy was told to treat the *"elder women as mothers."* Again, there is to be respect here. No matter who the *"older woman"* is, you are to treat her with the same respect you would treat your *"mother."*

Disrespect for Mothers Is Common

I realize that we are living in an age where *"mothers"* are not always respected. There is altogether too much disrespect shown to them by their children. They often talk back to their mothers. Some even curse them and others assault their *"mothers."* I certainly hope that you respect your *"mother"* if she is still living.

In our home, when I was growing up, if I did not respect my *"mother,"* I heard about it. I also felt it.

Pastor Timothy was also to treat *"the younger as sisters, with all purity."* The word for *"purity"* is HAGNEIA which comes from HAGNOS. It means: *"exciting reverence, venerable, sacred; pure; **pure from carnality, chaste**, modest; pure from every fault, immaculate; clean."*

The Sin of Incest Is Common Today

In too many homes today, *"sisters"* are violated by incest. There is no *"purity"* in those homes. This is not what Timothy was to do with the younger women.

I have two sisters, one two years older and one seven years younger, and though we would often have our disagreements, I treated them both with *"all purity."* My younger sister would often refer to me as her *"big bother"* instead of her *"big brother."* I was not even saved till I was sixteen years of age, but I was still taught to treat my sisters properly, and I did.

During several summers, while I was attending Dallas Theological Seminary, I was an American Red Cross Swimming Instructor at a Christian Pioneer Girls Camp in Ohio called Camp Cherith. I came upon this verse, and I practiced it. I treated these young girls *"with all purity,"* as I have always done with my own two sisters. As a pastor, Timothy was to practice this and teach others to do so in his church at Ephesus. With the pedophile activity among many of the Roman Catholic clergy and even among some in non-Roman Catholic churches, this admonition needs to be followed scrupulously.

1 Timothy 5:3

"Honour widows that are widows indeed."

We have several *"widows"* in connection with our church ministry here and around the country. We need to respect them, give them *"honour,"* and do what we can to help them. Since preaching this sermon on 1 Timothy some of them have passed on to Glory. The *"widows indeed"* will be defined in the next verses. The Bible says a number of things concerning *"widows."*

- **Exodus 22:22**
  Ye shall not afflict any widow, or fatherless child.
- **Deuteronomy 24:21**
  When thou gatherest the grapes of thy vineyard, **thou shalt not glean** *it* **afterward: it shall be** for the stranger, for the fatherless, and **for the widow**.
- **Deuteronomy 27:19**
  Cursed *be* **he that perverteth the judgment of the** stranger, fatherless, and **widow**. And all the people shall say, Amen.
- **Psalm 146:9**
  The LORD preserveth the strangers; **he relieveth the fatherless and widow:** but the way of the wicked he turneth upside down.

The Lord takes care of *"widows."* He is concerned about them.

- **Isaiah 1:17**
  Learn to do well; seek judgment, relieve the oppressed, judge the fatherless, **plead for the widow**.

The widow has lost her husband, the head of her home. She needs all the help she can get.

- **Zechariah 7:10**
  And **oppress not the widow**, nor the fatherless, the stranger, nor the poor; and let none of you imagine evil against his brother in your heart.

Some *"widows"* are rich because their husbands have left them money. Sometimes in this case, a man will get married to such a rich *"widow,"* not because he loves her and has good intentions, but because he wants her money. That is certainly one form of *"oppression"* of a *"widow."* Sometimes a salesman will come into the home of a *"widow"* and sell her something she should not get and cannot afford. This also is *"oppression"* of that *"widow."*

Widowhood Comes Unexpectedly

Who knows when women right here in our church, or someone reading this, will become a *"widow"* or a *"widower"*? We should give *"honour"* to any *"widow"* we meet.

---

1 Timothy 5:4

"But if any widow have children or nephews, let them learn first to shew piety at home, and to requite their parents: for that is good and acceptable before God."

In the last verse, Paul mentioned that the church was to *"honour"* those *"widows"* who are *"widows indeed."* If so, the church could then assist them financially. However, *"if any widow have children or nephews,"* then this changes the picture. The word for *"nephews"* is EKGONON. It means: *"sprung from one, born, begotten; a son, daughter, offspring, **children, descendants; grandchildren**."* This is a loose term for a number of different kinds of what we would now call "relatives." These relatives must *"shew piety at home, and to requite their parents."* The word *"requite"* is formed from two Greek words, APODIDOMI and AMOIBE. APODIDOMI has various meanings:

> *"to deliver, to give away for one's own profit what is one's own, to sell; to pay off, **discharge what is due**; a debt, wages, tribute, taxes, produce due; things promised under oath; conjugal duty; to render account; to give back, restore; to requite, recompense in a good or a bad sense."*

AMOIBE means: *"requital, recompence."* Some *"widows"* have no *"children"* or relatives, so they have nobody to take care of them. But if they do have relatives, these relatives should take care of and provide for their *"widows."* The parents have been taking care of these children and relatives for many years as they should, now it is the children's turn to care for their *"parents."* In the age of welfare, Medicaid, and social security, children are not taking today taking care of their widowed parent. They should stand ready to assist wherever possible.

- **2 Corinthians 12:14**
  Behold, the third time I am ready to come to you; and I will not be burdensome to you: for I seek not yours, but you: **for the children ought not to lay up for the parents, but the parents for the children.**

The parents should take care of the children. But if your father dies and your mother is a widow, then you as their child should switch roles. According to this verse, you should take care of your widowed mother. This is what God would have us to do.

Care For Relatives When Possible

I realize that sometimes, when your widowed parent gets to a certain age or poor health condition, it is impossible to care for them yourself. Just recently my wife's aunt, who was a widow in her 90's and was being taken care of by her children, had a change in her health conditions. They were unable to meet her needs. She had to be put into a nursing home. That may happen to any of us. As long as it is possible, you are to care for, *"requite,"* and *"give back"* to your parent.

If you do this, God says, that is *"good and acceptable."* He wants us and expects us to do this. My own mother was a widow in Naples, Florida. She had help to take care of her. My older sister went down there and took care of my mom in her own home. My Mom died and went home to be with the Lord in her own home. My dad was cared for in his home as long as he could be cared for, and then he went into a rest home. He lost his mind at the end. I do not know whether or not I will lose my mind like Dad, but that is in the Lord's caring and gracious hands. My dad was formerly a very brilliant chemical engineer with many abilities. When dementia takes over, the mind is changed greatly.

The last time I saw my dad alive was on a visit to his nursing home. When he saw me, the first words out of his mouth were *"I took Jesus as my Saviour."* He had not forgotten that. This brought me great joy and assurance. That is the most important thing a person can remember. My dad came to know the Lord Jesus Christ as his Saviour through our pastor when Dad was in Wills Eye Hospital for a glaucoma operation.

Yes, we as parents should take care of our children, but when we, as parents need to be cared for, we should be cared for by our children if they are able to do this. That is the Biblical requirement. I remember when I had Hodgkin's Disease back in 1985. I was ready to die and was preparing to go home to be with the Lord Jesus Christ. Our oldest son, D. A., Jr., bought a home and was intending to devote one room for my wife. He was willing and able to take care of this *"widow"* lady, his own mother. She will never forget this, nor will I. Many parents do not receive that kind of love, affection, and caring from their children. That is most unfortunate indeed.

1 Timothy 5:5

"Now she that is a widow indeed, and desolate, trusteth in God, and continueth in supplications and prayers night and day."

This verse describes a "*widow indeed.*"

Three Requirements For These Widows

[1] First, she must be a "*widow*" who is "*desolate.*" The word for "*desolate*" is MONOO. It means: "*to make single or solitary; leave alone, forsake.*" She has been "*left alone*" with no family to help her.

[2] Second, she must be a "*widow*" who "*trusteth in God.*" She must be a born-again "*widow*" who is "*trusting*" in the Lord Jesus Christ before the church should help her.

[3] Third, she must be a "*widow*" who "*continueth in supplications and prayers night and day.*" This would describe a "*widow*" who not only believes in prayer and "*supplications,*" but also exercises that belief and prays "*night and day.*" Not all "*widows*" would qualify on this basis. The death of a "*widow's*" husband should not stop her "*supplications and prayers.*" She should continue to trust the Lord and walk with Him "*night and day.*"

1 Timothy 5:6

"But she that liveth in pleasure is dead while she liveth."

The "*widow*" who is described here that "*liveth in pleasure*" is certainly not one who would qualify for the support of the church. She might be "*desolate,*" but it would not seem she would either be "*trusting*" in the Lord, or certainly not "*continuing in supplications and prayers night and day.*" The word for "*pleasure*" here is SPATALAO. It means: "*to live luxuriously, lead a voluptuous life, (give one's self to pleasure).*" Some "*widows*" even today feel that when their husband has died, they can be free to do as they please without the former restraining hand of their mate. She should be careful not to violate the warnings in this verse.

- **Proverbs 21:17**
  He that loveth pleasure *shall be* a poor man: he that loveth wine and oil shall not be rich.

"Pleasures" in this world are costly. If the *"widow"* is one who *"lives in pleasure"* and does not walk close to the Lord, this verse says that *"she is dead while she liveth."* She is spiritually *"dead"* to God and to His will. God does not want the widows to live in physical pleasures apart from His Word and His way. *"Death"* is a form of separation. In this case, this *"widow"* who chooses to live in *"pleasure"* has separated herself from the path God would have her to walk. This is a walking and living *"death"* indeed.

1 Timothy 5:7
"And these things give in charge, that they may be blameless."

The word for *"give in charge"* is PARAGGELLO. It means: *"to transmit a message along from one to another, to declare, announce; to command, order, charge."* Pastor Timothy was told *"to declare"* to these *"widows"* the standards concerning the *"widows."* The reason for this declaration is so they might be *"blameless"* before the Lord.   The word for *"blameless"* is ANEPILEPTOS. It means: *"not apprehended, that cannot be laid hold of; that __cannot be reprehended__, not open to censure, irreproachable."*

Widows Being Blameless

In order for them to be *"blameless,"* these widows should not be living in pleasure.   Instead, they should have genuine *"trust"* in the Lord and *"continue in supplications and prayers night and day."* This kind of life would make them to be *"blameless"* before the Lord. This is what He wants of all the those who are born-again Christians.

---

1 Timothy 5:8
"But if any provide not for his own, and specially for those of his own house, he hath denied the faith, and is worse than an infidel."

To what does *"any"* refer here? In the context, it could refer back to verse four and the *"children"* or *"nephews."* They are the ones to help their relatives who are *"widows."* This is probably the reference.

However, this verse has also been applied, standing alone, to refer to both husbands and fathers. If this is a possible interpretation, it can be applied in a wider sense. Paul told Pastor Timothy that these husbands and fathers should *"provide"* for their own families.   *"If any provide not for his own,"* there are some very important conclusions. The word for *"provide"* is PRONOEO. It means: *"to perceive before, foresee; to provide, think of beforehand; to provide for one; to take thought for, care for a thing."* The word for *"his own"* is IDIOS which means: *"pertaining to one's self, one's own, belonging to one's self."*

A Man Must Provide For His Family

A man must *"provide"* for the things that belong to him. He must have foresight and planning to do so. This is required of any godly father and husband.

The word *"provide"* does not only mean physical provisions such as the house, food, or clothes. *"Provide"* would also include *"provision"* for the spiritual teachings of the Scriptures. It would include Bible reading and bringing the children and the family up *"in the nurture and admonition of the Lord"* (Ephesians 6:4b). That is a very important part of the father and husband's *"provision"* for his family.

The word for *"house"* here is OIKEIOS. It means: *"belonging to a house or family, domestic, intimate; belonging to one's household, related by blood, kindred; belonging to the household of God; belonging, devoted to, adherents of a thing."*

The Husband Must Provide

The husband and father is to *"provide"* not only for *"his own"* personal things, but also for the things *"belonging to his household,"* which would include his wife and all his children. Since this is masculine in gender (*"his own"*), it would place the burden of provision upon the husband and father rather than upon the wife and mother. This should not be disregarded in our days of sometimes working women and shirking men.

Failing to *"provide"* for his own family, the man would have *"denied the faith"* and become *"worse than an infidel."* Since *"the faith"* has an article, it refers to the total body of doctrine and teachings of the Bible. This is serious. The man is also *"worse than an infidel."* The word for *"infidel"* is APISTOS. It means: *"unfaithful, faithless, (not to be trusted, perfidious); incredible; of things; unbelieving, incredulous; without trust (in God)."*

I remember in one of my classes that I taught in a Bible Institute in our area I had a young father who did not believe it was Christian to work. He felt like he was going to be in the Lord's work and he was going to let the government take care of him. He had the idea that the government owed him a living, and the best way to serve the Lord was to not work and get paychecks from the government. That way he could serve the Lord throughout the day. I could not make him understand anything differently.

Paul said in 2 Thessalonians 3:10b that *"if any would not work, neither should he eat."* If you take away food from somebody, pretty soon they are willing to work. If someone is unable to work, that is different. I am talking about people who are able to work and can work, but just refuse to work. That is who Paul is talking about. That man should not eat.

Spiritual Provision Is Also Needed

We who are husbands and fathers must *"provide"* for our wives and children (*"his own house"*) by encouraging them to read the Words of God and to cultivate spiritual things in their lives. We must make *"provision"* (seeing ahead of time and thinking ahead of time) not just materially but spiritually for our family. Unsaved people can provide materially for their children, and they do, but they cannot provide spiritually because they are lost.

1 Timothy 5:9

"Let not a widow be taken into the number under threescore years old, having been the wife of one man,"

Now we come to a section that has to do with helping the widows in the local church. In the early church there was a standard to assist those who were widows. There are a total of eight requirements if a widow were to be helped by the local church. The first two are given in this verse and the other six are in the next verse.

In the first part of this verse is says: *"Let not a widow be taken into the number."* This is a prohibition in the present tense which means that the church at Ephesus was to stop an action already in progress. It would mean, *"Stop taking in widows into the number"* unless these eight requirements were met. Apparently Pastor Timothy's church was taking in widows who did not meet these requirements.

[1] The first requirement for a local church to support a *"widow"* is that she had to be sixty years old or older.

[2] The second requirement for a local church to support a *"widow"* is that she must have been *"the wife of one man."*

1 Timothy 5:10

"Well reported of for good works; if she have brought up children, if she have lodged strangers, if she have washed the saints' feet, if she have relieved the afflicted, if she have diligently followed every good work."

[3] The third requirement for a local church to support a *"widow"* is that she must be *"well reported of for good works."* She should have a testimony of doing what is *"good."* Somebody who is a wicked widow and not godly cannot expect the church to assist her.

[4] The fourth requirement for a local church to support a *"widow"* is that she must have *"brought up children."* If the widow has not *"brought up children"* she cannot be supported by the church. The word for *"brought up children"* is TEKNOTROPHEO. It means: *"to bring up children."* It comes from TREPHO which means: *"to nourish, support; feed; to give suck, to fatten; to bring up, nurture."* This implies that the *"widow"* not only *"bring up"* and care for other mothers' children, but her own. She must be a mother herself.

[5] The fifth requirement for a local church to support a *"widow"* is that she must have *"lodged strangers."* The word for this is ZENODOCHEO. It means: *"to receive and entertain hospitably, to be hospitable."* The early Christians had no motels or hotels where visiting strangers could stay. When Christians went from town to town, they had to stay in the home of other believers. This widow should have been known for having given lodging to such *"strangers."*

[6] The sixth requirement for a local church to support a *"widow"* is that she must have *"washed the saints' feet."* When strangers came to stay with her she should have bent down and washed their feet. This was the custom for the hostess of the home. Most of the early Christians had to walk everywhere they went. Their feet were dusty and dirty because they wore sandals. . The *"widow"* should have done this as well.

[7] The seventh requirement for a local church to support a *"widow"* is that she must have *"relieved the afflicted."* The word for *"relieved"* is EPARKEO. It has many meanings: *"to avail or be strong enough for; to ward off or drive away, a thing for another's advantage; a thing from anyone, to defend; to aid, give assistance, relieve; **to give aid from one's own resources**."* What about those the *"widow"* is to *"relieve"*? The word for *"afflicted"* is THLIBO. It is a verb that means: *"to press (as grapes), press hard upon; a compressed way; narrow straitened, contracted; metaph. to trouble, afflict,* *distress.*" Those who are "*afflicted*" and troubled need aid and assistance. This widow has to have given aid "from her own resources" to those "*afflicted*" ones who were in trouble.

[8] The eighth requirement for a local church to support a "*widow*" is that she must have "*diligently followed every good work.*" The word for "*diligently followed*" is EPAKOLOUTHEO. It means: "*to follow (close) upon, follow after; to tread in one's footsteps i.e. to imitate his example.*" That word for "*diligently followed*" is not simply the normal word for follow which is AKOLOUTHEO. It has the preposition EPI before it. This is called a "*perfective*" addition showing that it is a specially "*diligent*" following. It is like when a son steps in the footsteps of his father when going through deep snow. He must "*diligently*" place his feet exactly in his father's steps so as to get through the deep snow successfully.

Two Different Words For "Good"

There are two different words in the Greek for "*good.*" One is KALOS which is used in verse 4 in the phrase "*good and acceptable.*" It is also used earlier in this verse 10 in the phrase "*well reported for good works.*" In those two verses, KALOS means "*good*" in the senses of: "*beautiful, handsome, excellent, eminent, choice, surpassing, precious, useful, suitable, commendable, admirable; beautiful to look at, shapely, magnificent*" among the various meanings. The emphasis is on the external goodness that people can see.

The present word for "*good*" is AGATHOS which means such things as: "*of good constitution or nature; useful, salutary; good, pleasant, agreeable, joyful, happy; excellent, distinguished; upright, honourable.*" There is a stress on the inner "*constitution or nature*" of a person rather than on external qualities.

---

1 Timothy 5:11

"But the younger widows refuse: for when they have begun to wax wanton against Christ, they will marry;"

The younger widows who were under sixty years of age and who did not meet all the other qualifications were not to be supported by the local church. The reason for this was that "*for when they have begun to wax wanton against Christ, they will marry.*" The Greek word for "*wax wanton against*" is KATASTRENIAO. It means: "*to feel the impulses of sexual desire.*" There is nothing wrong with this in the proper relationship with a marriage. If this is the case, they should seek another husband and marry him rather than be cared for by the local church. If these widows are under sixty, they will have the desire to marry and they will marry. And that is all right for them to do.

My wife's uncle married for the first time at the age of seventy-five. So, sometimes people marry even after sixty years of age. The reason for their declining to take care of the younger widows is because the church should have a continuous ministry by the older widows so that it is uninterrupted. This admonition is not against marrying, but it is just to get guidelines and qualifications for a local church's care of widows.

1 Timothy 5:12

"Having damnation, because they have cast off their first faith."

If the church provides for these younger widows and then they marry, the church is left without the ministry that these widows have been providing. The "*damnation*" or judgment upon them is for breaking their promise to the local church. Their "*first faith*" they have "*cast off*" is their solemn promise to help the local church in its various ministries for which they are qualified. This does not mean they will lose their salvation. God says to avoid taking in these younger widows for this reason.

The word for "*cast off*" is ATHETEO. It means: "*to do away with, to set aside, disregard; to thwart the efficacy of anything, nullify, make void, frustrate; to reject, to refuse, to slight.*" This is the "*faith*" or service that they had promised to perform. This is important that you have the older widows only to support and to help, and not the younger ones. When they marry, they break their agreement.

In the olden days you would say that "*My word is my bond.*" Now, we do not believe anybody's word. We put it in writing. Sometimes that is not even sufficient. People break their written word as well. These widows have contracted either verbally or in writing to help with the things in the local church in Ephesus, and God says through Paul writing to Pastor Timothy to be sure that you have all eight of these qualifications for widows before you take them into your church and help to support them from the church's money.

The Eight Rules For Widow Support

As they might be able, it is proper that the local church give support to the widows if they meet all eight of these qualifications:

(1) The widow is sixty years of age or older.

(2) The widow has been the *"wife of one man."*

(3) The widow is *"well reported of for good works."*

(4) The widow has *"brought up children."*

(5) The widow has *"lodged strangers."*

(6) The widow has *"washed the saints' feet."*

(7) The widow has *"relieved the afflicted."*

(8) The widow has *"diligently followed every good work."*

These are very difficult qualifications.

1 Timothy 5:13

"And withal they learn *to be* idle, wandering about from house to house; and not only idle, but tattlers also and busybodies, speaking things which they ought not."

Paul then tells Pastor Timothy that apparently younger widows can get into a lot of trouble if the church makes the mistake of helping them.

[1] First, the younger widows *"learn to be idle."* The word for *"idle"* is ARGOS. It means: *"free from labour, at leisure; lazy, shunning the labour which one ought to perform."*

[2] Second, the younger widows *"wander about from house to house."* They have no certain dwelling place. This indicates instability.

[3] Third, the younger widows are *"tattlers."* The word for this is PHLUAROS. It means: *"of persons uttering or doing silly things, garrulous, babbling; of things, foolish, trifling, vain."* They have no control of their tongues.

[4] Fourth, the younger widows are *"busybodies."* The word for this is PERIERGOS. It has various meanings: *"busy about trifles and neglectful of important matters; esp. busy about other folks' affairs, a busybody; of things: impertinent and superfluous; of magic arts."*

[5] Fifth, the younger widows are *"speaking things which they ought not."* These widows should not conduct themselves in this manner, nor should any Christian today.

God Is Concerned About Widows

You may wonder why any of us today should be so concerned about widows, whether younger or older. This teaching is part of the Scripture. God wants every one of us to be concerned about this. We have to prepare for the future. One day you, or someone you know, may be a widow. These things God wanted Timothy to be aware of so that he would have a properly functioning church.

As I *"preach the Word"* (2 Timothy 4:2), I come to these portions of Scripture that deal with certain different kind of subjects. I preach about them as well because they are a part of the Bible.

1 Timothy 5:14

"I will therefore that the younger women marry, bear children, guide the house, give none occasion to the adversary to speak reproachfully."

In this section of the chapter, we are going to be meeting six what I call *"stop signs."* By this I mean that we will see forms of various verbs that tell us to stop an action already in progress. The first *"stop sign"* is in this present verse. The other five are in verses 16, 19, 22, and 23.

In this verse, there are four injunctions that Paul tells young Pastor Timothy about *"younger women."*

[1] First, Paul desired the *"younger women"* to *"marry."* It is important to see that the *"will"* in this sentence is not simply an action in the future. The word is BOULOMAI. It means: *"to will deliberately, have a purpose, be minded; of willing as an affection, to desire."* There is nothing wrong with marriage. The Roman Catholic Church is wrong and ungodly in depriving marriage from their priests and nuns. Proper marriage is God's way.

● **Luke 20:34**
   And Jesus answering said unto them, **The children of this world marry, and are given in marriage:**
To say that marriage is a sin for the *"clergy"* is wrong.

● **1 Timothy 4:3**
   Forbidding to marry, *and commanding* to abstain from meats, which God hath created to be received with thanksgiving of them which believe and know the truth.
This is one of the signs of the last days.

- **Hebrews 13:4**
  Marriage *is* honourable in all, and the bed undefiled: but whoremongers and adulterers God will judge.

Not that all are married, but there is nothing wrong with marriage.

[2] Second, Paul desired the "*younger women*" to "*bear children*." This is a natural product of a good Christian marriage. I do not understand the unwillingness of some "*younger women*" to "*bear children*." It is both unnatural and even sinful, willful, and stubborn to reject this part of their marriage. If a couple is unable to have children, it is an entirely different matter.

- **Psalm 127:3**
  Lo, children *are* an heritage of the LORD: *and* the fruit of the womb *is his* reward.

- **Proverbs 13:22**
  A good *man* leaveth an inheritance to his children's children: and the wealth of the sinner *is* laid up for the just.

That inheritance is not only money it also includes a spiritual inheritance.

- **Proverbs 31:28**
  Her children arise up, and call her blessed; her husband *also,* and he praiseth her.

Some younger women cannot "*bear children*." They could adopt children if they wanted to.

[3] Third, Paul desired the "*younger women*" to "*guide the house*." The word for this is OIKODESPOTEO. It means: "*to be master (or head) of a house; to rule a household, manage family affairs.*" When they "*marry,*" these women are to "*manage*" and "*guide*" their households. This is a Scripturally-mandated duty for them. The last part of this Greek word is where we get our word "*despot.*" I realize that the husband is to be the one in charge of the family, and the wife is to submit to the husband as the leader. But in the area of the "*house,*" the wife has some specific tasks that she must undertake in this "*guidance*" of her "*house.*"

- **Psalm 32:8**
  I will instruct thee and teach thee in the way which thou shalt go: **I will guide thee with mine eye.**

Sometimes a father can just give an "*eye*" to their child, and that child knows exactly what is meant by that "*eye.*"

- **John 16:13**
  Howbeit when he, the Spirit of truth, is come, **he will guide you into all truth:** for he shall not speak of himself; but whatsoever he shall hear, *that* shall he speak: and he will shew you things to come.

[4]   Fourth, Paul desired the *"younger women"* to *"give none occasion to the adversary to speak reproachfully."* These *"younger women"* must *"toe the line"* as they say. Here is where the first stop sign appears. The verb in the clause *"give none occasion,"* is in the present tense. It is a negative command or a prohibition which in this tense means to stop an action already in progress. Apparently these younger women were giving occasion to the *"adversary"* to continue to be against them and to thus *"speak reproachfully"* against the name of the Lord. Paul told them to stop it!

- **1 Peter 5:8**
  Be sober, be vigilant; because **your adversary the devil, as a roaring lion, walketh about, seeking whom he may devour**:

Younger Women Must Watch Their Lives

The *"younger women"* must be careful to watch their lives so that the enemies of the gospel will not continue to *"speak reproachfully"* against the Lord.

---

1 Timothy 5:15
"For some are already turned aside after Satan."

Some of these *"younger women"* have *"turned aside after Satan."* Certainly there is a *"reproach"* there. Satan is the greatest *"adversary"* to Bible-believing Christians, but there are other enemies against the Lord and His people as well. If they are saved, they cannot be Satan's child, but maybe they are following Satan's techniques. The word for *"turned aside"* is EKTREPO. It means: *"to turn or twist out; in a medical sense used of dislocated limbs; to turn off or aside; to be turned aside; to turn aside; to turn away from, to shun a thing, to avoid meeting or associating with one."*

One of our friends twisted both of his ankles. He told us about it. Another friend of ours fell and tripped in her house and completely twisted her shoulder, dislocating it. She is now in a sling. This is the word that is used.

Do Not Turn Aside From the Lord

Any saved person who *"turns aside"* after the things of Satan is completely dislocated and is, in turn, *"turned aside"* from the Lord Jesus Christ.

I do not believe that any saved person can be lost. If you live for the Devil, walk too closely with the Devil's children , do what they do, and say what they say, you have "*turned aside*" after the devilish things, even though you may be saved. You are not following the things of Christ. That is for sure.

1 Timothy 5:16

"If any man or woman that believeth have widows, let them relieve them, and let not the church be charged; that it may relieve them that are widows indeed."

If a born-again Christian has a relative who is a "*widow,*" let him take care of that "*widow.*" The word for "*relieve*" is EPARKEO. It means: "*to avail or be strong enough for; to ward off or drive away, a thing for another's advantage; a thing from anyone, to defend;* **to aid, give assistance**, *relieve; to give aid from one's own resources.*" Even if they have to aid their "*widows*" from their "*own resources.*" If they have to dig down into their own pocket and take care of them then, let them do so.

In this verse we find a second "*stop sign.*" This comes in the clause where it says "*let not the church be charged.*" The word for "*charged*" is BAREO. It means: "*to burden, weigh down, depress.*" Since the verb is in the present tense, it indicates an action already in progress. Paul is saying, "*stop letting the church be burdened and weighed down.*" He said that so the church would be able to "*relieve them that are widows indeed.*"

Care Only For Qualified Widows

The church at Ephesus, where Timothy was the pastor, was burdened down with "*widows*" from whom they did not have to care. Some of these "*widows*" had believing relatives who should have been taking care of them rather than the church. The church's resources should be used to take care of genuine "*widows*" who meet all eight criteria mentioned in verses 9 and 10 above.

---

1 Timothy 5:17

"Let the elders that rule well be counted worthy of double honour, especially they who labour in the word and doctrine."

We must understand what the Bible teaches about "*elders.*" I realize that Presbyterians and others have a different view of "*elders*" than Baptists.

Pastor-Bishop-Elder--The Same Person

I believe that the Biblical view of *"elders"* is that the pastor-bishop-elder is all one and the same person. This is seen in the book of Acts and in the book of I Peter.

- **Acts 20:17**
  And from Miletus he sent to Ephesus, and **called the "*elders*" of the church.**

- **Acts 20:27**
  For I have not shunned **to declare unto you** all the counsel of God.

- **Acts 20:28**
  Take heed therefore unto yourselves, and to all the flock, over the which **the Holy Ghost hath made you overseers, to feed the church of God**, which he hath purchased with his own blood.

Paul is talking to the *"elders"* (PREBUTEROS) at Ephesus to *"take heed"* to themselves. Then he is telling the *"elders"* they are *"overseers."* This word is EPISCOPOS. It is also translated *"bishops"* whose duty is to *"oversee"* the church. The word for *"feed"* is POIMAINO which means *"to shepherd or pastor."* Here Paul talks to the elders who are also pastors and elders. The Bible does not say that the *"elders"* are something separate from the *"pastors"* or the *"bishops."* They are one and the same.

- **1 Peter 5:1-3**
  The elders which are among you I exhort, who am also an elder, and a witness of the sufferings of Christ, and also a partaker of the glory that shall be revealed: **Feed the flock** of God which is among you, **taking the oversight** *thereof*, not by constraint, but willingly; not for filthy lucre, but of a ready mind; Neither as being lords over *God's* heritage, but being ensamples to the flock.

Peter is talking to *"elders"* (PREBUTEROS). He was an *"elder"* himself. He tells these *"elders"* to *"feed the flock of God."* The word for *"feed"* is POIMAINO. It is the word for *"shepherd"* or *"pastor."* These *"elders"* and *"pastors"* are also to take the *"oversight."* This word is EPISCOPOS which means to be a *"bishop or overseer."* Peter agrees with the teaching in Acts 28 that the pastor-bishop-elder refers to one man with three different titles or designations. There very well might be more than one pastor-bishop-elder in one local church. One might be the main one, another might handle the music, and another visitation, and still another the youth programs.

The Presbyterians get the idea that wherever elders are plural there is to be a plurality of elders. They divide elders into ruling elders and teaching elders. No, I believe that wherever you have plural elders it means you have several churches possibly in the same city, or you have a large church that has assistant pastors-bishops-elders.

Paul talks about the *"elders that rule well be counted worthy of double honour."* *"Honour"* is the word TIME. It means:

> *"a valuing by which the price is fixed; of the price itself; of the price paid or received for a person or thing bought or sold; honour which belongs or is shown to one; of the honour which one has by reason of rank and state of office which he holds; deference, reverence"*

The Meaning of Double Honour

"Double honour" would mean that those who *"laboured in the Word and doctrine"* would be able to get a double salary for their labor in the Lord. TIME is the word for *"price."* I am afraid that this would leave many pastors out because they do not seem to be doing much in the line of *"labouring in the Word and doctrine."*

The word for *"labour"* is KOPIAO. It means: *"to grow weary, tired, exhausted (with toil or burdens or grief); to labour with wearisome effort, to toil; of bodily labour."*

If indeed the *"double honour"* means to have extra pay for extra work, it is going to be because of a *"toilsome labour."* It certainly does not mean to be given to a pastor who gives (and perhaps reads) only a twenty-or-thirty-minute sermon on Sunday morning and goes home for the rest of the week. Many preachers have forgotten that *"doctrine"* is what they need to preach with much *"labour."*

1 Timothy 5:18

"For the scripture saith, Thou shalt not muzzle the ox that treadeth out the corn. And, The labourer *is* worthy of his reward."

When Paul says, *"the Scripture saith,"* he uses the present tense which means that it is continually saying these words. This is Bible preservation.

Old Testament Words Are Preserved

Paul is writing to Timothy in about 60 A.D. He is quoting an Old Testament Scripture in the present tense, showing that the Scripture is still in existence after all these years. The Hebrew text was still there intact, in his day, and it is still with us, preserved plenarily and verbally for us today.

- 1 Corinthians 9:6-11
  Or I only and Barnabas, have not we power to forbear working?   **Who goeth a warfare any time at his own charges?** who planteth a vineyard, and eateth not of the fruit thereof? or who feedeth a flock, and eateth not of the milk of the flock?   Say I these things as a man? or saith not the law the same also?   For it is written in the law of Moses, **Thou shalt not muzzle the mouth of the ox that treadeth out the corn**. Doth God take care for oxen?   Or saith he *it* altogether for our sakes? For our sakes, no doubt, *this* is written: that he that ploweth should plow in hope; and that he that thresheth in hope should be partaker of his hope.   **If we have sown unto you spiritual things, *is it* a great thing if we reap your carnal things?**

Churches Must Support Their Pastors

These are verses that justify local churches financially supporting their pastors. Soldiers do not go to war on their own. The government pays their way. They give them their uniform. They give them their food. They give them their allowance. If you are a fighting solider they give you all the equipment needed for you to do battle.

If you plant a vineyard you eat of it. When the ox was "*treading out the corn,*" the Jews were not to put a "*muzzle*" on him. In other words, while the ox was working, they were not to put a "*muzzle*" on him. They were to let him eat the corn he was "*treading out.*" The word for "muzzle" is PHIMOO. It means:
> "*to close the mouth with a muzzle, to muzzle; metaph. to stop the mouth, make speechless, reduce to silence; to become speechless; to be kept in check.*"

A literal "*muzzle*" is something people put on dogs that are biters. Though I am ashamed to admit it, I used to bite people when I was a little boy. My dear mother told me if I kept this up, she was going to put a *"muzzle"* on me. I think I stopped biting people after that.

Speak Out Clearly on God's Words

Pastors-bishops-elders are those who should be speaking out clearly the great spiritual principles of God's Words in the Bible.

These faithful men of God should reap the offerings from the Lord's people. We receive offerings that are freely and willingly given both by people present in our local church and by those participating with us by way of the Internet. I have never pressured anyone to give. They give because the Lord has led them to do so. We do not pass any offering plates. We have an offering box at the rear of our church for people to give offerings if the Lord so leads them. Our Internet families, if the Lord so leads them, send their offerings by check or by Internet donation.

As in the case of the apostle Paul, I have never received any gifts from our local church, but have support from retirement and other support. Though some of our offerings are used for the various ministries of our local church, most of the offerings go to support our seven missionaries. Even though we are a small home church, as of this writing, this missionary support has been $1,200.00 each month. Our missionaries are in need, so we ask the Lord to guide and direct our people to give to their needs. The people have responded for which we praise and thank our Lord.

1 Timothy 5:19

"Against an elder receive not an accusation, but before two or three witnesses."

In this verse we have *"stop sign"* #3. It is a prohibition in the Greek present tense which means to stop an action already in progress.

The First Three Stop Signs

If you remember,

Stop Sign #1 is *"stop giving occasion to the adversary."*

Stop Sign #2 is *"stop having the church be responsible for unqualified widows."*

"Stop sign" #3 is *"stop receiving an accusation against an elder"* except *"before two or three witnesses."*

Notice, this does not prohibit bringing an *"accusation"* against a pastor-bishop-elder, but it demands that such an *"accusation"* be done in a proper manner. The requirement of *"two or three witnesses"* is repeated in many places in the Bible.

* **Matthew 18:16**
  But if he will not hear *thee,* then **take with thee one or two more, that in the mouth of two or three witnesses every word may be established.**
* **2 Corinthians 13:1**
  This *is* the third *time* I am coming to you. **In the mouth of two or three witnesses shall every word be established.**
* **Hebrews 10:28**
  He that despised Moses' law died without mercy **under two or three witnesses:**

In the Old Testament you could never have a person put to death by the mouth of one person. You had to have *"two or three witnesses."* Then you could condemn that person to death. Paul was telling Pastor Timothy to stop bringing an accusation against an elder unless there were two or three witnesses. It must be a credible charge.

The Bible Steps On Our Toes

It is easy for people to get upset at a preacher. Sometimes preachers *"step on the toes"* of the congregation. When I preach, if there is any toe-stepping, I want the Bible to do it, not I. Pastors must have a proper court-setting, or an *"accusation"* against him should not be *"received."*

1 Timothy 5:20

"Them that sin rebuke before all, that others also may fear."

This is referring to a pastor-bishop-elder who sins. The word for "*sin*" is HAMARTANO. It means: "*to be without a share in; to miss the mark; to err, be mistaken; to miss or wander from the path of uprightness and honour, to do or go wrong; to wander from the law of God, violate God's law, sin.*"

The Sins To Rebuke Before All

This refers, not only to "*sins*" of immorality, but also to "*sins*" of going wrong in doctrine.

This verb is in the present tense and implies a continuous sinning.

Billy Graham Must Be Rebuked

Billy Graham is an evangelist who should meet the qualifications of a pastor-bishop-elder. I believe Billy Graham is wrong in many areas of both doctrine and practice. As evidenced in his own words both in print, on audio tape, on video tape, and on television he has stated, among many other things, that: (1) He believes that people who do not hear the gospel of Christ can be saved. (2) He believes there is no real fire in Hell. (3) He believes we should fellowship with unbelievers and apostates. (4) He believes he should send his "converts" back to the churches whence they came, even if apostate Protestant churches, Roman Catholic churches, or Jewish churches. (5) He refuses to affirm that the Bible denies entrance into Heaven to those do come through the Lord Jesus Christ, but who continue to hold to the religious beliefs of the Jews, Hindus, Muslims, Buddhists, other world religions, and secular non-Christian people.

These and many other doctrines and practices are unscriptural and wrong. Because of this, he should be "*rebuked before all, that others also might fear.*"

The word for "*rebuke*" is ELEGCHO. It means:
"*to convict, refute, confute; generally with a suggestion of shame of the person convicted; by conviction to bring to the light, to expose; to find fault with, correct; by word; to reprehend severely, chide,*"

admonish, reprove; to call to account, show one his fault, demand an explanation; by deed; to chasten, to punish."

Pastor Timothy was to "*rebuke*" these sinning "*elders*" before all people so that others "*may fear.*" This is a proper doctrine and teaching. I have mentioned various sinning "*elders*" from time to time through the years. When I point out sinning pastors and name names, I am following this verse.

- **Proverbs 9:8**
  Reprove not a scorner, lest he hate thee: **rebuke a wise man, and he will love thee.**

- **Proverbs 13:1**
  A wise son *heareth* his father's instruction: but **a scorner heareth not rebuke.**

- **Proverbs 27:5**
  Open rebuke *is* better than secret love.

- **Ecclesiastes 7:5**
  It is **better to hear the rebuke of the wise**, than for a man to hear the song of fools.

- **2 Timothy 4:2**
  Preach the word; be instant in season, out of season; reprove, **rebuke,** exhort with all longsuffering and doctrine.

- **Titus 1:13**
  This witness is true. Wherefore **rebuke them sharply**, that they may be sound in the faith;

That is the hardest "*rebuke*" to take, a "*sharp rebuke.*" It is just like the point of an arrow or a pin.

- **Revelation 3:19**
  As many as I love, I rebuke and chasten: be zealous therefore, and repent.

The Purpose of Rebuking Sinning Elders

The Lord wants saved people to be on the line with the Lord Jesus Christ. The purpose of this "*rebuke*" of sinning "*elders*" is "*that others also may fear.*"

The word for "*fear*" is PHOBOS. It means: "*fear, dread, terror; that which strikes terror; reverence for one's husband.*"

When the pastor-bishop-elder knows his sin will be rebuked before all, he will hopefully think twice about getting involved with a sinful situation. Many times a pastor's sins are covered up. They go from one church where they have committed adultery, thievery, false doctrine, or whatever it may be. They then go to another church where that new church never asks questions about their past. Then the same sin often presents itself in the new church. This is wrong. Sinning pastors must be publicly rebuked in order to keep our local churches pure from such leaders.

1 Timothy 5:21

"I charge *thee* before God, and the Lord Jesus Christ, and the elect angels, that thou observe these things without preferring one before another, doing nothing by partiality."

Paul gives Pastor Timothy a strong *"charge"* before both God the Father and the Lord Jesus Christ. God the Father and God the Son are co-equal members of the Divine Trinity. They are both Deity and they are mentioned here in the same breath. The word for "charge" is DIAMARTUROMAI. It means:

> *"to testify; earnestly, religiously to charge; to attest, testify to, solemnly affirm; to give solemn testimony to one; to confirm a thing by testimony, to testify, cause it to be believed."*

"The elect angels" are in distinction to the fallen angels who followed Satan into his sin of rebellion against the Lord.

What Timothy Is To Observe

Paul tells Pastor Timothy *"that thou observe these things."* He is to follow Paul's teachings carefully. What things is he talking about? Let me list some of the things Paul refers to:

    (1)   Timothy is to stop bringing accusations against a pastor-bishop-elder except with two or three witnesses.

    (2)   Timothy is to *"rebuke before all"* those pastors-bishops-elders who sin.

    (3)   Timothy is to do this *"without preferring one before another."*

    (4)   Timothy is to do this by *"doing nothing by partiality."*

The word for *"without preferring one before another"* is PROKRIMA. It means: *"an opinion formed before the facts are known; a prejudgment, a prejudice."*

Just because a pastor-bishop-elder is well-known, or has money, this should not stop us from rebuking his sin. In the past, I have had various reactions to the case of the late Pastor Jack Hyles. Some thought he was a great man who did no wrong. Others believed he had done some very evil things. His popular status should not preclude any justifiable and needed "*rebuke.*"

The word for "*partiality*" is PROSKLISIS. It means: "*an inclination or proclivity of mind; a joining the party of one; partiality.*" If your best pastor-friend is a thief, or involved in adultery, or is a murderer, or is involved in some other sin, you are not to be "*partial*" to them. God says that in this verse.

1 Timothy 5:22

"Lay hands suddenly on no man, neither be partaker of other men's sins: keep thyself pure."

In this verse are found "*stop signs*" #4 and #5. There are two Greek present tense negative commands. As I have mentioned before, the present tense prohibition tells the reader to stop an action already in progress. The aorist tense prohibition tells the reader not even to begin an action. These two verbs are in the present tense.

"*Stop sign*" #4 is stop "*laying hands suddenly on any man.*" That means do not hastily ordain a pastor-bishop-elder for their ministry of the Lord.

Pastors Must Be Fully Qualified

Take time to be certain they are qualified in all areas of their life and ministry. The church was not following this wisdom, but was "*laying hands suddenly.*" Paul told Pastor Timothy to stop this wrong practice.

"*Stop sign*" #5 is stop "*being partakers of other men's sins.*" By "*laying hands suddenly*" on men whose lives were not ready for God's ministry and who let the Lord down by failure, Timothy was "*being a partaker of other men's sins*" by ordaining them "*suddenly.*" Here again the church was involved in this practice, and Paul told Timothy to stop it.

Paul told Pastor Timothy to "*keep thyself pure.*" Purity for pastors is essential, though, sad to say, it is not found among altogether too many pastors, evangelists, missionaries, and other Christian workers.

- Proverbs 30:5
  Every word of God *is* pure: he *is* a shield unto them that put their trust in him.
- Matthew 5:8
  Blessed *are* the pure in heart: for they shall see God.

- **Philippians 4:8**
  Finally, brethren, whatsoever things are true, whatsoever things *are* honest, whatsoever things *are* just, **whatsoever things *are* pure,** whatsoever things *are* lovely, whatsoever things *are* of good report; if *there be* any virtue, and if *there be* any praise, think on these things.
- **1 Timothy 3:9**
  Holding the mystery of the faith **in a pure conscience**.
- **2 Timothy 2:22**
  Flee also youthful lusts: but follow righteousness, faith, charity, peace, with them that call on the Lord **out of a pure heart.**

Our hearts must be pure as we pray and call upon the Lord.

- **Titus 1:15**
  Unto the pure all things *are* pure: but unto them that are defiled and unbelieving *is* **nothing pure**; but even their mind and conscience is defiled.
- **1 Peter 1:22**
  Seeing ye have purified your souls in obeying the truth through the Spirit unto unfeigned love of the brethren, *see that ye* **love one another with a pure heart fervently:**

Believers are to love one another with a "*pure*" heart.

- **2 Peter 3:1**
  This second epistle, beloved, I now write unto you; in *both* which **I stir up your pure minds** by way of remembrance:
- **1 John 3:3**
  And every man that hath this hope in him **purifieth himself, even as he is pure.**

1 Timothy 5:23

"Drink no longer water, but use a little wine for thy stomach's sake and thine often infirmities."

In this verse there is "*stop sign*" #6. Evidently, Pastor Timothy was drinking polluted water. Paul told him to stop it. He suggested instead that he "*use a little wine for thy stomach's sake*" and other "*often infirmities.*" Timothy had a "*stomach*" problem.

No Justification For Drinking Alcohol

People have used this verse to say that Christians today should be able to drink a "*little wine*" and therefore drink in moderation. That is not what this verse is saying. The word for "*wine*" is OINOS. Unless specified in the context, "*wine*" is the "*fruit of the vine*" which is grape juice.

That is why the Lord Jesus Christ said that he would no longer drink of the "*fruit of the vine*" until He does it in the Millennial kingdom (Matthew 26:29; Mark 14:25; Luke 22:18). I believe that this verse talks about grape juice, the "*fruit of the vine*" and not intoxicating wine. Grape juice is from the grape and would not partake of the apparent pollution found in the water in Ephesus. Paul was telling Timothy to take some grape juice to help his stomach. The Nazarites of the Old Testament could not partake of anything that came from the vine.

- Numbers 6:3-4
  He shall separate *himself* **from wine and strong drink,** and shall drink no vinegar of wine, or vinegar of strong drink, **neither shall he drink any liquor of grapes, nor eat moist grapes, or dried. All the days of his separation shall he eat nothing that is made of the vine tree, from the kernels even to the husk**.

Paul was not telling Timothy either to drink intoxicating "*wine*" or to become an alcoholic. I used to preach often in a church on the West Coast. I stopped preaching in that church because I learned that the pastor drinks alcoholic beverages. When I questioned him about his drinking, he did not like it. I gave him seven verses of Scripture that use the word NEPHO or NEPHALEOS which tell us not to drink anything with alcohol in it. I sent him those verses. He broke fellowship with me thereafter. I put in **bold** font and **underlined** the word which is translated in English from either NEPHO or NEPHALEOS. NEPHALEOS means: "*sober, temperate; abstaining from wine, either entirely or at least from its immoderate use; of things free from all wine, as vessels, offerings.*" Here are those seven verses that teach total abstinence from all alcoholic beverages for all Christians.

Verses Against Alcoholic Drinks

- **1 Thessalonians 5:6**

  Therefore let us not sleep, as *do* others; but let us watch and be **sober**.

This verse is talking to ordinary Christians. It does not only apply to pastors, deacons, missionaries, and other Christian workers.

- **1 Thessalonians 5:8**

  But let us, who are of the day, be **sober**, putting on the breastplate of faith and love; and for an helmet, the hope of salvation.

- **1 Timothy 3:2**

  A bishop then must be blameless, the husband of one wife, **vigilant**, sober, of good behaviour, given to hospitality, apt to teach;

- **1 Timothy 3:11**

  Even so *must their* wives *be* grave, not slanderers, **sober**, faithful in all things.

This verse is referring to deacon's wives as needing to abstain from alcohol.

- **2 Timothy 4:5**

  But **watch** thou in all things, endure afflictions, do the work of an evangelist, make full proof of thy ministry.

- **Titus 2:2**

  That the aged men be **sober**, grave, temperate, sound in faith, in charity, in patience.

The older men are told to abstain from alcohol.

- **1 Peter 1:13**

  Wherefore gird up the loins of your mind, be **sober**, and hope to the end for the grace that is to be brought unto you at the revelation of Jesus Christ;

These seven verses are not simply total abstention requirements for pastors or church officers only. These apply to all Christians.

Christ Turned Water to Grape Juice

I believe that in John Chapter 2 when the Lord Jesus turned the water into *"wine"* it was OINOS, or the fruit of the vine. It was grape juice. It was not fermented.

There is a book that we have in our **Bible For Today** ministry entitled *Wines and the Laws of Fermentation* (**BFT #514**). It shows conclusively that whenever the Scriptures in the Old or New Testaments speak of *"wine,"* it is **always** unfermented **unless** the context indicates clearly otherwise. Timothy's stomach needed something other than polluted water, so Paul told Timothy to drink a little of the *"fruit of the vine."*

When Mrs. Waite and I were in West Africa during three separate Bible Conferences, we asked them to boil our drinking water, and they did. We did not have a single bit of stomach problem the three times we were over there because we were very careful. We were there each time for two weeks or so, and were fine.

1 Timothy 5:24

"Some men's sins are open beforehand, going before to judgment; and some *men* they follow after."

I believe he is talking here about the *"open"* sins committed while these men were living. Some men and women's *"sins"* are *"open"* in the sense that it can be observed by all. Anyone can see they are wicked and corrupt sinners. On the other hand, some men and women are able to conceal their secret *"sins."* A person cannot see them. Unsaved people will have their secret *"sins"* judged by the Lord Jesus Christ at the Great White Throne Judgment. Then they will be cast into the lake of fire. The known, unconfessed secret *"sins"* of the saved will be judged at the Judgment seat of Christ.

1 Timothy 5:25

"Likewise also the good works *of some* are manifest beforehand; and they that are otherwise cannot be hid."

Some *"good works"* can be seen or *"manifest"* while the person is alive. Those works which are wicked and corrupt *"cannot be hid."* You can hide them for a little while and deceive, but after awhile, they cannot *"be hid."* As the Old Testament verse says: *"Be sure your sin will find you out."* (Numbers 32:23)

Various Presidents and Congressmen have had serious *"sins"* that were kept quiet for a long time. Liberace was a very famous pianist. After he died of AIDS it was published that he was a homosexual. The press knew this before his death, but it was hidden from the general public. The same is true of the movie actor Rock Hudson who died of AIDS. His homosexuality was kept secret by the press until he died. Some men's "*sins*" cannot be hid. I hope that every one of us will manifest our "*good works*" openly while we are living to please the Lord Jesus Christ. "*Living for Jesus a life that is true, striving to please Him in all that I do.*" That is what God wants us to do that we may be worthy of His praise.

"Living For Jesus"

Living for Jesus and walking His way
Living for Jesus each hour of the day
Living for Jesus and telling His praise
Living for Jesus thru all of my days.

Living for Jesus in joy and in tears
Living for Jesus until He appears
Living for Jesus for soon He will come'
Living for Jesus to hear His 'well done.'

Living for Jesus my wonderful Lord
Living for Jesus believing His Word
Living for Jesus my wonderful Friend
Living for Jesus right unto the end.

By Gertrude G. Sanborn
With Tears in My Heart

First Timothy Chapter Six

1 Timothy 6:1

"Let as many servants as are under the yoke count their own masters worthy of all honour, that the name of God and *his* doctrine be not blasphemed."

Paul is speaking to Pastor Timothy, the pastor at Ephesus, and to *"servants."* As *"servants"* they were *"under the yoke."* These who were under bondage were to *"count their own masters worthy of all honour."* Their masters may have been bad *"masters,"* but these *"servants"* were to count their *"masters worthy."* Many *"servants"* are nasty. Also those who work for others can be mean, nasty, and rude. If we are Christians and we work for other people, we should count our *"masters"* to be *"worthy of honour."*

A while back there was a presentation on television called *"Driving Miss Daisy."* It was about an old battle-axe-of-a-woman who was very bitter. She had a man who drove her car and served her every whim. She was rude and horrible to that man, yet he never answered her back unkindly. Unfortunately, many people are not that way to those for whom they work.

Why should *"servants"* be sure to *"count their own masters worthy of all honour"*? The reason is given in this verse. It is in order *"that the name of God and his doctrine be not blasphemed."* When one *"blasphemes,"* he reviles the Name of God and causes Him to be evil spoken of. *"Servants"* are spoken of many times in the Bible.

- **John 15:15**
  Henceforth **I call you not servants; for the servant knoweth not what his lord doeth**: but I have called you friends; for all things that I have heard of my Father I have made known unto you.
- **Acts 16:17**
  The same followed Paul and us, and cried, saying, **These men are the servants of the most high God**, which shew unto us the way of salvation.

Paul and Silas were representatives and *"servants"* of the most high God. They were *"servants"* who were honoring to the Lord.

- **Romans 6:17**
  But God be thanked, that **ye were the servants of sin**, but ye have obeyed from the heart that form of doctrine which was delivered you.

Before we were saved we used to be *"servants of sin."*

- **Romans 6:22**
  But now being made free from sin, and **become servants to God**, ye have your fruit unto holiness, and the end everlasting life.

That is what God wants us to be--*"servants"* for Him. He wants us to do what He wants us to do.

- **1 Corinthians 7:23**
  Ye are bought with a price; **be not ye the servants of men**.

We are to be *"servants"* of God, and not *"servants"* of men.

- **Ephesians 6:5**
  Servants, be obedient to them that are *your* masters according to the flesh, with fear and trembling, in singleness of your heart, as unto Christ;

- **Ephesians 6:6**
  Not with eyeservice, as menpleasers; but **as the servants of Christ, doing the will of God from the heart**;

Serve As Unto Christ

We should *"serve"* those for whom we work as if we were working for the Lord Jesus Christ.

- **Colossians 3:22**
  Servants, obey in all things *your* masters according to the flesh; not with eyeservice, as menpleasers; but in singleness of heart, fearing God:

- **Colossians 4:1**
  Masters, give unto *your* servants that which is just and equal; knowing that ye also have a Master in heaven.

The *"masters"* ought to treat their *"servants"* right also.

- **Titus 2:9**
  Exhort **servants to be obedient unto their own masters**, *and* to please *them* well in all *things*; not answering again;

That means that there should be no disputing and arguing with the *"masters."*

- **1 Peter 2:18**
  Servants, *be* subject to *your* masters with all fear; not only to the good and gentle, but also to the froward.
- **Revelation 22:3**
  And there shall be no more curse: but the throne of God and of the Lamb shall be in it; and **his servants shall serve him:**

If we are saved we are going to "*serve*" the Lamb of God for all eternity.

1 Timothy 6:2

"And they that have believing masters, let them not despise *them*, because they are brethren; but rather do *them* service, because they are faithful and beloved, partakers of the benefit. These things teach and exhort.

Apparently the earlier verse was talking about "*servants*" who had unbelieving "*masters.*" This verse is dealing with "*masters*" who are saved. Here is the "*stop sign*" in this verse. From the structure of this present tense prohibition, these "*servants*" were "*despising*" their believing Christian "*masters.*" Paul told them here to stop it.

There are many references to "*despising*" in the Scripture. This word is KATAPHRONEO. It means: "*to contemn, despise, disdain, think little or nothing of.*"

- **Proverbs 1:30**
  They would none of my counsel: **they despised all my reproof**.

If we do not take God's "*counsel,*" we are going to be in trouble. We should not "*despise*" His "*reproof.*"

- **Proverbs 3:11**
  My son, **despise not the chastening of the LORD;** neither be weary of his correction:
- **Proverbs 14:2**
  He that walketh in his uprightness feareth the LORD: but *he that is* perverse in his ways despiseth him.

Those who are perverse "*despise*" the Lord. They do not want anything to do with him.

- **Proverbs 15:5**
  A fool despiseth his father's instruction: but he that regardeth reproof is prudent.

Sons should listen to their fathers.

- **Proverbs 15:20**
  A wise son maketh a glad father: but **a foolish man despiseth his mother**.

We are not to "*despise*" our mothers. If we do, we are fools.

● **Luke 10:16**
He that heareth you heareth me; and **he that despiseth you despiseth me; and he that despiseth me despiseth him that sent me**.

If we know the Lord Jesus Christ as our Saviour and people "*despise*" us, they are "*despising*" Christ as well.

● **1 Timothy 4:12**
Let no man despise thy youth; but be thou an example of the believers, in word, in conversation, in charity, in spirit, in faith, in purity.

Timothy was not to be "*despised*" because he was young.

● **2 Timothy 3:3**
Without natural affection, trucebreakers, false accusers, incontinent, fierce, **despisers of those that are good**,

● **Hebrews 12:5**
And ye have forgotten the exhortation which speaketh unto you as unto children, My son, **despise not thou the chastening of the Lord**, nor faint when thou art rebuked of him:

These "*servants*" should give these "*masters*" service because they are "*brethren.*" Being saved, they are "*partakers of the benefit*" of salvation and eternal life. Born-again Christians are "*partakers*" in many areas.

● **Colossians 1:12**
Giving thanks unto the Father, **which hath made us meet to be partakers of the inheritance of the saints in light**:

Those of us who are saved are "*partakers of the inheritance*" of Heaven.

● **Hebrews 3:1**
Wherefore, holy brethren, **partakers of the heavenly calling**, consider the Apostle and High Priest of our profession, Christ Jesus;

● **Hebrews 12:10**
For they verily for a few days chastened *us* after their own pleasure; but he for *our* profit, **that *we* might be partakers of his holiness.**

God wants the believers to be "*partakers of His holiness.*"

● **1 Peter 5:1**
The elders which are among you I exhort, who am also an elder, and a witness of the sufferings of Christ, and also **a partaker of the glory that shall be revealed:**

All of us who are saved will one day be "*partaking*" of the glory of the Lord Jesus Christ. It will not be too long for some of us.

Bible Doctrines Are To Be Taught

These doctrines and practices Pastor Timothy was to *"teach and exhort."* It should be a part of the preaching of the Words of God in his church at Ephesus and, by application, in all churches in that day and in ours as well.

"Do It Unto Him"

Do it unto the Lord for He understands;
Do it all to His Name and be blessed.
No matter if others regard it as small,
No matter if anyone sees it at all.
Do it unto the Lord.

Do it unto the Lord; He knoweth your strength;
He knoweth each effort and seeth each length.
He watches each testing and appraiseth the cause;
He lists our endurance and maketh each pause.
Do it unto the Lord.

Do it unto the Lord; it bringeth sweet peace,
A balm for aloneness and wondrous release.
He measures our lack and He knoweth our frame;
And He giveth contentment when it's done in His Name.
Do it unto the Lord

By Gertrude G. Sanborn
With Tears In My Heart

1 Timothy 6:3

"If any man teach otherwise, and consent not to wholesome words, *even* the Words of our Lord Jesus Christ, and to the doctrine which is according to godliness;

The words *"teach otherwise"* are taken from one Greek word, HETRODIDASKALEO. It means: *"to teach other or different doctrine; deviating from the truth."* This would refer to anyone who was deviating from the truth, or teaching something different from what Paul had been teaching here which, in turn, were *"wholesome words, even the Words of our Lord Jesus Christ."*

What are included in the *"Words of our Lord Jesus Christ"*? I believe they are not only what He spoke while on earth, but I believe that the Lord Jesus Christ is the Author of all the New Testament Greek Words and all the Old Testament Hebrew and Aramaic Words.

Knowing We Have God's Words

How do we have and know all the *"Words of our Lord Jesus Christ"*? Two things are required for this.

(1) We must have every one of those original Hebrew, Aramaic, and Greek Words preserved for us.

(2) We must have an accurate translation of those preserved original Words available to people in their own language all over the world such as has been done in our English King James Bible.

Where Are God's Original Words?

(1) I believe the Hebrew, Aramaic, and Greek Words underlying our King James Bible are the exact, original, plenarily, verbally inspired, inerrant, and preserved Words.

(2) I also believe that our King James Bible has accurately translated those preserved inerrant Words into our English language.

These preserved original Hebrew, Aramaic, and Greek Words must be used as the basis for accurate translation into all the languages of the world, whether English, Spanish, French, German, Italian, or any other language.

There is a recently-published book that tells a translator in detail how to translate the Bible in a proper manner. It was written by Dr. H. D. Williams. The title is *Word-For-Word Translating of The Received Texts--Verbal Plenary Translating.* It is a fully-indexed, perfect-bound book of 296 pages. It is **BFT #3302 @ $10.00 + $5.00 S&H** and can be obtained by writing **Bible For Today**, 900 Park Avenue, Collingswood, NJ 08108 or by calling 856-854-4452 with credit card. There is nothing like this book among all of the other books about how to translate the Bible.

Even some of the major fundamentalist schools and institutions doubt that we really do have the *"Words of our Lord Jesus Christ"* preserved for us today. The leading Fundamentalist schools teaching this heresy are Bob Jones University, Detroit Baptist Seminary, Central Baptist Seminary, Calvary Baptist Seminary, Maranatha Baptist Bible College, Northland Baptist Bible College, and others. **They teach their students that they cannot believe that God has even promised to preserve His Hebrew, Aramaic, and Greek Words. They therefore deny that He has done so.**

We Must Consent to Christ's Words

Paul warns against the kind of people who *"teach otherwise, and consent not to wholesome words, even the words of our Lord Jesus Christ, . . ."*

The President of Central Baptist Seminary in the Minneapolis area, Kevin Bauder, in the book, *One Bible Only?* stated:

"Even with regard to written words, it is demonstrably true that

when someone's spoken words were later recorded in Scripture, the 'exact' words spoken were not necessarily the very words that were used in Scripture." (p. 159, quoted in my book, *Fuzzy Facts From Fundamentalists*, p. 62 (**BFT #3064BK, @ $8.00 + S&H**)

This would mean that he does not even know for sure if the *"Words of the Lord Jesus Christ"* were properly written down in our Bibles. This is an apostate and a heretical position!! He is therefore not absolutely **CERTAIN** of such gospel verses as John 1:10-13; 3:16; 4:14; 5:24; 6:35; 10:9; 14:1-3, 14:6 and many, many more *"Words of our Lord Jesus Christ."* We must stand for the all the *"Words of our Lord Jesus Christ."*

Paul told Pastor Timothy that he should also be interested in *"the doctrine which is according to godliness."* This *"doctrine"* is that which is found in the Bible and should be believed and preached. *"Godliness"* is God's goal for every born-again Christian.

- 1 Timothy 2:2
  For kings, and *for* all that are in authority; **that we may lead a quiet and peaceable life in all godliness and honesty**.
- 1 Timothy 4:7
  But refuse profane and old wives' fables, and **exercise thyself** *rather* **unto godliness**.
- 1 Timothy 6:11
  But thou, O man of God, flee these things; and **follow after righteousness, godliness,** faith, love, patience, meekness.

Those who deny the *"Words of the Lord Jesus Christ"* have something seriously wrong with them.

1 Timothy 6:4

"He is proud, knowing nothing, but doting about questions and strifes of words, whereof cometh envy, strife, railings, evil surmisings,

In this verse there are the eight of the eleven things that are true about these pastors and other individuals who do not *"consent"* to the *"Words of our Lord Jesus Christ"* and the *"doctrine which is according to godliness."* There are three more things mentioned in the next verse making a total of eleven.

Some Are Proud

[1] The non-consenters are *"proud."*

The word for *"proud"* is TOPHOO. It means:
"to raise a smoke, to wrap in a mist; metaph. to make proud, puff up with pride, render insolent; to be puffed up with haughtiness or pride; to blind with pride or conceit, to render foolish or stupid; beclouded, besotted."

This is God's description of what those people are who are not following the *"Words of our Lord Jesus Christ."* If they do not have all the *"Words,"* how can they follow them?

Some Are Knowing-Nothing

[2] The non-consenters are *"Knowing nothing."*

They think they know things, but they do not.

Some Dote About Questions

[3] The non-consenters are *"doting about questions."*

The word for *"doting"* is NOSEO. It means: *"to be sick; metaph. of any ailment of the mind; to be taken with such an interest in a thing as amounts to a disease, to have a morbid fondness for."* There are some people who have many questions. They are subject to debates and controversy whether it is over the five-points of hyper Calvinism or some another kind of debates.

Some Dote About Strifes of Words

[4] The non-consenters are *"doting"* about *"strifes of words."*

This would indicate a wrangling about trifling matters involving definitions of certain words.

Some Have Envy

[5] The non-consenters have *"envy."*

If all these people are doing is *"striving,"* they are going to have *"envy"* one with another.

Some Have Strife

[6] The non-consenters have *"strife."*

Some Have Railings

[7] The non-consenters have *"railings."*

The word for *"railings"* is BLASPHEMIA. It means: *"slander, detraction, speech injurious, to another's good name; impious and reproachful speech injurious to divine majesty."*

Some Have Evil Surmisings

[8] The non-consenters have *"evil surmisings."*

These people have very *"evil"* thoughts and imaginations which are only guesses and ideas not based on facts. Evolution is one such *"evil surmising."* The assumed superiority of the Gnostic manuscripts of the Vatican and Sinai ("B" and "Aleph") is another such *"evil surmising."*

1 Timothy 6:5

"Perverse disputings of men of corrupt minds, and destitute of the truth, supposing that gain is godliness: from such withdraw thyself.

Some Have Perverse Disputings

[9]   The non-consenters have *"perverse disputings of men of corrupt minds."*

We have all kinds of perverse and twisted individuals. Sexual perverts are increasing daily. The Internet pornography sites are easy sources for those of *"corrupt minds."*

Some Are Destitute of the Truth

[10] The non-consenters are *"destitute of the truth."*

As I said before, I believe the Lord Jesus Christ was the Author not only of all the New Testament Greek Words (John 16:12-14), but also, by extension as the Logos or Revelator, of all the Old Testament Hebrew and Aramaic Words. He told the Holy Spirit of God what to tell the writers of both the Old and New Testaments what to write down.

Some Suppose Gain Is Godliness

[11] The non-consenters are *"supposing that gain is godliness."*

The word for "gain" is PORISMOS. It means: *"acquisition, gain; source of gain."* Mere *"acquisition"* of things is considered as *"gain"* by these non-consenters. The Bible speaks often about *"gain."*

- **Proverbs 15:27**
  He that is greedy of gain troubleth his own house; but he that hateth gifts shall live.

- Mark 8:36
For what shall it profit a man, if he shall gain the whole world, and lose his own soul?
Fanny Crosby wrote a hymn called *"Take the World, But Give Me Jesus."* The Lord is of far more value and *"gain"* than the world.
- **Philippians 1:21**
For to me to live *is* Christ, and to die *is* gain.
If we are saved, going Home to be with the Lord is *"gain."*
- **Philippians 3:7**
But **what things were gain to me, those I counted loss for Christ.**
Paul was a Hebrew of the Hebrews. He was a Pharisee. He was profiting in the Jewish religion before the Lord Jesus Christ saved him.

Notice what pastors and other born-again Christians are ordered to do with these people who are guilty of *"not consenting to the Words of the Lord Jesus Christ and godly doctrine,"* and are therefore guilty of all eleven of the above failures. *"From such withdraw thyself."* The Greek word for *"withdraw"* is APHISTEMI. It means:

"to make stand off, cause to withdraw, to remove; to excite to revolt; to stand off, to stand aloof; to go away, to depart from anyone; to desert, withdraw from one; to fall away, become faithless; to shun, flee from; to cease to vex one; to withdraw one's self from, to fall away; to keep one's self from, absent one's self from."

Just get away from them. If you do not *"withdraw"* from these people, then they will pull you down.

Schools Use False Greek Words

It is interesting to note that the major *"separatist"* schools [such as Bob Jones University, Detroit Baptist Seminary, Central Baptist Seminary, Calvary Baptist Seminary, and others] have adopted a Westcott/Hort, Nestle/Aland, United Bible Societies Critical Greek text which omits entirely *"from such withdraw thyself."* Hence one of the major verses for Biblical separation is omitted from most modern English and other language versions, some of which they prefer. It is gone from the ASV, the NASV, the NIV, the TNIV, the ESV, the RSV, the NRSV, the CEV, and most of the other modern perversions.

- **2 Thessalonians 3:6**
  Now we command you, brethren, in the name of our Lord Jesus Christ, that ye **withdraw yourselves from every brother that walketh disorderly, and not after the tradition which he received of us.**
  Sometimes we have to *"withdraw"* ourselves even from saved people if they are *"walking disorderly."* God commands that we do that.

Abundance Not Always Gain

This idea of *"gain"* also can be looked at as *"abundance."* The Lord Jesus told a story about a man who was seeking abundance and *"gain."*

- **Luke 12:15-21**
  And he said unto them, Take heed, and beware of covetousness: for **a man's life consisteth not in the abundance of the things which he possesseth.** And he spake a parable unto them, saying, The ground of **a certain rich man brought forth plentifully**: And he thought within himself, saying, What shall I do, because I have no room where to bestow my fruits? And he said, This will I do: I will pull down my barns, and build greater; and there will I bestow all my fruits and my goods. And I will say to my soul, **Soul, thou hast much goods laid up for many years;** take thine ease, eat, drink, *and* be merry. But God said unto him, *Thou* fool, this night thy soul shall be required of thee: then whose shall those things be, which thou hast provided? **So** *is* **he that layeth up treasure for himself,** and is not rich toward God.

The Rich Fool

God called this man a *"fool"* because he had plenty of goods but was not thinking of tomorrow. When we die, our goods are left behind. We must never fail to be rich toward God. Do not be a *"fool."*

1 Timothy 6:6

"But godliness with contentment is great gain."

"*Gain*" is not "*godliness*." On the other hand, "*godliness with contentment is great gain*" as this verse declares. God wants saved people to be content.

- **Luke 3:14**
  And the soldiers likewise demanded of him, saying, And what shall we do? And he said unto them, Do violence to no man, neither accuse *any* falsely; and **be content with your wages**.

- **Philippians 4:11**
  Not that I speak in respect of want: for **I have learned, in whatsoever state I am, *therewith* to be content**.

  Paul had many wants and needs being in prison. If every one of us could take what Paul said and apply it to our lives, we would have "*gain*."

- **Hebrews 13:5**
  Let your conversation *be* without covetousness; *and **be content with such things as ye have**: for he hath said, I will never leave thee, nor forsake thee.

  If you do not have much of this world's goods and you live for the Lord in peace with "*contentment*"? How is that a "*gain*"? It is a "*gain*" because God says it is a "*gain*." He is the One who keeps score as to "*gains*." It is not a "*gain*" to the world. The world does not want us to be "*content*" with anything. The world says we need to not be "*content*" with our wages, our homes, our clothes, or anything else in our lives. The world does not like "*contentment*." They equate "*contentment*" with laziness or not having a drive to get ahead. God says to be content because "*contentment*" is great "*gain*."

  The word for "*contentment*" is AUTARCHEIA. It means:
  "*a perfect condition of life in which no aid or support is needed; sufficiency of the necessities of life; a mind contented with its lot, contentment.*"

Be Content With God's Provision

Do you have food on your table? Do you have a roof over your head? Do you have clothes to wear? Is it warm where you live? Do you have a measure of health? If these things are true of you, you should be "*content*" with God's gracious provision.

1 Timothy 6:7

"For we brought nothing into *this* world, *and it is* certain we can carry nothing out."

This is a simple and a true statement. Think of all the things we did **not** bring "*into this world.*" Did you bring any speech into the world when you were born? No, you made noise, but you could not talk. Could you walk when you came into the world? No, you could not even crawl. Did you bring any clothes when you were born? No you had no clothes, suits, or even shoes. Did you bring any money with you? No, you had no money either. You were penniless. The only thing you had was your mother and your father. They took care of you. Did you bring a house into the world when you were born? Did you bring a car with you? If you had one you could not have driven it. Did you bring a boat with you when you were brought into this world? Did you bring any skills with you? You could not operate a computer. You could not read or write. You brought nothing into this world. Did you bring any friends with you? No, you brought no friends into this world. You make friends. It says in Scripture that if you want friends you must show yourself friendly. Friends are made. Some friends are good, some friends are bad. Did you bring salvation with you when you came into the world? No, you did not bring salvation with you.

"*And it is certain we can carry nothing out.*" As it is certain that we "*brought nothing into this world,*" it is even more "*certain*" that "*we can carry nothing out.*" That is a certainty. You are not going to be able to take your speech as we know it here. You are going to leave all your clothes behind you when you leave this world. You are not going to take any money with you. I do not care if you make several millions of dollars. The richest men in the world will leave all their money here. You cannot take your house with you.

You Can't Take It With You

When Mrs. Smith sold us our home in 1965, we knew that when we died we would leave our house behind just as Mrs. Smith did. When my wife's dad went home to be with the Lord, he left us his car. He could not take it with him, and we will not take ours with us either. We will leave all our friends here on this earth. The only thing we can take with us is the things we have done for the glory of our Lord Jesus Christ.

All of us have an "*appointment*" that we must keep, whenever it is scheduled.

• **Hebrews 9:27**
And as **it is appointed unto men once to die,** but after this the judgment:

We must trust the Lord Jesus Christ while we are living so that we can avoid the Great White Throne judgment? We will all die unless the Lord Jesus comes back and the rapture takes the saved ones Home to Heaven. Every one of us will be "on time" for death's "*appointment.*"

1 Timothy 6:8

"And having food and raiment let us be therewith content."

If we have "*food and raiment*" we are exhorted to be "*content.*" As we said before, "*Godliness with contentment is great gain*" (1 Timothy 6:6) The word for "*content*" is ARKEO. It means: "*to be possessed of unfailing strength; to be strong, to suffice, to be enough; to defend, ward off; to be satisfied, to be contented.*"

The Lord Jesus often talked about "*contentment*" as far as "*food and raiment*" are concerned.

- Matthew 6:25-34

Wherefore I say unto you, **Take no thought for your life, what ye shall eat, or what ye shall drink; nor yet for your body, what ye shall put on. Is not the life more than meat, and the body than raiment?**

Behold the fowls of the air: for they sow not, neither do they reap, nor gather into barns; yet your heavenly Father feedeth them. Are ye not much better than they?

Which of you by taking thought can add one cubit unto his stature? And why take ye thought for raiment? Consider the lilies of the field, how they grow; they toil not, neither do they spin: And yet I say unto you, That even Solomon in all his glory was not arrayed like one of these.

Wherefore, **if God so clothe the grass of the field, which to day is, and to morrow is cast into the oven, *shall he* not much more *clothe* you, O ye of little faith? Therefore take no thought, saying, What shall we eat? or, What shall we drink? or, Wherewithal shall we be clothed?**

(For after all these things do the Gentiles seek:) **for your heavenly Father knoweth that ye have need of all these things. But seek ye first the kingdom of God, and his righteousness; and all these things shall be added unto you.**

Take therefore no thought for the morrow: for the morrow shall take thought for the things of itself. Sufficient unto the day *is* the evil thereof.

The first thing we are to seek is the *"Kingdom of God."* Remember what the Lord Jesus Christ said about entering the *"Kingdom of God."*

- John 3:3

Jesus answered and said unto him, Verily, verily, I say unto thee, **Except a man be born again, he cannot see the kingdom of God.**

Receive the Lord Jesus Christ Now

The only way we can *"see"* or *"enter"* into the *"Kingdom of God"* is to repent of our   sins and genuinely receive the Lord Jesus Christ as our Saviour and Redeemer Who died for our sins. Once we have sought Him and found Him as our Saviour, all these needs that He mentioned, according to His promise, *"shall be added unto you."*

That does not seem to be acceptable to the 21st Century man or woman. They say they are not going to be "*content*" with just "*food and raiment.*" They say they must have much more than that for "*contentment.*" God can give us other things, but even if we do not have them, we are still to be "*content*" if we have only "*food and raiment.*" These things that God says should bring "*contentment*" find a disagreement in the heart of the person in the world, and, sad to say, in the heart of too many born-again Christians!

1 Timothy 6:9

"But they that will be rich fall into temptation and a snare, and *into* many foolish and hurtful lusts, which drown men in destruction and perdition.

Many times in our King James Bible, when we see the word "*will*," it is an indication of the future tense. But in this verse, this is not the case. In this verse, the word for "*will*" is BOULOMAI. It means: "*to will deliberately, have a purpose, be minded; of willing as an affection, to desire.*" These people are going to have riches no matter what else happens.

Rich Desires and Temptation

God says that men who have that one supreme desire to "*be rich*" will "*fall into temptation.*" The word for "*temptation*" is PEIRASMOS.

It means a variety of things:

> "*an experiment, attempt, trial, proving; the trial made of you by my bodily condition, since condition served as to test the love of the Galatians toward Paul (Gal. 4:14); the trial of man's fidelity, integrity, virtue, constancy; **an enticement to sin**, temptation, **whether arising from the desires or from the outward circumstances; an internal temptation to sin;** of the temptation by which the devil sought to divert Jesus the Messiah from his divine errand; of the condition of things, or a mental state, by which we are enticed to sin, or to a lapse from the faith and holiness; adversity, affliction, trouble: sent by God and serving to test or prove one's character, faith, holiness; temptation (i.e. trial) of God by men; rebellion against God, by which his power and justice are, as it were, put to the proof and challenged to show themselves.*"

This is "*an enticement to sin*" either from within the person or outside the person.

Rich Desires and Snares

Notice a second thing about those who have a strong desire *"to be rich."*
They are going to fall into *"a snare."*

This word is PAGIDA. It means:

> *"snare, trap, noose; of snares in which birds are **entangled and
> caught; implies unexpectedly, suddenly,** because birds and beasts
> are caught unawares; a snare, i.e. whatever brings peril, loss,
> destruction; of a sudden and unexpected deadly peril; of the
> allurements and seductions of sin; the allurements to sin by which
> the devil holds one bound; the snares of love."*

Notice that the *"snare"* catches *"unexpectedly or suddenly."* The trap of those
who are willing and desirous to be rich is first, a secret and sudden trap that they
cannot get out. They who are wanting *"to be rich"* will have these *"snares."*
These men and women will most likely go to all the places where the rich
people go. Waiting for these *"rich"* people are *"snares and traps."*

In addition to these other dangers, those having a strong desire *"to be rich"*
will fall into *"many foolish and hurtful lusts, which drown men in destruction
and perdition."* The word for *"perdition"* is APOLEIA. It has various
meanings: *"destroying, utter destruction; of vessels; a perishing, ruin,
destruction; of money; the destruction which consists of eternal misery in hell."*
Quite often, those who strongly desire *"to be rich"* have no time for God
or the Lord Jesus Christ.

"No Time For God"

No time for God?
What fools we are, to clutter up
Our lives with common things
And leave without heart's gate
The Lord of life and Life itself--Our God!

No time for God?
As soon t say no time
To eat or sleep or love or die.
Take time for God,
Or you shall dwarf your soul,
And when the angel death
Comes knocking at your door,
A poor misshapen thing you'll be
To step into eternity!

No time for God?
That day when sickness comes
Or trouble finds you out
And you cry out for God,
Will He have time for you?

No time for God?
Some day you'll lay aside
This mortal self and make your way
To worlds anew,
And when you meet Him face to face
Will He have time for you?

By Norman L. Trott

The Bible has many things to say concerning *"riches."*

- **Proverbs 10:22**

  The blessing of the LORD, **it maketh rich**, and he addeth no sorrow with it.

- **Proverbs 13:7**

  There is that **maketh himself rich**, yet *hath* nothing: *there is* that maketh himself poor, **yet *hath* great riches**.

Rich men may not have the true *"riches"* of Heaven, and the poor men may have the eternal lasting *"riches"* of the Lord Jesus Christ.

- **Proverbs 14:20**

  The poor is hated even of his own neighbour: but **the rich *hath* many friends.**

What kind of *"friends"* are they? As long as the money holds out the friends stay around, but as soon as your riches are gone so are your friends.

- **Proverbs 22:2**

  The rich and poor meet together: the LORD *is* the maker of them all.

If both are saved, they are brothers in Christ.

- **Proverbs 23:4**

  Labour not to be rich: cease from thine own wisdom.

- **Proverbs 28:6**

  Better *is* the poor that walketh in his uprightness, than *he that is* perverse *in his* ways, **though he *be* rich.**

- **Ecclesiastes 5:12**

  The sleep of a labouring man *is* sweet, whether he eat little or much: but **the abundance of the rich will not suffer him to sleep**.

When you are *"rich,"* you have so many things you have to guard.

- **Jeremiah 9:23**

  Thus saith the LORD, Let not the wise *man* glory in his wisdom, neither let the mighty *man* glory in his might, **let not the rich *man* glory in his riches:**

Don't Glory in Riches

If the Lord has given you *"riches,"* praise the Lord for those riches, but don't glory in them.

- **2 Corinthians 6:10**

  As sorrowful, yet alway rejoicing; as poor, **yet making many rich**; as having nothing, and *yet* possessing all things.

  Paul was poor in his own life, but *"rich"* in the riches of the Lord.

- **2 Corinthians 8:9**

  For ye know the grace of our Lord Jesus Christ, that, **though he was rich, yet for your sakes he became poor, that ye through his poverty might be rich.**

True Riches

Trusting in Christ is true riches.

- **1 Timothy 6:17**

  Charge them that are rich in this world, that they be not highminded, **nor trust in uncertain riches**, but in the living God, who giveth us richly all things to enjoy;

  "Riches" truly are *"uncertain."* Look at the stock market if you do not believe me. A person who used to have a million dollars a few years ago, had less than $500,000 a few years later after a crash of the market. It was gone.

- **Revelation 3:17**

  Because thou sayest, **I am rich**, and increased with goods, and have need of nothing; and knowest not that thou art wretched, and miserable, and poor, and blind, and naked:

  We must find in the Lord Jesus Christ and in God our Father the *"riches"* of His grace and the *"riches"* of Heaven.

1 Timothy 6:10

"For the love of money is the root of all evil: which while some coveted after, they have erred from the faith, and pierced themselves through with many sorrows."

Money Itself Is Not Evil

This *"love of money"* is indeed the *"root of all evil."* It is the strong desire of the previous verse *"to be rich."* This does not mean that *"money"* itself is *"evil."* It is the *"love of money"* which is the *"root"* of *"all evil"* and many sins.

The word for *"evil"* is KAKOS. It means: *"of a bad nature; not such as it ought to be; of a mode of thinking, feeling, acting; base, wrong, wicked; troublesome, injurious, pernicious, destructive, baneful."*

The Sinfulness of Covetousness

"Covetousness" is a sinful thing.

The word for *"covet"* is OREGOMAI. It means: *"to stretch one's self out in order to touch or to grasp something, to reach after or desire something; to give one's self up to the love of money."* If this is their condition, *"they have erred from the faith and pierced themselves through with many sorrows."*

"The" Faith Refers to Bible Doctrine

"The faith," when used with the article in Greek, refers to the doctrines taught in the Bible.

To *"err from the faith"* means to go astray from the Words of God. That is a terrible price to pay is it not? If you work for money, seven days a week, in order *"to be rich,"* there is little time to go to church, to read the Bible, to pray or to have strong fellowship with the Lord. Those who have this *"love of money"* have also *"pierced themselves through with many sorrows."* The word for "pierced" is PERIPEIRO. It means: "*to pierce through; metaph. to torture one's soul with sorrows.*"

Godly Contentment Is Great Gain

Our God wants us to be "*content*" with the things that we have. He wants to remind us that "*godliness with contentment is great gain*" (1 Timothy 6:6). The world may not think that this is "*great gain,*" but God does. He reminds us that we brought nothing into this world and we will take nothing out. God wants us to have the riches of God in Christ Jesus, and to glorify Him with our life.

---

1 Timothy 6:11

"But thou, O man of God, flee these things; and follow after righteousness, godliness, faith, love, patience, meekness."

Pastor Timothy is to "*flee these things*" mentioned before. He is especially to "*flee*" from the "*love of money.*"   Sometimes we are to "*flee*" unto things but more often we are to "*flee*" from things.

- **Psalm 143:9**
  Deliver me, O LORD, from mine enemies: **I flee unto thee** to hide me.

We should "*flee*" from evil, but "*flee*" unto the Lord.

- **Matthew 3:7**
  But when he saw many of the Pharisees and Sadducees come to his baptism, he said unto them, O generation of vipers, **who hath warned you to flee from the wrath to come?**

- **1 Corinthians 6:18**
  Flee fornication. Every sin that a man doeth is without the body; but he that committeth fornication sinneth against his own body.

God tells us to "*flee*" sexual sin.

- **Genesis 39:12**
  And she caught him by his garment, saying, Lie with me: and **he left his garment in her hand, and fled, and got him out.**

We are to "*flee*" from adultery and fornication.

- **2 Timothy 2:22**
  Flee also youthful lusts: but follow righteousness, faith, charity, peace, with them that call on the Lord out of a pure heart.

After telling Pastor Timothy to "*flee*" from evil, he reminds him that he is to "*follow after*" some things. All six of these things are important.

Fellowship With the Lord & Virtues

He wrote him to "*follow after righteousness, godliness, faith, love, patience, meekness.*" All these virtues are the result of close fellowship with the Lord Jesus Christ and allowing God the Holy Spirit Who indwells every believer to produce His fruit. Such fruit is not likely to be produced in someone who has a strong lust "*to be rich*" and to "*love money.*"

The Bible mentions many other things that deal with "*following.*"

- **Matthew 4:19**
  And he saith unto them, **Follow me**, and I will make you fishers of men.
- **John 10:27**
  My sheep hear my voice, and I know them, and **they follow me**:

If you are one of His sheep, you "*follow*" Him.

- **John 12:26**
  If any man serve me, let him follow me; and where I am, there shall also my servant be: if any man serve me, him will *my* Father honour.

Fleeing Without Following Is Empty

It does not do any good to "*flee*" things if we do not "*follow.*" By the same token, it does not do any good to "*follow*" if we do not "*flee.*" We should not want to take our sins with us.

- **2 Timothy 2:22**
  Flee also youthful lusts: **but follow righteousness, faith, charity, peace,** with them that call on the Lord out of a pure heart.

In the present verse eleven, Paul lists six different things for Pastor Timothy to *"follow."* He was the Pastor in the city of Ephesus. Ephesus was a large seaport in Asia Minor, which is now Turkey.

Timothy Was to Follow Righteousness

(1) First, Timothy was to preach the word and *"follow righteousness."*

Ephesus was wicked. There was much idolatry in the city. Despite this, Timothy was told to *"follow righteousness"* in the midst of unrighteousness.

Timothy Was to Follow Godliness

(2) Second, Timothy was to *"follow godliness."*

He was not to get into the sin, wickedness, and ungodliness of the city of Ephesus around him.

Timothy Was to Follow Faith

(3) Third, Timothy was to *"follow faith."*

Even though it might have looked bleak and dark for this pastor, his trust and *"faith"* in the Lord Jesus Christ must be *"followed."*

Timothy Was to Follow Love

(4) Fourth, Timothy was to *"follow love."*

No matter how many people might have hated him or his *"love"* of the truth, he was to show *"love,"* even, and especially, toward his enemies.

Timothy Was to Follow Patience

(5) Fifth, Timothy was to *"follow patience."*

No matter how strong the desire is to get things over quickly, this pastor was to *"follow patience"* and wait for God to solve his problems.

Timothy Was to Follow Meekness

(6) Sixth, Timothy was to *"follow meekness."*

He was not to be rude and egotistical. He was not to brag or boast.

We who are born-again Christians living in our time should *"follow after"* these same six things.

The word used for *"follow after"* is DIOKO. Depending on the context, it has various meanings:

"to make to run or flee, put to flight, drive away; to run swiftly in order to catch a person or thing, to run after; to press on: figuratively of one who in a race runs swiftly to reach the goal; to pursue (in a hostile manner); in any way whatever to harass, trouble, molest one; to persecute; to be mistreated, suffer persecution on account of something; without the idea of hostility, to run after, follow after: someone; metaph., to pursue; to seek after eagerly, earnestly endeavour to acquire."

1 Timothy 6:12

"Fight the good fight of faith, lay hold on eternal life, whereunto thou art also called, and hast professed a good profession before many witnesses."

In our present verse 12, we come back to the phrase, *"lay hold on eternal life whereunto thou art also called."*

The word for *"lay hold on"* is EPILAMBANOMAI. It means:

"to take in addition, to lay hold of, take possession of, overtake, attain, attain to; to lay hold of or to seize upon anything with the hands, to take hold of, lay hold of; metaph. to rescue one from peril, to help, succour."

We must *"lay hold"* of that *"eternal life"* that we have been given when we trusted the Lord Jesus Christ as our Saviour.

In our morning church services we often sing the chorus called, "*Faithful to the Fight*." This is a song written by Gertrude Grace Sanborn, my wife's mother. She dedicated it to me, her son-in-law. When we sing it, it brings to mind this verse where Paul commands Pastor Timothy to "*fight the good fight of faith*."

"Faithful to the Fight"

Faithful to the fight
Faithful to the faith
Faithful to the finish for God.

Faithful to the right
Faithful in His might
Faithful to the Word of God

Faithful in the fray
Faithful every day
Faithful in the fight for the faith

Faithful to the fight
Faithful to the faith
Faithful to the finish for God

By Gertrude G. Sanborn
With Tears In My Heart

In this verse the word "*faith*" is used with the article in Greek. Timothy is to "*fight the good fight of* [**the**] *faith*." When the article is used in Greek, it refers to the entire body of doctrine that God has revealed to us in the Bible. That doctrine is what we are to "*fight*" for. The verb for "*fight*" is AGONIZOMAI. It means:

> "*to enter a contest: contend in the gymnastic games; to contend with adversaries, fight; metaph. to contend, struggle, with difficulties and dangers; to endeavour with strenuous zeal, strive: to obtain something.*"

Some people do not "*fight*" for anything. Pastor Timothy was to "*fight the good fight of* [**the**] *faith*." Since this is in the present tense in Greek, it is to be a continuous, unending "*fight*" and battle for **the** faith and doctrines of the Bible. He was not to let any one stop him. It is also in the imperative mood and is therefore a command rather than merely a suggestion.

Notice, this "*fight*" is "*good*." The word for "*good*" is KALOS. In various contexts, it means:

"*beautiful, handsome, excellent, eminent, choice, surpassing, precious, useful, suitable, commendable, admirable; beautiful to look at, shapely, magnificent; good, excellent in its nature and characteristics, and therefore well adapted to its ends; genuine, approved; precious; joined to names of men designated by their office, competent, able, such as one ought to be; praiseworthy, noble; beautiful by reason of purity of heart and life, and hence praiseworthy; morally good, noble; honourable, conferring honour; affecting the mind agreeably, comforting and confirming.*"

Often, those who speak or write about those of us who "*contend for the faith*" (Jude 1:3b) say we are doing something that is ugly or evil. In this verse, God Himself calls this "*fight*" something that is "*beautiful, good, and excellent in its nature and characteristics.*" We should never be ashamed of carrying out this "*charge*" and "*command*" if we do it in a Scriptural manner.

Our Fight for the Faith Today

The battle was raging in Paul's day, and perhaps it is even worse today. "*The faith*" is being denied. "*The faith*" in the Lord Jesus' Virgin Birth is being denied. Around Christmas time, preachers talk about Jesus being born, but many of them leave out His Virgin Birth. "*The faith*" in the bodily resurrection of Jesus Christ is being denied. "*The faith*" in God's preservation of the original Hebrew, Aramaic, and Greek Words of the Bible is being denied, even by many prominent Fundamentalists. There are battles all over regarding "*the faith.*" Timothy was told in his day to continue to fight for "*the faith.*" We should do so in our day.

There are a number of verses concerning "*fighting.*"
*   **Psalm 144:1**
    <<*A Psalm* of David.>> Blessed *be* the LORD my strength, which **teacheth my hands to war,** *and* **my fingers to fight:**
    My mother-in-law always said that "*my fingers to fight*" could be applied to the use of our "*fingers*" to write or type faithful materials that exalt the Lord.

That is why I praise God that I can use my fingers to write and to fight for the doctrines of "*the faith.*".

- **1 Samuel 17:32**
  And David said to Saul, Let no man's heart fail because of him; **thy servant will go and fight with this Philistine**.

  David was a youth with a great "*faith*" and a great "*fight.*" As others have wisely said, "*It's not the size of the dog in the fight that counts, but the size of the fight in the dog.*" This dog, David, had plenty of fight. He had the faith of the Lord God of Heaven and earth and he was determined, by God's help, to slay that giant, and he did.

- **1 Corinthians 9:26**
  I therefore so run, not as uncertainly; **so fight I**, not as one that beateth the air:

  This is a spiritual battle we are in.

- **2 Timothy 4:7**
  I have fought a good fight, I have finished *my* course, I have kept the faith:

  This is the verse that is the basis of the chorus "*Faithful to the Fight.*" Paul wrote the book of 2 Timothy during his second Roman imprisonment. It was the last book he penned. Paul the apostle wrote to that young preacher Timothy and encouraged him to "*fight*" the same "*fight.*" We who are born-again Christians are in a battle today just as Paul and Timothy were in a battle in their day.

Don't Neglect The Fight for the Faith

It is very sad that many today seek to become spiritual "*conscientious objectors*" to the battle for "*the faith*" and do not "*fight the good fight of* [the] *faith.*"

- **1 Corinthians 14:8**
  For if the trumpet give an uncertain sound, **who shall prepare himself to the battle**?

  Our 𝕭ible 𝔉or 𝔗oday 𝕭aptist 𝕮hurch gives a "*certain sound.*" That is how we prepare ourselves for "*the battle.*" Every person who knows anything about us is aware of which side of the many "*battles*" for "*the faith*" we are on because our "*trumpet gives*" a certain "*sound.*" Pray that it will ever be so!

  The Scriptures also talk about "*warfare.*"

- **2 Corinthians 10:4**
  (For **the weapons of our warfare** *are* **not carnal**, but mighty through God to the pulling down of strong holds;)
- **1 Timothy 1:18**
  This charge I commit unto thee, son Timothy, according to the prophecies which went before on thee, **that thou by them mightest war a good warfare;**
  Then there are verses about being a solider.

- **2 Timothy 2:3-4**
  Thou therefore **endure hardness, as a good soldier of Jesus Christ. No man that warreth entangleth himself with the affairs of** *this* **life; that he may please him who hath chosen him to be a soldier.**

Born-Again Christians Are Soldiers

Every born-again Christian, whether they are a pastor like Timothy or not, is a *"solider"* for the Lord Jesus Christ. We must please Christ *"who has chosen us to be a soldier."*

There is a hymn, written by Isaac Watts, which sums up the Christian's work of a Christian *"soldier."* It asks many important questions for us today:

Am I a Soldier of the Cross?

"Am I a soldier of the cross? A follower of the Lamb?
And shall I fear to own His cause, Or blush to speak His name?
Must I be carried to the skies, On flowery beds of ease,
While others fought to win the prize, And sailed thru bloody seas?
Are there no foes for me to face? Must I not stem the flood?
Is this vile world a friend to grace, To help me on to God?
Sure I must fight if I would reign--Increase my courage, Lord!
I'll bear the toil, endure the pain, Supported by Thy Word."

Any *"soldier"* in a battle where he is fighting must have enemies. Otherwise, there is no need to *"fight."* I was given an interesting poem recently that asks an important question. It was written by Charles McKay.

"No Enemies?"

You have no enemies, you say at last?
My friend, the boast is poor.
He who has mingled in the fray
Of duty that the brave endure,
Must have made foes.
If you have none,
Small is the work that you have done.
You've hit no traitor on the hip.
You've dashed no cup from perjured lip.
You've never turned the wrong to right.
You've been a coward in the fight!"

By Charles McKay

This is an interesting poem to think about. We must not be *"cowards"* in the *"fight for the faith."* Let me clarify the spiritual *"fight," "battle,"* and *"warfare"* that we're in today. It is one thing to fight the Roman Catholic Church with all their errors. It is one thing to fight the modernists and liberals who deny almost everything the Bible teaches. It is one thing to fight the neo-evangelicals who compromise vital points of the Christian faith.

Even Fundamentalists Can Be Wrong

But, it is quite a different thing to have to *"fight"* our Fundamentalist brethren who are with us in many areas of doctrine, including Biblical separation, yet are in completely unscriptural territory in the area of Theology known as Bibliology--the doctrine of the Bible. In this area, we are miles apart. That is the important *"fight"* for *"the faith"* that I and others are battling at this time. It means we must be earnest in our contention for truth and honesty.

It reminds me of the United States Army Oath regarding loyalty to the U. S. Constitution, which reads:

"I (insert name), having been appointed a (insert rank) in the U.S. Army under the conditions indicated in this document, do accept such appointment and do solemnly swear (or affirm) that I will support and defend the Constitution of the United States against all enemies, foreign and domestic, that I will bear true faith and allegiance to the same; that I take this obligation freely, without any mental reservation or purpose of evasion; and that I will well and faithfully discharge the duties of the office on which I am about to enter, so help me God."

A similar oath that should be taken by all Bible-believing born-again pastors and all saved people generally would read:

"I will support and defend the King James Bible and its underlying Hebrew, Aramaic, and Greek Words against all enemies, foreign [unsaved] and domestic [saved]."

What a *"good fight of* [the] *faith"* this would be, even against such *"domestic"* enemies of this truth, that is, saved people whose *"bibles"* are on a foundation of drifting and sinking *"sand"* (cf.. Matthew 7:26-27)

1 Timothy 6:13

"I give thee charge in the sight of God, who quickeneth all things, and *before* Christ Jesus, who before Pontius Pilate witnessed a good confession;"

Here is Paul's *"charge"* or command to Pastor Timothy *"in the sight of God"* the Father and *"before Christ Jesus"* God's Son. The specifics of the *"charge"* are given in the next verse. Our God does *"quicken"* or make alive all things. Even after our Lord's crucifixion, God the Father raised Him up bodily from the grave.

Pontius Pilate was the sixth Roman Procurator of Judea. Under his permission, the Romans crucified the Lord Jesus Christ. Our Saviour *"witnessed a good confession"* before him, regardless of the cost.

- **Mark 15:2**
  And Pilate asked him, **Art thou the King of the Jews? And he answering said unto him, Thou sayest *it*.**
- **Mark 15:3**
  And **the chief priests accused him of many things: but he answered nothing.**

Certain things the Lord Jesus answered and certain things He did not, but He *"witnessed a good profession"* before many witnesses. We who are born-again by His grace must do the same.

1 Timothy 6:14

"That thou keep *this* commandment without spot, unrebukeable, until the appearing of our Lord Jesus Christ:"

The *"charge"* or *"commandment"* of God the Father and God the Son from the previous verse is given here. What is this *"charge"*? The word is PARAGGELO. It means: *"to transmit a message along from one to another, to declare, announce; or command, order, charge."*

The *"charge"* in verse 13 is a synonym for *"commandment"* in this verse. The word for *"commandment"* is ENTOLE. In various contexts, it means: *"an order, command, charge, precept, injunction; **that which is prescribed to one by reason of his office**; a commandment; a prescribed rule in accordance with which a thing is done; a precept relating to lineage, of the Mosaic precept concerning the priesthood; ethically used of the commandments in the Mosaic law or Jewish tradition."*

What is this *"commandment"* that Paul wants Pastor Timothy to *"keep"*? The only *"commandment"* in the context is found in verse 12. I believe that it is to *"Fight the good fight of* [the] *faith."* The word for *"keep"* is TEREO. It means: *"to attend to carefully, **take care of; to guard**; metaph. to keep, one in the state in which he is; to observe; to reserve: to undergo something."* Pastor Timothy, all pastors, and all Christians today, by application, are commanded to *"take care of and to guard"* the *"faith"* which is all the doctrines of the Bible.

Without Spot and Unrebukeable

How carefully was Timothy to *"keep"* this *"commandment"*? It was to be both *"without spot"* and *"unrebukeable."* The word for *"without spot"* is ASPILOS. It means: *"spotless; metaph. free from censure, irreproachable; free from vice, unsullied."* The word for *"unrebukeable"* is ANEPILEPTOS. It means: *"not apprehended, that cannot be laid hold of; that cannot be reprehended, not open to censure, irreproachable."*

The *"keeping"* and guarding of God's doctrines as revealed in the Bible must be thorough and **"free from censure."**

The phrase, *"without spot,"* is only used eleven times in our King James Bible. Here are a few illustrations of it.

- **Numbers 28:3**
  And thou shalt say unto them, This *is* the offering made by fire which ye shall offer unto the LORD; **two lambs of the first year without spot day by day**, *for* a continual burnt offering.
- **Hebrews 9:14**
  How much more shall the blood of Christ, who through the eternal Spirit **offered himself without spot to God**, purge your conscience from dead works to serve the living God?
- **1 Peter 1:19**
  But with the precious blood of Christ, **as of a lamb without blemish and without spot:**

We have a sinless, perfect Saviour, otherwise He could not save us from our sins.

- **2 Peter 3:14**
  Wherefore, beloved, seeing that ye look for such things, be diligent **that ye may be found of him in peace, without spot**, and blameless.

Notice the duration of the command to continuously "*fight the good fight of* [the] *faith*." The "*fight*" and battle must be "*until the appearing of our Lord Jesus Christ.*" I believe this refers to the coming of the Lord Jesus Christ in the Rapture of the born-again Christians. When will He "*appear*"? We do not know. We are to keep fighting that "*good fight of faith*" either until the Lord Jesus Christ appears in the Rapture (if we are saved), or He calls us Home to Heaven.

1 Timothy 6:15

"Which in his times he shall shew, *who is* the blessed and only Potentate, the King of kings, and Lord of lords;"

The Lord Jesus Christ, mentioned in verse 14, is the One Who will "*show*" Who this Person is. The word for "*potentate*" is DUNASTES. It means: "*a prince, a potentate; a courtier, high officer, royal minister of great authority.*" This only Potentate is someone Who is in charge. The Lord will show Who it is. Though this refers to the omnipotent God, the term has been used of secular kings as well in the Old Testament.

- **Ezra 7:12**
  Artaxerxes, **king of kings**, unto Ezra the priest, a scribe of the law of the God of heaven, perfect *peace*, and at such a time.

This means he is the king over all the other kings. He is the lead king.

- **Ezekiel 26:7**
  For thus saith the Lord GOD; Behold, I will bring upon Tyrus
  Nebuchadrezzar king of Babylon, **a king of kings**, from the
  north, with horses, and with chariots, and with horsemen, and
  companies, and much people.
- **Daniel 2:37**
  Thou, **O king, *art* a king of kings**: for the God of heaven hath
  given thee a kingdom, power, and strength, and glory.

  The Lord Jesus is the real *"King of kings."* The others are only rulers of
this earth as mentioned in the New Testament.
- **Revelation 17:14**
  These shall make war with the Lamb, and the Lamb shall
  overcome them: for he is **Lord of lords, and King of kings**:
  and they that are with him *are* called, and chosen, and faithful.
- **Revelation 19:16**
  And he hath on *his* vesture and on his thigh a name written,
  KING OF KINGS, AND LORD OF LORDS.

  In The Old Testament also *"Lord of lords"* is an expression used of the
Lord Himself.
- **Deuteronomy 10:17**
  For the LORD your God *is* **God of gods, and Lord of lords**,
  a great God, a mighty, and a terrible, which regardeth not
  persons, nor taketh reward:
- **Psalm 136:3**
  O give thanks to **the Lord of lords**: for his mercy *endureth* for
  ever.

  One day, in God's own time, He will show Who is the One and only
"Potentate." At that time, all the men, women, boys, and girls who have ever
lived will bow down to the Lord Jesus Christ and *"every tongue should confess
that Jesus Christ is Lord to the glory of God the Father"* (Philippians 2:11).
This includes those who crucified the Lord Jesus Christ and all those who have
rejected Him as their Saviour. They did not want Him to rule over them while
they were alive, but one day they must bow to Him. One day God is going to
show everyone without any question who is the *"King of kings and the Lord of
lords."* People did not care about Jesus when He was born in a manger, because
there was no room for Him in the Inn. Today, sad to say there is no room for
Him in the hearts of multitudes of people.

1 Timothy 6:16

"Who only hath immortality, dwelling in the light which no man can approach unto; whom no man hath seen, nor can see: to whom *be* honour and power everlasting. Amen."

The Lord Jesus Christ, God the Father, and God the Holy Spirit are the only Beings Who have had *"immortality"* from all eternity past. The word for *"immortality"* is ATHANASIA. It means: *"undying, everlasting."* The English word, like the Greek word, means *"no death."* A *"mortal"* is a person who is subject to death. A *"mortician"* is one who takes care of people who are dead.

God the Father is *"immortal"* and can never die. God the Holy Spirit is *"immortal"* and can never die. God the Son is *"immortal"* and can never die. But when God the Son became perfect Man by the miracle of the virgin birth, He was able to die for the sins of the world, and He did so. He took upon Himself our nature and was made *"in the likeness of sinful flesh"* (Romans 8:3b) yet He was absolutely sinless. He was perfect Man as well as perfect God. He experienced death not for His sins, but for the sins of the world. As to the Deity of Christ, it was immortal and deathless. We human beings are mortal, that is, subject to death.

● **1 Corinthians 15:53**
  For this corruptible must put on incorruption, and **this mortal must put on immortality.**

● **2 Timothy 1:10**
  But is now made manifest by the appearing of our Saviour Jesus Christ, who hath abolished death, and **hath brought life and immortality to light through the gospel:**

We who are born-again have a destiny to be *"immortal"* if we are saved. Right now we are *"mortal,"* but if we are *"in Christ"* we will put on *"immortality"* and there will be no more death. That is one of the truths that the book of Revelation tells us about Heaven. There is no night, no death, no sin, nor curse there, for the former things have passed away (Revelation 21:4).

Our God, Father, Son, and Holy Spirit are said to be *"dwelling in the light."* The attribute of *"light"* is found in many places referring to one of the Persons of the Godhead.

● **John 1:4**
  In him was life; and **the life was the light of men**.

The Lord Jesus was light and life.

● **1 John 1:5**

This then is the message which we have heard of him, and declare unto you, that **God is light, and in him is no darkness at all.**

There is not a single speck of "*darkness*" in the God of the Bible.

- **1 John 1:7**

  But if we walk in the light, **as he is in the light**, we have fellowship one with another, and the blood of Jesus Christ his Son cleanseth us from all sin.

  It is stated of this "*immortal*" God, is One "*Whom no man hath seen, nor can see.*" That is true.

- **Exodus 33:22**

  And it shall come to pass, **while my glory passeth by, that I will put thee in a clift of the rock, and will cover thee with my hand while I pass by:**

- **John 1:18**

  No man hath seen God at any time; the only begotten Son, which is in the bosom of the Father, he hath declared *him*.

- **John 6:46**

  Not that any man hath seen the Father, save he which is of God, he hath seen the Father.

The Lord Jesus Christ is the only One Who has seen God the Father.

- **John 14:9**

  Jesus saith unto him, Have I been so long time with you, and yet hast thou not known me, Philip? **he that hath seen me hath seen the Father;** and how sayest thou *then*, Shew us the Father?

- **1 John 4:12**

  No man hath seen God at any time. If we love one another, God dwelleth in us, and his love is perfected in us.

- **1 John 4:20**

  If a man say, I love God, and hateth his brother, he is a liar: for he that loveth not his brother whom he hath seen, **how can he love God whom he hath not seen?**

When we who are saved get new bodies, we will see the resurrected Saviour in Heaven, and we will be like Him. This is the Deity we will see in our resurrected bodies.

"*Honour and glory everlasting*" should be given to the Triune God.

1 Timothy 6:17

"Charge them that are rich in this world, that they be not highminded, nor trust in uncertain riches, but in the living God, who giveth us richly all things to enjoy;"

Pastor Timothy was to *"charge"* some of his congregation about a number of things. The word for *"charge"* is PARAGGELLO. It means: *"to transmit a message along from one to another, to declare, announce; to command, order, charge."* Being in the Greek present tense, it would mean that Timothy was constantly to declare or announce these things to *"them that are rich in this world."*

There are two parts to this *"charge."* Both of these parts are what I have referred to as *"stop signs."* I call them that because of the Greek structure. Both verbs are in the present tense and both are negative commands or prohibitions. The present tense prohibition in Greek means to stop an action already in progress.

What Greek Present Prohibitions Mean

A literal translation, therefore, would be:

1. Stop being *"highminded,"* and

2. Stop *"trusting"* in *"uncertain riches."*

The word for *"highminded"* is HUPSELOPHONEO which means: *"to be high minded, proud."*

Pride Must Be Stopped

Pride must be stopped on the part of these *"rich"* ones.

Secondly, they were to stop putting their *"trust"* in *"uncertain riches."* The word for "riches" is PLOUTOS. It means: *"riches, wealth; abundance of external possessions; fulness, abundance, plenitude; a good i.e. that with which one is enriched."*

Uncertain Riches

Such *"riches"* are *"uncertain"* because they can be taken away at a
moment's notice by a number of different kinds of reverses.

On the contrary, these *"rich"* people should *"trust"* in *"the living God
Who giveth us richly all things to enjoy."* The God of the Bible is indeed the
True Giver of eternal *"riches."* If we are truly saved, we have many rich and
wonderful blessings from our God and His Son, the Lord Jesus Christ.

While I was a pastor in New England in the 1960's, someone told us a
humorous story about pride and highmindedness to illustrate a point. There are
two very prominent families there in New England--the Cabots and the Lodges.
They did not wish to associate with or speak to any of the more common people.
As the story goes, "the Cabots spoke only to the Lodges, and the Lodges spoke
only to God." God warns against being *"highminded."*

- **Romans 11:20**
  Well; because of unbelief they were broken off, and thou
  standest by faith. **Be not highminded, but fear:**
- **2 Timothy 3:4**
  Traitors, heady, **highminded,** lovers of pleasures more than
  lovers of God;

Being *"highminded"* is one of the sins of the *"last days"* (2 Timothy 3:1).
Our *"trust"* must be in the living God.

- **Job 13:15**
  Though he slay me, yet will I trust in him: but I will maintain
  mine own ways before him.

Job knew what *"trust"* was.

- **Psalm 5:11**
  But **let all those that put their trust in thee rejoice:** let them
  ever shout for joy, because thou defendest them: let them also
  that love thy name be joyful in thee.

There is a rejoicing in *"trusting"* in the Lord.

- **Psalm 20:7**
  Some *trust* in chariots, and some in horses: but we will
  remember the name of the LORD our God.
- **Psalm 37:5**
  Commit thy way unto the LORD; **trust also in him;** and he
  shall bring *it* to pass.

- **Psalm 40:4**
  Blessed *is* **that man that maketh the LORD his trust**, and respecteth not the proud, nor such as turn aside to lies.
- **Psalm 49:6**
  They that trust in their wealth, and boast themselves in the multitude of their riches;
- **1 Peter 1:18**
  Forasmuch as ye know that **ye were not redeemed with corruptible things,** *as* **silver and gold**, from your vain conversation *received* by tradition from your fathers;
- **Psalm 62:8**
  Trust in him at all times; *ye* people, pour out your heart before him: God *is* a refuge for us. Selah.

Trust in the Lord Always

When we who are saved feel down-and-out, look up to the Lord. When we are penniless, look up. When we are sick, look up. When we are out of a job, look up. We must *"trust in Him at all times."*

- **Psalm 118:8**
  It is **better to trust in the LORD** than to put confidence in man.

He will never let you down. Men and women will let us down many times.

- **Isaiah 26:4**
  Trust ye in the LORD for ever: for in the LORD JEHOVAH *is* everlasting strength:
- **Mark 10:24**
  And the disciples were astonished at his words. But Jesus answereth again, and saith unto them, Children, **how hard is it for them that trust in riches to enter into the kingdom of God!**
- **2 Corinthians 1:9**
  But we had the sentence of death in ourselves, that **we should not trust in ourselves, but in God** which raiseth the dead:

Paul Faced Death Constantly

Paul was ready to die. He was condemned. Paul faced death many times. Remember the storm on the Mediterranean Sea? Paul said that he believed God (Acts 27:25). Paul and all the other prisoners were delivered from that storm. Remember the first Roman imprisonment when Paul was sentenced to death? During this imprisonment he wrote Ephesians, Philippians, Colossians, and Philemon. (My verse-by-verse books on each of these are available.) These are known as the four *"prison epistles."* The Lord delivered Paul from that imprisonment as well.

1 Timothy 6:18

"That they do good, that they be rich in good works, ready to distribute, willing to communicate;"

Paul tells Pastor Timothy four more things that these *"rich"* people must do.

3. *"That they do good."* This verb, as well as the two that follow, are in the present tense and imply that the action is to be continuous. These *"rich"* people must continue to *"do good."*

"Do good" is one word in Greek--AGATHAERGEO. The root word for *"good"* here is AGATHOS. It means: *"of good constitution or nature; useful, salutary; good, pleasant, agreeable, joyful, happy; excellent, distinguished; upright, honourable."* Trench's *Synonyms* book points out that AGATHOS is essential goodness, while KALOS is external goodness.

4. *"That they be rich in good works."*

Good Works Are Riches

Their wealth must not be limited to money or what money can buy. They must also continue to be *"rich"* in the area of *"good works."*

The word for *"good"* here is KALOS. It means variously:
"beautiful, handsome, excellent, eminent, choice, surpassing, precious, useful, suitable, commendable, admirable; beautiful to look at, shapely, magnificent; good, excellent in its nature and characteristics, and therefore well adapted to its ends; genuine,

approved; precious; joined to names of men designated by their office, competent, able, such as one ought to be; praiseworthy, noble; beautiful by reason of purity of heart and life, and hence praiseworthy; morally good, noble; honourable, conferring honour; affecting the mind agreeably, comforting and confirming."

This is a difficult task to perform in any of the various meanings of the word *"good."* It is nevertheless a command that should be continued to be obeyed by these *"rich"* people, and by application to every born-again Christian.

5. **That they be *"ready to distribute*."** The word for *"ready to distribute"* is EUMETADOLOS. It means: *"ready or free to impart; liberal."*

The Rich Must Be Givers

They are continuously to be ready to impart to others in need from their wealth.

---

6. **That they be *"willing to communicate*."** *"Willing to communicate"* is one word also. It is KOINONIKOS. It means: *"social, sociable, ready and apt to form and maintain communion and fellowship; inclined to make others sharers in one's possessions, inclined to impart, free in giving, liberal."*

The Rich Must Have Fellowship

In addition to the former command to *"impart one's possessions"* as needed, there is a second part to this word. It means that these *"rich"* people are not to be snobs or aloof, but *"maintain communion and fellowship"* with others who are less fortunate.

There are a number of verses that apply to one or the other of these four *"charges"* Paul gave to Pastor Timothy.

- **Matthew 5:16**
  Let your light so shine before men, **that they may see your good works**, and glorify your Father which is in heaven.

- **Acts 9:36**
  Now there was at Joppa a certain disciple named Tabitha, which by interpretation is called Dorcas: **this woman was full of good works** and almsdeeds which she did.

- Ephesians 2:8-10
  For by grace are ye saved through faith; and that not of yourselves: *is* the gift of God: Not of works, lest any man should boast. For **we are his workmanship, created in Christ Jesus unto good works**, which God hath before ordained that we should walk in them.
- 1 Timothy 2:10
  But (which becometh women professing godliness) **with good works**.
- 1 Timothy 5:10
  Well reported of for good works; if she have brought up children, if she have lodged strangers, if she have washed the saints' feet, if she have relieved the afflicted, if she have diligently followed every good work.
- 2 Timothy 3:17
  That the man of God may be perfect, **throughly furnished unto all good works.**

The Bible Furnishes Good Works

The Bible is given to us Christians because we need to be completely *"furnished"* with *"good works"* to follow.

- Titus 2:7
  In all things shewing thyself a pattern of good works: in doctrine *shewing* uncorruptness, gravity, sincerity,
  The preacher Titus and every Christian should be a *"pattern of good works."*
- Titus 2:14
  Who gave himself for us, that he might redeem us from all iniquity, and purify unto himself **a peculiar people, zealous of good works.**

Zealous of Good Works

What makes Christians *"peculiar"* is that they must be *"zealous of good works."* They should not want to do evil works but *"good works."*

- **Titus 3:8**
  This is a faithful saying, and these things I will that thou affirm constantly, that **they which have believed in God might be careful to maintain good works**. These things are good and profitable unto men.

Good Works Must Be Visible

If people who do not know the Lord Jesus Christ as their Saviour see "*good works*" they may be more willing to listen about Christ. But if they see Christians doing evil works they may not listen.

- **Titus 3:14**
  And **let ours also learn to maintain good works** for necessary uses, that they be not unfruitful.
- **Hebrews 10:24**
  And **let us consider one another to provoke unto love and to good works**:

We need to urge each other to do "*good works*."

- **1 Peter 2:12**
  Having your conversation honest among the Gentiles: that, whereas they speak against you as evildoers, they may **by your good works**, which they shall behold, glorify God in the day of visitation.

So much for the various verses that deal with the believers' doing "*good works*."

Let us look at some verses that speak of communicating, giving, and sharing.

- **Luke 18:22**
  Now when Jesus heard these things, he said unto him, Yet lackest thou one thing: **sell all that thou hast, and distribute unto the poor, and thou shalt have treasure in heaven**: and come, follow me.
- **Galatians 6:6**
  Let him that is taught in the word communicate unto him that teacheth in all good things.

That means that those who are "*taught*" should give money to those who "*teach*" them.

- **Philippians 4:14**
  Notwithstanding ye have well done, that **ye did communicate with my affliction**.
- **Hebrews 13:16**
  But **to do good and to communicate forget not**: for with such sacrifices God is well pleased.

The *"rich"* were *"to do good"* and be *"willing to distribute"* to others out of their abundance.

1 Timothy 6:19

"Laying up in store for themselves a good foundation against the time to come, that they may lay hold on eternal life."

By following the command in the previous verse, the *"rich"* people will be *"laying up in store for themselves a good foundation against the time to come."* This is a *"good foundation against the time to come."* Every saved person will appear one day before the *"Judgment Seat of Christ"* (2 Corinthians 5:10) where their works will be judged and where rewards, or lack of rewards will be determined. Paul told Timothy to urge these *"rich"* people to *"lay up in store for themselves a good foundation."* The word for *"laying up in store"* is APOTHESAURIZO. It means: *"to put away, lay by in store, to treasure away; to store up abundance for future use."* It is indeed a plan for the future.

Here are some verses that speak of *"laying up in store"* and *"foundations."*

- **2 Kings 20:17**
  Behold, the days come, that all that *is* in thine house, and that which **thy fathers have laid up in store** unto this day, shall be carried into Babylon: nothing shall be left, saith the LORD.

The Babylonians stole all the wealth of God's beautiful temple.

- **1 Corinthians 16:2**
  Upon the first *day* of the week let every one of you **lay by him in store,** as *God* hath prospered him, that there be no gatherings when I come.

The *"first day of the week"* is Sunday. That is when we give gifts to the Lord.

- **Luke 6:47-48**
  Whosoever cometh to me, and heareth my sayings, and doeth them, I will shew you to whom he is like: He is like a man which built an house, and digged deep, and **laid the foundation on a rock:** and when the flood arose, the stream beat vehemently upon that house, and could not shake it: for it was founded upon a rock.

- **Luke 14:28-29**
  For which of you, intending to build a tower, sitteth not down first, and counteth the cost, whether he have *sufficient* to finish *it*? Lest haply, **after he hath laid the foundation**, and is not able to finish *it*, all that behold *it* begin to mock him,

- **1 Corinthians 3:10**
  According to the grace of God which is given unto me, as a wise masterbuilder, **I have laid the foundation**, and another buildeth thereon. But let every man take heed how he buildeth thereupon.

God Knows Who Are His

- **2 Timothy 2:19**
  Nevertheless the foundation of God standeth sure, having this seal, The Lord knoweth them that are his. And, Let every one that nameth the name of Christ depart from iniquity.

We do not know who is the Lord's. Only He knows. I can look at everybody who is sitting in this room, and I don't know for sure if you are the Lord's or if you are not the Lord's. He alone knows. But God's *"foundation"* stands *"sure."*

---

1 Timothy 6:20

"O Timothy, keep that which is committed to thy trust, avoiding profane *and* vain babblings, and oppositions of science falsely so called:)"

This is the third time Paul mentions Timothy by name. (The other two places are in 1 Timothy 1:2, and 18.) Here Paul is charging Pastor Timothy to *"keep that which is committed to thy trust."* The word for *"keep"* is PHULASSO. It has various meanings:

> *"to guard; to watch, keep watch; **to guard or watch, have an eye upon**: lest he escape; to guard a person (or thing) that he may remain safe; lest he suffer violence, be despoiled, etc. to protect; to protect one from a person or thing; to keep from being snatched away, preserve safe and unimpaired; to guard from being lost or perishing; to guard one's self from a thing; to guard i.e. care for, take care not to violate; to observe; to observe for one's self*

something to escape; to avoid, shun flee from; to guard for one's self (i.e. for one's safety's sake) so as not to violate, i.e. to keep, observe (the precepts of the Mosaic law)."

The thing that Timothy is to *"guard or watch, or have an eye upon"* is *"that which is committed to thy trust."* The one word for the clause, *"that which is committed to thy trust,"* is PARAKATATHEKE. It means:

"a deposit, a trust or thing consigned to one's faithful keeping; used of the correct knowledge and pure doctrine of the gospel, to be held firmly and faithfully, and to be conscientiously delivered unto others."

What is this *"deposit"*? I believe it is everything that Paul taught Timothy including the gospel of the Lord Jesus Christ and all the other doctrines in the Bible that either were already written or would be written. Timothy followed Paul all over the then-known-world in his missionary journeys.

Guarding God's Written Words

As a pastor, Timothy had to be trustworthy concerning every doctrine found in God's written Words. That is also what I have to do as a pastor, and what you have to do as Christians. We must keep and guard that which is committed to our trust.

Two Negative Actions

In protecting and guarding this *"trust,"* Timothy was to remember two negative actions:

1.   Avoid profane and vain babblings.
2.   Avoid oppositions of science falsely so called.

1.   He was to be *"avoiding profane and vain babblings."* Since this verb for *"avoiding"* is in the Greek present tense, it means that this *"avoiding"* is to be continuous and without letup. He was to avoid both *"profane and worldly babblings."* The word for *"profane"* is BEBELOS. It means: *"accessible, lawful to be trodden; of places; **profane; unhallowed**, common, public place; of men, ungodly."*

Avoid Empty Discussion

The word for *"vain babblings"* is KENOPHONIA which means: *"empty discussion, discussion of vain and useless matters."* These words speak for themselves. If they are to be avoided by a pastor in Paul's day, they should be avoided by pastors (and other Christians) in our day by application.

2. He was to avoid *"oppositions of science falsely so called."* The word for "science" is GNOSIS. Though some feel that Gnosticism was not present in Paul's day, I disagree. Here is evidence of it right in this verse. The word means:

"knowledge signifies in general intelligence, understanding; the general knowledge of Christian religion; **the deeper more perfect and enlarged knowledge** *of this religion, such as belongs to the more advanced; esp. of **things lawful and unlawful for Christians;** moral wisdom, such as is seen in right living."*

Gnosticism's Heresies--Alive Today

Gnosticism has raised its ugly and wicked head in the *DaVinci Code* by Dan Brown and the so-called *Gospel of Judas*, and in other Gnostic false books.

"Atheistic or theistic evolution" is a *"science falsely so called"* as well. This parades as a *"science,"* but is established on hypotheses rather than observable facts. It is guesswork taught as truth.

1 Timothy 6:21

"Which some professing have erred concerning the faith. Grace *be* with thee. Amen.

Serious Erring About The Faith

Some of those in Timothy's day have evidently *"professed"* this Gnostic/science which is false and ungodly. Because of this, they *"erred concerning the faith."*

The word for "*erred*" is ASTOCHEO. It means: "*to deviate from, miss (the mark).*"These people have twisted themselves out of the orbit of the faith. They have missed the mark, have deviated from the faith because they have listened to the "*profane and vain babblings*" of this heresy.

The Faith=All the Biblical Doctrines

"*The faith*" has the Greek article and thus refers to the entire body of the doctrines of the Bible.

This "*science*" or GNOSIS was used by the Gnostics in the early church as well as those today. The Gnostics thought they knew everything. Be careful about those who think they know everything. That is indicative of something. To say they know everything means that they are proud, arrogant and boasters. That is sin.

What Gnostics Deny, Then & Now

As to the specifics of their "*erring concerning the faith,*" the Gnostics:

1. deny the Virgin Birth of the Lord Jesus Christ.
2. deny the Deity of the Lord Jesus Christ.
3. deny the bodily resurrection of the Lord Jesus Christ.
4. deny the bodily return of the Lord Jesus Christ.
5. deny that the Lord Jesus Christ is One Person.

Don't follow them. This is only a beginning enumeration of the heretical "*errors*" of this group. Modern-day Gnostic apostates deny the same things.

At the end of the book is "*grace be with thee. Amen.*"

That word "*Amen*" is a descriptive term. It is a transliteration of a Hebrew word into Greek. It means:

> "*firm; metaph. faithful; verily, amen; at the beginning of a discourse -surely, truly, of a truth; at the end - so it is, so be it, may it be fulfilled. It was a custom, which passed over from the synagogues to the Christian assemblies, that when he who had read or discoursed, had offered up solemn prayer to God, the others responded Amen, and thus made the substance of what was uttered their own.*

Amen, a Universal Word

The word 'amen' is a most remarkable word. It was transliterated directly from the Hebrew into the Greek of the New Testament, then into Latin and into English and many other languages, so that it is practically a universal word. It has been called the best known word in human speech. The word is directly related -- in fact, almost identical -- to the Hebrew word for 'believe' (amam), or faithful. Thus, it came to mean 'sure' or 'truly,' an expression of absolute trust and confidence. -- HMM"

When Abraham believed God, he said *"Amen,"* or *"I believe it."*

It is a great thing that we who are born-again Christians have. Let us keep on the battle for *"the faith."* Let's keep fighting, though trying not to be *"contentious"* even though people might think us to be. The *"weapons of warfare are not carnal, but mighty through God"* (2 Corinthians 10:4).

Never Stop Fighting for The Faith

Let us never stop fighting *"the good fight"* for THE FAITH (1 Timothy 6:12). Let us also *"earnestly contend for the faith which was once delivered unto the saints"* (Jude 3b).

Fight and contend for *"the faith"* in your own corner of the world, wherever it is needed. Stand fast for the Words of God and all the doctrines of Scripture.

"Don't Let Your Vision Grow Dim"

Don't let your vision grow dim;
Don't tire of the toil and the task.
Don't let the cost of your heavenly call
Keep you from following Him.

Don't let the vision grow dim;
Don't let your purpose grow faint.
Don't let the yearnings recede from your heart;
Don't let your vision grow dim.

Don't let your vision grow dim;
Don't let the fire burn low,
Forget not the plight of those souls lost in sin;
Don't let your vision grow dim.

By Gertrude G. Sanborn
With Tears In My Heart

Index of Words and Phrases

About the Author

The author of this book, Dr. D. A. Waite, received a B.A. (Bachelor of Arts) in classical Greek and Latin from the University of Michigan in 1948, a Th.M. (Master of Theology), with high honors, in New Testament Greek Literature and Exegesis from Dallas Theological Seminary in 1952, an M.A. (Master of Arts) in Speech from Southern Methodist University in 1953, a Th.D. (Doctor of Theology), with honors, in Bible Exposition from Dallas Theological Seminary in 1955, and a Ph.D. in Speech from Purdue University in 1961. He holds both New Jersey and Pennsylvania teacher certificates in Greek and Language Arts.

He has been a teacher in the areas of Greek, Hebrew, Bible, Speech, and English for over thirty-five years in ten schools, including one junior high, one senior high, four Bible institutes, two colleges, two universities, and one seminary. He served his country as a Navy Chaplain for five years on active duty; pastored three churches; was Chairman and Director of the Radio and Audio-Film Commission of the American Council of Christian Churches; since 1969, has been Founder, President, and Director of THE BIBLE FOR TODAY; since 1978, has been President of the DEAN BURGON SOCIETY; has produced over 700 other studies, books, cassettes, VHS's, CD's, or VCR's on various topics; and is heard on both a five-minute daily and thirty-minute weekly radio program IN DEFENSE OF TRADITIONAL BIBLE TEXTS, on radio, shortwave, and streaming on the Internet at BibleForToday.org, 24/7/365. Dr. and Mrs. Waite have been married since 1948; they have four sons, one daughter, and, at present, eight grandchildren, and five great-grandchildren. Since October 4, 1998, he has been the Pastor of The Bible For Today Baptist Church in Collngswood, New Jersey.

Order Blank (p. 1)

Name:_____

Address:_____

City & State:_____Zip:_____

*Credit Card #:*_____*Expires:*_____

[ ] Send 1 Timothy--Preaching Verse by Verse, by Pastor D. A. Waite, 296 pages, hardback ($14+$5 S&H) fully indexed.

[ ] Send *Word-For-Word Translating of The Received Texts* by Dr. H. D. Williams, 288 pages, paperback ($10+$5 S&H).

The Most Recently Published Books

[ ] Send *8,000 Differences Between Textus Receptus & Critical Text* by Dr. J. A. Moorman, 544 pp., hd.back ($20+$5+ S&H)

[ ] *Early Manuscripts, Church Fathers, & the Authorized Version* by Dr. Jack Moorman, $18+$5 S&H. Hardback

[ ] Send *The LIE That Changed the Modern World* by Dr. H. D. Williams ($16+$5 S&H) Hardback book

[ ] Send *With Tears in My Heart* by Gertrude G. Sanborn. Hardback 414 pp. ($25+$5 S&H) 400 Christian Poems

Preaching Verse by Verse Books

[ ] Send *Romans--Preaching Verse by Verse* by Pastor D. A. Waite 736 pp. Hardback ($25+$5 S&H) fully indexed

[ ] Send *Colossians & Philemon--Preaching Verse by Verse* by Pastor D. A. Waite ($12+$5 S&H) hardback, 240 pages.

[ ] Send *Philippians--Preaching Verse by Verse* by Pastor D. A. Waite ($10+$5 S&H) hardback, 176 pages.

[ ] Send *Ephesians--Preaching Verse by Verse* by Pastor D. A. Waite ($12+$5 S&H) hardback, 224 pages.

[ ] Send *Galatians--Preaching Verse By Verse* by Pastor D. A. Waite ($12+$5 S&H) hardback, 216 pages.

[ ] Send *First Peter--Preaching Verse By Verse* by Pastor D. A. Waite ($10+$5 S&H) hardback, 176 pages.

Send or Call Orders to:
THE BIBLE FOR TODAY
900 Park Ave., Collingswood, NJ 08108
Phone: 856-854-4452; FAX:--2464; Orders: 1-800 JOHN 10:9
E-Mail Orders: BFT@BibleForToday.org; Credit Cards OK

Order Blank (p. 2)

Name:_____

Address:_____

City & State:_____Zip:_____

Credit Card #:_____Expires:_____

Books on Bible Texts & Translations

[ ] Send *Defending the King James Bible* by Dr. Waite ($12+$5
   S&H) A hardback book, indexed with study questions.
[ ] Send *BJU's Errors on Bible Preservation* by Dr. D. A.
   Waite, 110 pages, paperback ($8+$4 S&H) fully indexed
[ ] Send *Fundamentalist Deception on Bible Preservation* by
   Dr.Waite, ($8+$4 S&H), paperback, fully indexed
[ ] Send *Fundamentalist MIS-INFORMATION on Bible Ver-
   sions* by Dr. Waite ($7+$4 S&H) perfect bound, 136 pages
[ ] Send *Fundamentalist Distortions on Bible Versions* by Dr.
   Waite ($6+$3 S&H) A perfect bound book, 80 pages
[ ] Send *Fuzzy Facts From Fundamentalists* by Dr. D. A.
   Waite ($8.00 + $4.00) printed booklet
[ ] Send *Foes of the King James Bible Refuted* by DAW ($10
   +$4 S&H) A perfect bound book, 164 pages in length.
[ ] Send *Central Seminary Refuted on Bible Versions* by Dr.
   Waite ($10+$4 S&H) A perfect bound book, 184 pages
[ ] Send *The Case for the King James Bible* by DAW ($7
   +$3 S&H) A perfect bound book, 112 pages in length.
[ ] Send *Theological Heresies of Westcott and Hort* by Dr. D.
   A. Waite, ($7+$3 S&H) A printed booklet.
[ ] Send *Westcott's Denial of Resurrection*, Dr. Waite ($4+$3)
[ ] Send *Four Reasons for Defending KJB* by DAW ($3+$3)

Send or Call Orders to:
THE BIBLE FOR TODAY
900 Park Ave., Collingswood, NJ 08108
Phone: 856-854-4452; FAX:--2464; Orders: 1-800 JOHN 10:9
E-Mail Orders: BFT@BibleForToday.org; Credit Cards OK

Order Blank (p. 3)

Name:_____

Address:_____

City & State:_____Zip:_____

Credit Card #:_____Expires:_____

More Books on Texts & Translations

[ ] Send *Holes in the Holman Christian Standard Bible* by Dr. Waite ($3+$2 S&H) A printed booklet, 40 pages
[ ] Send *Contemporary Eng. Version Exposed*, DAW ($3+$2)
[ ] Send *NIV Inclusive Language Exposed* by DAW ($5+$3)
[ ] Send *26 Hours of KJB Seminar* (4 videos) by DAW ($50.00)

Books By Dr. Jack Moorman

[ ] *Early Manuscripts, Church Fathers, & the Authorized Version* by Dr. Jack Moorman, $18+$5 S&H. Hardback
[ ] Send *Forever Settled--Bible Documents & History Survey* by Dr. Jack Moorman, $20+$5 S&H. Hardback book.
[ ] Send *When the KJB Departs from the So-Called "Majority Text"* by Dr. Jack Moorman, $16+$5 S&H
[ ] Send *Missing in Modern Bibles--Nestle-Aland & NIV Errors* by Dr. Jack Moorman, $8+$4 S&H
[ ] Send *The Doctrinal Heart of the Bible--Removed from Modern Versions* by Dr. Jack Moorman, VCR, $15 +$4 S&H
[ ] Send *Modern Bibles--The Dark Secret* by Dr. Jack Moorman, $5+$3 S&H
[ ] Send *Samuel P. Tregelles--The Man Who Made the Critical Text Acceptable to Bible Believers* by Dr. Moorman ($2+$1)
[ ] Send *8,000 Differences Between TR & CT* by Dr. Jack Moorman [$65 + $7.50 S&H] Over 500-large-pages of data
[ ] Send *356 Doctrinal Erors in the NIV & Other Modern Versions*, 100-large-pages, $10.00+$6 S&H.

Send or Call Orders to:
THE BIBLE FOR TODAY
900 Park Ave., Collingswood, NJ 08108
Phone: 856-854-4452; FAX:--2464; Orders: 1-800 JOHN 10:9
E-Mail Orders: BFT@BibleForToday.org; Credit Cards OK

Order Blank (p. 4)

Name:_____

Address:_____

City & State:_____Zip:_____

Credit Card #:_____Expires:_____

Books By or About Dean Burgon

[ ] Send *The Revision Revised* by Dean Burgon ($25 + $5
S&H) A hardback book, 640 pages in length.

[ ] Send *The Last 12 verses of Mark* by Dean Burgon ($15+$5
S&H) A hardback book 400 pages.

[ ] Send *The Traditional Text* hardback by Burgon ($16+$5
S&H) A hardback book, 384 pages in length.

[ ] Send *Causes of Corruption* by Burgon ($15+$5 S&H)
A hardback book, 360 pages in length.

[ ] Send *Inspiration and Interpretation*, Dean Burgon ($25+$5
S&H) A hardback book, 610 pages in length.

[ ] Send *Burgon's Warnings on Revision* by DAW ($7+$4
S&H) A perfect bound book, 120 pages in length.

] Send *Westcott & Hort's Greek Text & Theory Refuted by
Burgon's Revision Revised--Summarized* by Dr. D. A.
Waite ($7.00+$4 S&H), 120 pages, perfect bound.

[ ] Send *Dean Burgon's Confidence in KJB* by DAW ($3+$3)

[ ] Send *Vindicating Mark 16:9-20* by Dr. Waite ($3+$3 S&H)

[ ] Send *Summary of Traditional Text* by Dr. Waite ($3 +$3)

[ ] Send *Summary of Causes of Corruption*, DAW ($3+$3)

[ ] Send *Summary of Inspiration* by Dr. Waite ($3+$3 S&H)

Send or Call Orders to:
THE BIBLE FOR TODAY
900 Park Ave., Collingswood, NJ 08108
Phone: 856-854-4452; FAX:--2464; Orders: 1-800 JOHN 10:9
E-Mail Orders: BFT@BibleForToday.org; Credit Cards OK

Order Blank (p. 5)

Name:_____

Address:_____

City & State:_____Zip:_____

Credit Card #:_____Expires:_____

Books by D. A. Waite, Jr.

[ ] Send *Readability of A.V. (KJB)* by D. A. Waite, Jr. ($6+$3)
[ ] Send *4,114 Definitions from the Defined King James Bible*
    by D. A. Waite, Jr. ($7.00+$4.00 S&H)
[ ] Send *The Doctored New Testament* by D. A. Waite, Jr.
    ($25+$5 S&H) Greek MSS differences shown, hardback
[ ] Send *Defined King James Bible* lg. prt. leather ($40+$7.50)
[ ] Send *Defined King James Bible* med. prt. leather ($35+$6)

Miscellaneous Authors

[ ] Send *Guide to Textual Criticism* by Edward Miller ($7+$4)
    Hardback book
[ ] Send *Scrivener's Greek New Testament Underlying the King*
    James Bible, hardback, ($14+$5 S&H)
[ ] Send *Scrivener's Annotated Greek New Testament*, by Dr.
    Frederick Scrivener: Hardback--($35+$5 S&H);
    Genuine Leather--($45+$5 S&H)
[ ] Send *Why Not the King James Bible?--An Answer to James*
    White's KJVO Book by Dr. K. D. DiVietro, $10+$5 S&H
[ ] Send Brochure #1: "*1000 Titles Defending KJB/TR*"(N.C.)

More Books by Dr. D. A. Waite

[ ] Send *Making Marriage Melodious* by Pastor D. A. Waite
    ($7+$4 S&H), perfect bound, 112 pages.

Send or Call Orders to:
THE BIBLE FOR TODAY
900 Park Ave., Collingswood, NJ 08108
Phone: 856-854-4452; FAX:--2464; Orders: 1-800 JOHN 10:9
E-Mail Orders: BFT@BibleForToday.org; Credit Cards OK